Vintage Base Ball's Enduring Legacy

Jack Pelikan

Pocol Press
Punxsutawney, PA

POCOL PRESS
Published in the United States of America
by Pocol Press
320 Sutton Street
Punxsutawney, PA 15767
www.pocolpress.com

By Jack Pelikan

All rights reserved. No part of this book may be reproduced in any form whatsoever without the express written consent of Pocol Press.
Exceptions are made for brief quotations for criticism and reviews.

Publisher's cataloging-in-publication

Names: Pelikan, Jack, author.
Title: Vintage base ball's enduring legacy / Jack Pelikan.
Description: Punxsutawney, PA: Pocol Press, 2023.
Identifiers: ISBN 979-8-9852820-7-8
Subjects: LCSH Baseball--United States--History--19th century. | Baseball teams--United States--History. | BISAC SPORTS & RECREATION / Baseball / History
Classification: LCC GV877 .P45 2023 | DDC 796.357/0973--dc23

Library of Congress Control Number: 2023937387

Cover photo:
Billy "Bulldog" Gay pitches against the Addison Mountain Stars at the 2020 Akron Cup on their home field at picturesque Stan Hywet Hall and Gardens. Photo courtesy of the Akron Black Stockings.

To Lauren, Maddie and John for bringing me inspiration and joy each day.

In memoriam of vintage base ball legends Mike "Ace" Adrian and Jonathan "Charlie Brown" Farris.

Table of Contents

Prologue – What Year is it Again?   **1**

Part I: Niche to National Pastime – Origin and Ascent of America's Game (c. 1840-1870)   **5**

1: Humble Origins   5

2: Early Rules   25

3: Gaining Momentum   47

Part II: Passed by the Pro's – Commercialization, Corruption and Adaptation   **69**

4: Meteoric Rise, Commercialization and Scandal   69

5: Free Agency, Tanking and Analytics, Oh My!   83

Part III: Alive and Well – Vintage Base Ball's Revival   **97**

6: Back to Basics: Reemergence of Vintage Base Ball   97

7: Mountain Athletic Club (Fleischmanns, NY)   112

8: Akron Black Stockings (Akron, OH)   136

9: Lafayette Square Cyclone (St. Louis, MO)   157

10: Ohio Village Diamonds Ladies Vintage Base Ball Club (Columbus, OH)   172

11: Westward Expansion: Fort Verde Excelsiors (Camp Verde, AZ) & Whatcom Aces (Bellingham, WA)   189

Epilogue – Those Were and These Are the Days 209

Appendix – Vintage Base Ball Terminology 213

Bibliography   229

Index   249

Prologue – What Year is it Again?

I awoke on a blazing, summer Saturday in 2013, or so I thought when my wife and I left our apartment just southwest of downtown St. Louis. With both the temperature and humidity pushing triple-digits and conditions resembling your local gym's steam room, we had every excuse to stay in, but we needed the fresh air. Staying close, we walked the surrounding Lafayette Square neighborhood, a nationally renowned preservationist community known for its iconic "Painted Lady" Victorian row houses and centerpiece Lafayette Park, the oldest city park west of the Mississippi. Consistent with the surrounding homes, Lafayette Park is meticulously preserved to its mid-19th century origin, from its wrought iron fences, gatehouse and bronze statues to the intentional omission of common park amenities like power lines, light towers, bleachers and backstops. While the park's natural settings and backdrop of pristine Victorian homes may give anyone pause to recall the current year, this day proved especially difficult.

After reaching the park's northwest corner, where a group of men dressed in full-length wool uniforms reminiscent of the Civil War appeared to be playing some primitive baseball game, I briefly convinced myself that I was either hallucinating from the heat or traveling through time. After slapping my cheeks and checking my trusty cell phone, I realized it was still in fact 2013 and that this exhibition must be a historical reenactment.

Bewilderment quickly shifted to curiosity as I continued to watch. I even wanted to intervene at one point and correct an egregious missed call when an inning ended after the outfielder picked up a bloop single on a high hop. How did the umpire miss that? I knew he was the only official and had poor visibility from far away home plate, but that ball bounced over three feet! While I could empathize with that poor barehanded outfielder, and recall selling my fair share of traps as catches back in my playing days, I was outraged by the opposing team's utter lack of outrage. Were they not watching the same game? Maybe I really was hallucinating. Or maybe it was the passionate and bitter St. Louis Cardinals fan in me, still seeking justice from the 1985 World Series Game 6 when Royals' pinch hitter Jorge Orta was errantly awarded first while his club trailed 1-0 in the bottom of the ninth despite being clearly beaten to the bag by Cardinals pitcher Todd

Worrell (watch the clip and judge for yourself), which led to an epic implosion that ultimately lost the game and eventually the series. Either way, I had to make my voice heard.

While I knew better than to disrupt this refreshingly civil contest, I, much to the frustration of my sunburnt bride, was unwilling to leave without a clear explanation. Luckily, a gentleman in similar period attire stood nearby waiting to play the next game. Without hesitation, I approached him, abandoning all pleasantries, and bluntly asked what we were watching. As if he'd heard this question hundreds of times, he merely chuckled and proceeded with a 15-minute crash course on vintage base ball.

As you can presume from this book, I instantly became a fan. What wasn't to like? For starters, he introduced himself by his vintage nickname "Charlie Brown"[1] and referred to himself as a "ballist", the 19th century term for player. Note that vintage jargon is used throughout the book. If not defined directly in the text, the Appendix contains a dictionary of common vintage terms like bounders (bouncers), corkers (hard hits) and daisy cutters (sharp grounders).

If the 1860's attire, nicknames and lingo hadn't sold me already, Charlie's explanations of the vintage rules were the icing on the cake. He began with an overview of early 1860's rules and gameplay (detailed in Chapter 2), including how an out can be registered by catching the ball on the fly or after a single bounce, which is often the preferred option since gloves were not part of the original game. He also explained how the strike zone, perhaps the most controversial topic in today's game and leading cause of arguments and ejections, was not part of the 1860's game as strikers (hitters) were allowed to take pitches, which were delivered underhand, until hit or missed three times and secured by the catcher on the fly or single bounce.

Luckily, Charlie's tutorial even included etiquette which, like the rules, has not deviated from the 1860's. For example, rolling up your sleeves on a hot day, while a logical and natural impulse, is considered improper without permission from the ladies in the audience. And while both teams that day were playing with the utmost class and sportsmanship, Charlie informed me that disciplinary measures remain in place. While my mind gravitated to the vast and dubious collection of modern baseball outbursts like Baltimore's Roberto Alomar spitting in umpire John Hirschbeck's face after a called third strike in 1996 or even Braves' minor league manager Phil Wellman's prolonged 2007 tirade involving a buried home plate and two literally stolen bases, the infractions in the vintage game are far more subdued and commonly pertain to ungentlemanly behavior like spitting on the ground or cursing. One can only imagine the millions, if not billions, levied on today's professionals for such common behaviors. Fortunately for today's vintage ballists, fines are not pegged to inflation and enforced at their original 19th century prices, which rarely exceed a quarter.

Fifteen minutes were not nearly enough to learn the vintage game. After bidding adieu to Charlie, I vowed to learn more and watch vintage ball every chance I could. A decade later, the vintage game still evokes that same sense of curiosity, intrigue and nostalgia as it did on that scorcher in 2013. And while the game has grown to over 400 clubs since its humble origins on Long Island in 1979, it remains relatively unknown to most sports fans.

To broaden awareness of this largely hidden treasure, chronicle its origins and revival, and share some of the compelling stories of the women and men who carry on the vintage game, I embarked on a scholarly journey through interviews, books, periodicals and the internet that culminated in this work. The book is divided into three parts. Part I establishes context through exploration of the game's origins, including the mid-19th century "Pioneer Era", which remains the standard for most of today's vintage clubs. Part II chronicles the game's rapid ascent as the national pastime in the late 19th century and resulting Golden Era. And while the book's focus remains the history and revival of the vintage game, Part II also explores the modern game's commercialization, scandals and landmark shifts including free agency, data analytics and competitive balancing measures (i.e., tanking) that have, for better or worse, irreversibly shaped today's game and motivated some to resurrect the vintage game. Lastly, Part III offers previously untold accounts of today's vintage base ball community, told through the lenses of various clubs across the country.

While it has been a long and arduous quest involving paperbacks, callbacks, emails, elaborate tales, caffeine and magazines, I have remained steadfast in my mission to shine a brighter light on this unheralded yet essential piece of Americana. My only hope is that after reading this book, you will also come to appreciate the hidden gem that is vintage base ball by supporting or even starting your local club and spreading the word (via Pony Express or text). As vintage ballists say after a match, "Huzzah!"²

Part I: Niche to National Pastime – Origin and Ascent of America's Game (c. 1840-1870)

1: Humble Origins

"The one constant through all the years, Ray, has been baseball. America has rolled by like an army of steamrollers. It has been erased like a blackboard, rebuilt and erased again. But baseball has marked the time. This field, this game — it's a part of our past, Ray. It reminds us of all that once was good and it could be again."

- James Earl Jones as Terence Mann in the 1989 film
Field of Dreams

Not Always America's Pastime

While the fictional Terence Mann's iconic speech in the beloved film *Field of Dreams* still resonates with baseball and movie fans over 30 years later, it also downplays the game's nearly two centuries of transformation. Beginning with its precursors like England's stoolball, cricket and rounders followed by America's wicket and town ball, and the niche following during the Knickerbocker Era of the 1840's and 50's, the initial version of baseball (or "base ball" as it was commonly referred until consolidated in the 1880's) paled in comparison to today's roughly $11 billion Major League Baseball (MLB) empire. And while Chapter 2 analyzes various aspects of early gameplay and rules, many of which have withstood the test of time, subsequent chapters chronologically profile various eras and explore how the game has continuously adapted, including the adoption of free agency, analytics and competitive balancing, to meet the everchanging needs of its stakeholders including owners, players, agents, media and fans.

To fully understand the extent and impact of baseball's ongoing transformation, one must first understand the game's primitive and humble origins and the underlying factors that led to its ascent and continued reign as America's Pastime. And while the fictional Terence Mann's assertion that "the one constant through all these years has been baseball" is poetic and inspiring, it Is also (as the following chapters will reveal) misleading, as baseball has been anything but constant throughout its dynamic history.

Early Bat and Ball Games

Although baseball's origins can be traced to the mid-19th century, most notably with New York's Knickerbocker Club, who formally published rules in 1845 and played the first official game the following year (a 23-1 dismantling at the hands of the New York Nine at Hoboken, New Jersey's Elysian Fields), the origin and evolution of bat and ball games are less clear.

While one can easily (and amusingly) visualize prehistoric cave men launching rocks with wooden clubs, historians must rely upon verifiable evidence, most notably through early writing and art. Perhaps the earliest accounts of this concept stem from Ancient Egypt's *seker-hemat* (loosely translated to "batting the ball") around 2400 B.C. Based on inscriptions found within pyramids, Egyptologists like Dr. Peter Piccione of the College of Charleston have cited images of pharaohs like Thutmose III and their priests playing catch and even batting balls. Yet *seker-hemat* was no mere game, but rather a religious ritual most commonly performed in the spring, where the ball is believed to have represented the eye of Apopi, the great serpent of chaos in ancient Egyptian religion, and the pharaoh or priests' act of hitting the ball was symbolic of overcoming evil, restoring universal balance and renewing creation.[3]

Another early bat and ball game is the Viking's *knattleikr*. which potentially dates back to 9th century A.D. Iceland. While the game's history is generally limited to family sagas and the details of gameplay are broadly interpreted, prevailing accounts maintain that players used wooden bats to either hit or fling balls tossed at them, thus also drawing comparisons to Irish hurling or American lacrosse. The comparisons to modern baseball largely end there however, as it is widely believed the game was occasionally played on ice and involved frequent violence.[4]

English Precursors: Stoolball, Cricket and Rounders

Even though baseball's lineage to the earliest bat and ball games is speculative due to limited historical evidence, the game's linkage to its more contemporary precursors, particularly those in England, is undeniable.

One of baseball's earliest, documented links is the English game "Doutee Stool" or stoolball. The game is commonly believed to date back to at least 1330 A.D. when Winkfield clergyman William Pagula wrote a Latin poem urging priests to restrict bat and ball games from being played in church yards.[5] Originally, stoolball was played with a bat, ball and three-legged milking stool. The bowler (pitcher) attempts to hit the stool with the ball (similar to the stumps in cricket) while the defender (batter) earns points for batting the ball and protecting the stool. Once the stool is hit, the turn is over and players change sides. Over time, the game evolved into a team sport with two stools, where batters ran to one another's stations after hit balls to score additional points. If the fielding opponents are able to hit either stool (via tagging or throwing) before the runner reaches, they are declared out. While stoolball remains a niche pastime in England, primarily for female scholastic competitions, it's best known for its significance as a forerunner of cricket.

Like stoolball, the exact origins of cricket remain highly debated. However, the International Cricket Council maintains that while cricket may have been invented by children in the woodlands of southeast England as early as the Saxon period (c. 410-1066 A.D.), the first written reference to adults playing cricket did not occur until 1611, when two men were fined for failing to attend Easter services due to a cricket match. Cricket, emerging from the Old English or Saxon term "cryce" meaning stick or staff, remained largely a recreational game played in the countryside until the 18th century when the game rose to national and (by virtue of their colonial reach) global prominence, thanks largely to the formation of prestigious clubs like the Hambledon and Marylebone Cricket Clubs, the latter of which still maintains the Laws of Cricket and resides at Lord's Cricket Ground in London, the game's most storied venue.

While cricket has ascended to become Britain's and ultimately the world's second most popular sport with over 2.5 billion fans today, trailing only soccer's 3.5 billion, the sport has struggled to remain relevant in America especially since the Civil War.[6] This sentiment was perhaps best articulated in a March 10, 1868 edition of New York's *Spirit of the Times*:

"Cricket we have always had, as an exotic. It has been played for years at Hoboken and other retired localities, but chiefly by Englishmen, and it is still regarded even by American players, as an English game."[7]

Regardless of whether American apathy towards cricket is a byproduct of baseball's emergence or postwar dissociation from British customs, the stark contrast in how Americans perceive the two games further dispels the prevailing myth that baseball emerged directly from cricket. And while cricket and baseball share some commonalities with respect to batting, baserunning and defense, England's lesser-known game of rounders is far closer to baseball.

Dating back to the Tudor period (c. 1485-1603), rounders began and largely remains a recreational youth game as the premise and rules are simple. Two teams generally ranging from six to 15 players each compete on a field marked with a batting square and four posts arranged in a pentagonal formation. Unlike the baseball diamond, the fourth post, where runs are scored, sits on a straight line roughly 30 feet below the third post and 30 feet to the left of the batting square, which sits below the pitching square and second post and diagonal from the first and third posts. The bowler or feeder (pitcher) provides an underhand delivery from the box in the middle of the formation roughly 25 feet from the batter. Once hit, regardless of the location as there is no foul territory, the batter runs to the first post and can continue to advance unless the ball is caught, runner is tagged or the ball reaches the post before the runner (known as "stumped"). Once the ball is returned to the bowler in the square, the runners must remain at their current stations until bowled to a new batter. Also note that in some earlier versions, runners were declared out if struck with the ball while running between posts. Teams continue to score via multi-post hits and safely reaching the fourth post. A side is retired once all batters or runners are declared out. However, in earlier versions, sides that were down to their final two players had the opportunity to restore all of their batters should one of them hit one of three deliveries and run all the way to the fourth post in a single play.[8]

While believed to have been around as a children's game for centuries, rounders' earliest documented reference, where it is interestingly referred to as "Base-Ball", resides in John

Newberry's 1744 children's classic *A Pretty Little Pocket Book* in the following passage:

"Base-Ball. The Ball once struck off, Away Flies the Boy, To the next destin'd Post, and then Home with Joy."[9]

Note that the text alone does not indicate how many posts the boy must pass, but the illustration at the end of the chapter reveals that there are at least three stations (as opposed to cricket's two), which are arranged in either a triangular or diamond formation.

In addition to the aforementioned literary reference, the linkage to rounders is reinforced by predominant baseball authorities, most notably the "Father of Baseball" and Hall of Fame writer Henry Chadwick, who acknowledges the following in his *1860 Beadle's Dime Base-Ball Player* rulebook:

"As we propose briefly to note the progress of Base Ball from its origin, we deem it appropriate to introduce the rules for playing the English Game of Rounders, from which Base Ball is derived."[10]

But Chadwick's credit to the English game largely ends there as he proceeds to assert base ball as the superior game:

"The above (rounders) is a very simple game, and one designed only for relaxation during the intervals from study in schools, and is entirely devoid of the manly features that characterize Base Ball as played in this country. Boys and even girls can play Rounders without difficulty; but Base Ball, to be played thoroughly, requires the possession of muscular strength, great agility, quickness of eye, readiness of hand, and many other faculties of mind and body that mark the man of nerve. But it is needless further to comment on the meritorious features of our American game, suffice it to say that it is a recreation that any one may be proud to excel in, as in order to do so, he must possess the characteristics of true manhood to a considerable degree."

To fully comprehend Chadwick's viewpoint, one must first understand the early American adaptations of cricket and rounders.

Early American Adaptations: Wicket and Town Ball

While Americans had played cricket since Britain's occupation in the early 17th century and the game enjoyed some early success particularly at the collegiate level, the need to establish a homegrown game intensified after the American Revolution and War of 1812. Naturally, the adaptation was gradual, likely beginning with Connecticut's 1830 version of wicket.

As implied by its name, wicket was designed in the image of cricket, including the bowling and batting styles, the two-inning format and the circular field with two running stations. However, wicket was customized to add more flexibility and give it a distinctive American flavor. Most notably, equipment was adapted to promote more offense including usage of a larger bat and ball and smaller stumps to reduce the hitting area. Additionally, while eleven cricketers (including the bowler and wicketkeeper) stand on defense, wicket did not have such limits as upwards of 30 players were occasionally seen in the field. Further, as wicket contests were often organized haphazardly in urban areas like Bristol, Connecticut (the future birthplace of ESPN), games could be played in streets as opposed to the country fields and manicured grounds synonymous with English cricket. Lastly, as wicket was commonly regarded as "a game for fun and exercise only, affording little scope for what is called scientific play," minimal statistics and records beyond the final scores were kept.11

While wicket remained popular in Connecticut and gained traction in random outposts like Western Michigan through the 1850's, other parts of the country were simultaneously adapting other bat and ball games. For example, the Massachusetts Game consisted of four bases arranged in a square with the striker (hitter) situated between the first and fourth (home) bases, similar to rounders, and the balls and bats were considerably smaller than those used in wicket. Unlike baseball, runners were often put out by "soaking" or being pelted with the ball. A similar game emerged in rural Virginia known as round-town. Eventually, these regional varieties were consolidated under a common umbrella known simply as town ball.

Most commonly associated with Philadelphia's Olympic Ball Club, town ball became the country's most popular sport thanks largely to the formal organization of clubs and documentation of rules and results. In fact, the Olympic Club had their own clubhouse and (by 1838) their own constitution, of which a rare copy was sold at auction in 2007 for $141,000. And because of the vast similarities between 1830's town ball and the Knickerbockers' 1840's version of base ball, historians continue to debate whether the Olympic Club was actually the first ever organized base ball club.[12]

However, the Olympic Club's formation was not without its share of adversity. For starters, gaining enough adult members to consistently play games, which were entirely intrasquad scrimmages until other clubs emerged, proved challenging not only because of the prevailing sentiment that such games were juvenile, but also because games were frequently played on Sundays, which ran counter to various religious and local blue laws. These issues were exacerbated by the reality that Philadelphia was a bustling urban center with limited public transportation at the time and even more limited greenspace.

Yet the fledgling club and its determined founders were able to navigate these challenges and build an institution that lasted for over 50 years. To begin, the original club from 1831 was down to just four members before merging with another in 1833 and convincing others to try this entertaining new game. Additionally, to secure adequate playing grounds that were also open on Sundays, the club took 15-minute ferry rides into undeveloped Camden, New Jersey, where they played rent-free in front of large, growing crowds. Lastly, with the building of a clubhouse and ratification of bylaws in 1838, the Olympic Club evolved from a childish club to a legitimate organization that would attract over 100 members in the coming years. The club's success inspired others to follow suit and, by the 1860's, the city had over 100 organized ball clubs.[13]

But the success of town ball was not limited to Philadelphia or the east coast for that matter. In fact, town ball spread west in the 1840's and thrived in cities like St. Louis, Cincinnati and Davenport. In fact, town ball became so popular that even Abraham Lincoln was known to have played the game in his younger days in 1840's Springfield, as noted by his neighbor James Gourley:

"We played the old-fashioned game of town ball – jumped – ran – fought and danced. Lincoln played town ball – he hopped well

– in 3 hops he would go 40.2 (feet) on a dead level...He was a good player – could catch a ball."[14]

Abner Doubleday & The Great Myth

If you've ever wondered why the National Baseball Hall of Fame and Museum resides in the charming yet small rural Upstate New York Village of Cooperstown, you're not alone. However, the decision to build the Hall there in 1939 was far from random. In fact, the prevailing myth at the time was that the first baseball game had been played there one hundred years earlier involving a future major general in the Union Army and Civil War hero Abner Doubleday. If you've visited Cooperstown or recall watching MLB's Hall of Fame Games or Classics, you will also recall the adjacent stadium is named Doubleday Field, which stands on a former cow pasture and alleged site of the first game.

The basis for this claim? A 1905 commission (and subsequent report) established by former player and sporting goods magnate Albert Goodwill (A.G.) Spalding to investigate baseball's origins. The commission included National League president Abraham G. (A.G.) Mills; US Senator (CT) and former National League president Morgan Bulkeley; AAU president James Sullivan; former players Al Reach, George Wright and Arthur Gorman; and former league president Nicholas E. Young. In addition to the national publicity and marketing opportunities the project afforded Spalding and his business, the commission was likely spurred by legendary writer and the oft-proclaimed "Father of Baseball" Henry Chadwick's 1903 article linking baseball directly to England's rounders. Chadwick's sentiment was hardly new as he made the same assertion in his rulebook *1860 Beadle's Dime Base-Ball Player*. However, Spalding remained either unconvinced or unwilling to accept the national pastime as a British holdover.

Despite the commission's impressive credentials and three years of "research" before publishing the report in *Spalding's Official Base Ball Guide 1908*, the results were almost immediately called into question by various media outlets. As one would expect at the dawn of the 20th century, the journalistic burden of proof was far lighter than in today's culture of extreme skepticism. In fact, the commission's most impactful conclusion that the first game was played in Cooperstown in 1839 hinged on a letter from a septuagenarian mining engineer in Colorado named Abner Graves, who claimed to have been schoolmates with Doubleday at Green's Select School in Cooperstown, where he allegedly witnessed Doubleday draw up the first baseball field and team formation. Graves' letter was in response to the commission's open call for information published in Akron's *Beacon Journal,* which also published Graves' response under the title "Abner Doubleday Invented Base Ball."

One of the Spalding report's most immediate and vocal detractors was *Collier's* Will Irwin, whose 1909 article proved that Doubleday was still a cadet at West Point in 1839 with no record of taking leave that year. Other critics later pointed out other glaring flaws in Graves' account including a 15-year age difference between the alleged schoolmates, evidence that Doubleday's family left Cooperstown two years prior and the lack of any corroborating accounts from Doubleday or his inner circle, which included 30-year friend and commission member A.G. Mills. Others even went as far as to say that Graves' account had mistaken the general for another Doubleday residing in Michigan. These counterclaims were not without merit as Graves, who had no interactions with the Mills Commission and a long history of sensationalism, spent his final days in 1926 in a Colorado state asylum after being declared criminally insane upon his conviction in the shooting death of his second wife Minnie.

Despite the preponderance of evidence to the contrary, the Doubleday Myth endured for decades thereafter. Nearly 30 years after the commission's report, Cooperstown resident and millionaire heir of the Singer Sewing Machine fortune Stephen C. Clark, inspired by his discovery of an antique ball allegedly linked to Doubleday that was purchased from Graves' relative outside of Cooperstown, amplified the myth, using it as a springboard for tourism and an ultimately successful bid to land the Hall in 1939.[15]

Nevertheless, the Doubleday Myth has been so widely discredited over the years that even the National Baseball Hall of Fame and Museum has since acknowledged (and embraced) its inaccuracy, thus explaining the absence of his bronze plaque there. In a 2010 article titled "The Doubleday Myth is Cooperstown's Gain", Hall official Craig Muder wrote:

"Doubleday was at West Point in 1839, yet 'The Myth' has grown so strong that the facts will never deter the spirit of Cooperstown."[16]

Despite the overwhelming preponderance of evidence to the contrary, both the commission and general public largely accepted Doubleday as the game's founder for decades in a phenomenon best articulated by historian David Block:

"These critics carried little weight compared to the towering influence of Spalding and his commission, and the American public was quick to welcome Abner Doubleday as the nation's newest icon. The Cooperstown tale rapidly found its way into children's schoolbooks, taking its place alongside other historical anecdotes like Ben Franklin and his kite, and George Washington and the cherry tree. The debate over baseball's origins quietly slid into the shadows. In part, this peace was due to the passing of those two old warriors, Chadwick and Spalding [in 1908 and 1915, respectively], whose personalities and friendly rivalry had so long fueled the controversy. More to the point, in the minds of most observers, there was nothing left to debate."[17]

To the credit of Abner Doubleday, who passed away 15 years prior to Spalding's report, there is no verifiable evidence that he ever claimed to have invented baseball or even played in the alleged game in 1839. Even though Doubleday did not invent the game, he certainly supported it, as evidenced by his 1871 letter to his commanding officers requesting baseball supplies for the enjoyment of his African American regiment in Texas. And while Doubleday will forever be associated with a popular albeit apocryphal baseball origin story, his true legacy will be that of an American hero for his courageous service and leadership in both the Mexican-American and Civil War, where he fought in landmark battles at Fort Sumter, Antietam and Gettysburg.

The Knickerbocker Base Ball Club

Since the discreditation of the Doubleday Myth in the early 20th century, New York's Knickerbocker Base Ball Club has been widely regarded as the first organized base ball club due to their publication of the game's first set of standardized rules in

1845 and their participation in the first official game in 1846. While that claim remains contested by those that view town ball as a raw form of base ball instead of a precursor, the magnitude of the Knickerbockers' impact on the game is irrefutable.

The club, named after Manhattan's volunteer Knickerbocker (fire) Engine Company where several members served, began playing intrasquad scrimmages as early as 1842 before formally organizing in 1845 under club president and Harvard-educated physician Daniel Lucious "Doc" Adams and bank clerk Alexander Cartwright Jr. As part of the club's organization, a constitution and bylaws were ratified including a set of 20 rules for gameplay. While the rules themselves were hardly revolutionary, borrowing largely from elements of rounders and town ball, the very act of recording and disseminating standardized rules helped to unify a patchwork of regional bat and ball games into what would initially be known as the "New York Game" and eventually America's Game.

While not fundamentally different from the informal rules of its precursors, the 1845 Knickerbocker Rules introduced some new wrinkles that forever shaped the game. Most notably, the practice of soaking, or pelting your opponent to register an out, was abolished in favor of force-outs and tags (Rule 13), which in all likelihood was intended to curb the frequent injuries synonymous with town ball. As another safety measure, fielders were permitted to make an out by catching the ball on a single bounce (Rule 12). The field itself changed from the five-station square to a diamond by consolidating home plate and the striker's (batter) box and spacing the bases equally at 42 paces apart (Rule 4). Additionally, lines were drawn from home to first and third, and balls hit outside of those areas were considered foul (Rule 10). Lastly, provisions were put in place to limit match duration including three outs per side each inning (Rule 15) and the 21-run requirement to win the match (Rule 8), as opposed to Massachusetts town ball's 100. Nevertheless, the 21-run requirement can still lead to some long and exhausting games, as noted by current vintage ballists that have played 1845-style games, which are typically reserved for special occasions.[18] Note that the Knickerbockers published updated rules in 1854, this time in conjunction with two other area clubs (Gotham and Eagle), that were largely consistent with the 1845 version but for the removal of three prior rules unrelated to gameplay and the addition of specifications on pitching distance (15 paces) and ball dimensions (5.5-6 ounces and 2.75-3.5 inches in diameter). While very similar to the 1845 rules, the 1854 edition was significant in that it was agreed upon with other clubs and even published in local and national newspapers, which ultimately helped the New York Game become America's Game.

Beyond authoring and publicizing the game's first set of rules, the Knickerbockers were renowned for their play. Due to the lack of greenspace in dense, bustling Manhattan, the club resuscitated the former cricket grounds at Hoboken, New Jersey's Elysian Fields. And while the Knickerbockers did not formally organize until their 1845 constitution, various members had been playing ball together for years. Despite the presence of documented rules, Knickerbocker intrasquad games were often informal and improvised with varying roster sizes and scores, including some where the combined tallies exceeded 100. Naturally, experimentation was a key component of these informal contests, some of which permanently shaped the nascent game. Perhaps most notably, Doc Adams is credited with creating the shortstop position around 1850. His rationale was to establish a roaming infielder to relay balls thrown from the outfield, thus introducing the fundamental concept of the cut-off man.[19]

The Knickerbockers played exclusively intrasquad until 1851 with some notable exceptions including their June 19, 1846 contest against the New York Nine (also referred to as the New Yorks or Gothams) at the Elysian Fields, an event widely recognized as baseball's first official game since it featured different clubs and was played in accordance with the Knickerbocker's 1845 Rules. Despite playing by their rules, the Knickerbockers were overwhelmed by their talented opponents, whose prior bat and ball game experience clearly translated into a 23-1 laugher over four innings, which Knickerbocker president Duncan Curry later described as:

"An awful beating you could say at our own game, but, you see, the majority of the New York Club's players were cricketers, and clever ones at that game, and their batting was the feature of their work. The chief trouble was that we had held our opponents too cheaply and few of us had practiced any prior to the contest, thinking that we knew more about the game than they did... The pitcher of the New York nine was a cricket bowler of some note,

and while one could use only the straight arm delivery, he could pitch an awfully speedy ball. The game was in a crude state. No balls were called on the pitcher and that was a great advantage to him, and when he did get them over the plate, they came in so fast our batsmen could not see them."[20]

    Undeterred by the setback, the Knickerbockers returned to the Elysian Fields the very next day, albeit in intrasquad competition. Continuing with the experimentation, the club even introduced uniforms in 1849, which consisted of blue wool pants, white flannel shirts and straw hats, a decision prompted by comfort and mobility over style.[21]

    By 1851, the Knickerbockers resumed external competition and their "rivalry" with the Gothams. Unlike in 1846, the Knickerbockers were more adept at their own game taking down the host Gothams (then known as the Washingtons) in Harlem by a score of 21-11. The Knickerbockers continued their dominance over the Gothams, sweeping annual home-and-home series until the Gothams prevailed again in 1854. Over the following years, the Knickerbockers played select clubs across the area including New York's Eagles and Empires and Brooklyn's Excelsiors.

    Meanwhile, the Knickerbocker game, then referred to as the "New York Game" due to the abundance of competing town ball varieties in other areas like Massachusetts and Philadelphia, was becoming far more than a local phenomenon thanks in large part to the power of the press. After the Knickerbockers published their 1854 rules with a field diagram, practice schedules and locations in the nationally distributed *Sunday Mercury* in 1855, other papers like the *Syracuse Standard* followed suit. In addition to publishing rules, papers began covering games in the 1850's, including the Knickerbockers' 21-12 triumph over the Gothams in 1853. By 1856, New York boasted over a dozen base ball clubs and local presses like *Porter's Spirit of the Times* and the *New York Mercury* began using the terms "national game" and "national pastime", respectively.[22] Even so, press coverage of the early game had been intermittent, at least until the arrival of legendary sportswriter and oft anointed "Father of Baseball" Henry Chadwick, whose contributions from over 50 years covering the game include development of the official box score, invention of earned runs and batting average statistics, rules reformation including elimination of the bound catch out in fair territory, and combating rampant gambling and corruption. Note that Chadwick's contributions are further profiled in Chapter 2.

The Case for Doc Adams

Rather than bring clarity to base ball's true origin story and identity of its creators, the early 20th century disproval of the Doubleday Myth seemed to breed more controversy. In his *SABR* article "Doc Adams", Official Historian of Major League Baseball John Thorn notes of this predicament:

"The history of baseball is a lie from beginning to end, from its creation myth to its rosy models of commerce, community, and fair play. The conventional tale of the game's birth is substantially incorrect — not just the Doubleday fable, pointless to attack, but even the scarcely less legendary development of the Knickerbocker game, ostensibly sired by Alexander Cartwright."[23]

The Knickerbocker's Alexander Joy Cartwright, Jr. is widely regarded as a "Father of Modern Base Ball" with those very words inscribed on his 1938 Cooperstown plaque, which also credits him with setting the bases 90 feet apart, establishing nine inning games with nine players each, organizing the Knickerbocker Base Ball Club and spreading baseball to the Pacific Coast and Hawaii. The latter claims of his Knickerbocker involvement and western travels are not disputed. In fact, Cartwright was a founding member of the club and served in leadership roles from 1846-1849 before leaving New York to partake in the Gold Rush before permanently settling in Hawaii, where he served as a fire chief, government advisor and philanthropist. While with the Knickerbockers, Cartwright is credited with authoring the club's original 1845 rules, even though none of which pertain to those on his Cooperstown plaque, and officiating the aforementioned "first base ball game" between the Knickerbockers and New York Nine in 1846.

Rather, the controversy lies not with Cartwright himself, but the circumstances around his posthumous induction into the Hall and the enduring omission of his former teammate, Knickerbocker co-founder and president Daniel "Doc" Adams. To understand this controversy, one must harken back to the aftermath of the Doubleday Myth. From 1935 to 1938, prior to the Hall's 1939 opening and centennial commemoration of baseball's mythical first game and over four decades after Alexander Cartwright's passing, his grandson Bruce Cartwright Jr. teamed up with the Honolulu Chamber of Commerce to write a series of letters to the Hall decrying the planned Doubleday celebrations while campaigning for his grandfather's recognition as the true Father of Baseball.

In a likely act of contrition and truce, Hall Secretary Alexander Cleland finally wrote a letter to John Hamilton, Manager of the Honolulu Chamber of Congress, dated July 6, 1938 containing the following parts:

"The fact that the celebration will center in Cooperstown will be allowed in no way to minimize the importance of any of the great personalities connected with its history, much less that of Alexander J. Cartwright, Jr. It is universally conceded that Mr. Cartwright organized the Knickerbocker Club in 1845; that this was the world's first organized baseball club, and that Mr. Cartwright was the 'Father of Organized Baseball.'... Your letter has forced our hands to some extent but we feel that you have a right to advanced information and are willing to say, in strict confidence, that we expect to hold a special Cartwright Day as one of the principal features of the celebration, commemorating the organization of the Knickerbockers, and Mr. Cartwright's part in the development of the game. On this day it is planned to unveil a bronze plaque in memory of Mr. Cartwright in the Hall of Fame, and produce a pageant delineating his journey across the continent, organizing clubs as he went."[24]

Similar to the Doubleday Myth, journalists and historians called the Cartwright assertions into question, most notably due to the inherent bias of Cartwright's grandson and the Hall's reliance on his word and self-furnished evidence. Unlike the Doubleday Myth, which was debunked by journalists almost immediately, Cartwright's letters remained largely unquestioned for over half a century. In her 2009 book *Alexander Cartwright: The Life Behind the Baseball Legend,* Monica Nucciarone, through usage of handwriting experts, has dismissed the baseball references in Alexander Cartwright's 1849 Goldrush journal as forgeries entered by his grandson to supplement his campaign.

More importantly, Bruce Cartwright's assertions that his grandfather revolutionized gameplay by introducing landmark changes including 90-feet base paths, nine inning games and nine player limits, remained unchallenged by both the Hall and general public for nearly a century, likely due to a combination of Cartwright's association with the original 1845 rules and the lack of evidence to the contrary. That is until 2015, when a memorabilia collector (with the assistance of baseball historian John Thorn) uncovered drafts of an 1857 manuscript titled "Laws of Baseball", which was authored by Knickerbocker executives Doc Adams and William Grenelle and confirmed by Adams himself in an 1896 interview with the *Sporting News*. The document, considered by Thorn as baseball's "Magna Carta",[25] was ratified by 14 New York clubs at their first convention in 1857. More importantly, the document is far more comprehensive than the Knickerbockers' basic 17 rules from 1854 and introduces fundamental changes that remain in place today. Most notably, the distance between bases, which had been vaguely specified in the prior Knickerbocker rules as 42 paces, were fixed to 30 yards or 90 feet, and the pitcher's distance to 45 feet (later moved to 60.5 feet in the 1890's due to overhand pitching). Further, matches were no longer determined by the first club to reach 21 runs but rather the highest scorer after nine innings totaling 27 outs per side. Additionally, lineups were fixed at nine players, representing a stark contrast to precursors like wicket and town ball where sides would often exceed 30 players.

Despite being arguably the most significant document in baseball history, it was literally left in a drawer for over a century. In 1967, Grenelle's granddaughter stumbled upon the document, which had remained in the family since the 1857 convention. Unfortunately, the document went back in the drawer for another 32 years after she decided the heirloom was too valuable to donate. After resurfacing at a 1999 auction in New York, where a buyer paid $12,650, the document was again tucked away until a hunch in 2015 provoked the buyer to contact Sotheby's and consultant John Thorn regarding its value and authenticity. After the breakthrough study, the document was again auctioned in 2016, this time for $3.3 million, and loaned to the Library of Congress.

The document's rediscovery and related publications seemed to have come at the perfect time as Doc Adams joined ten others on the Hall's 2016 Pre-Integration Era Ballot. And while Adams led all candidates with ten votes, he fell two votes shy of the requisite 75%. To exacerbate matters, Adams did not return to the ballot the subsequent year, as is the case for modern players that accumulate at least 5% of votes, rather Adams' Pre-Integration Era category was reorganized into the larger Early Baseball Era Ballot which votes only once a decade, the first of which in 2022 did not even include Adams.

While the next eligible ballot, now under the pre-1980 Classical Baseball Era category, will not be cast until 2025, the advocacy for Doc Adams' enshrinement continues. Adams' greatest advocate was his great granddaughter Marjorie Adams, who led a decades-long, national campaign to broaden awareness of her great grandfather's contributions and continually lobbied for his enshrinement. And while she tragically succumbed to lung cancer in 2021, her memorable words have inspired others to carry on her cause:

"I will not let this rest. I will continue to work toward what I want to see: Doc's plaque at the Hall. This quest is as much for my father and grandfather as it is for Doc, and none of those gentlemen would approve if I gave up. Imagine how baseball might be now if Doc had given up in the early years of the Knickerbockers."[26]

Resuming Marjorie's tireless work, the growing list of outspoken advocates like MLB historian John Thorn, SABR's Peter Mancuso, AP writer and Hall voter Hal Bock and the Vintage Base Ball Association provides continued hope that Adams will one day assume his long overdue place in Cooperstown.

National Association of Base Ball Players

Contrary to some outspoken media outlets like New York's *Mercury* and *Porter's Spirit of the Times*, base ball was still a regional phenomenon in the mid-1850's. And while the 1857 convention was a major turning point that united New York's prominent clubs under Doc Adams and William Grenelle's "Laws of Base Ball", outsiders were more reluctant to embrace the "New York Game".

The following year, in a largely symbolic gesture, the convention reorganized, under the leadership of Doc Adams, as the National Association of Base Ball Players or "NABBP". Contrary to its title, the association was not for individual players but member clubs, all of which were based in the New York area. Nonetheless, the organization broadened the game's geographic appeal, added structure under a common rulebook and annual convention and supported future growth, as evidenced by the spike in clubs represented at the convention, which grew from around 20 in 1858 to roughly 60 in 1860, including one from Detroit.

And while the establishment of a national organization with abundant media coverage (thanks to writers like Henry Chadwick) broadened interest, expansion was ultimately fueled by various word-of-mouth and grassroots campaigns like Brooklyn transplant Merritt Griswold's successful persuasion of a reluctant St. Louis town ball club to try the New York game in 1860 (covered more in Chapter 9). Even Philadelphia's (and the nation's) most legendary town ball squad, the Olympic Club, had switched over to the new game by 1860.

Not only did the NABBP provide centralized rules, governance and annual conventions to solicit feedback and continually improve the game, but it also established a competitive league structure that recognized champions each year beginning (at least officially) with the Brooklyn Atlantics, who went 11-1 in 1859. Yet the rise in competition inevitably led to rampant professionalism, and the National Association of Base Ball Players gave way to the National Association of Professional Base Ball Players in 1871 and ultimately the enduring National League in 1876.

And while the National Association of Base Ball Players' rapid expansion and intensified competition effectively ended the gentlemanly Knickerbocker Era, Doc Adams reflected on the game's growth and his club's contributions with pride when he remarked:

"I resigned in 1862, but not before thousands were present to witness matches, and any number of outside players standing ready to take a hand on regular playing days. But we pioneers never expected the game to be universal as it had now become."[27]

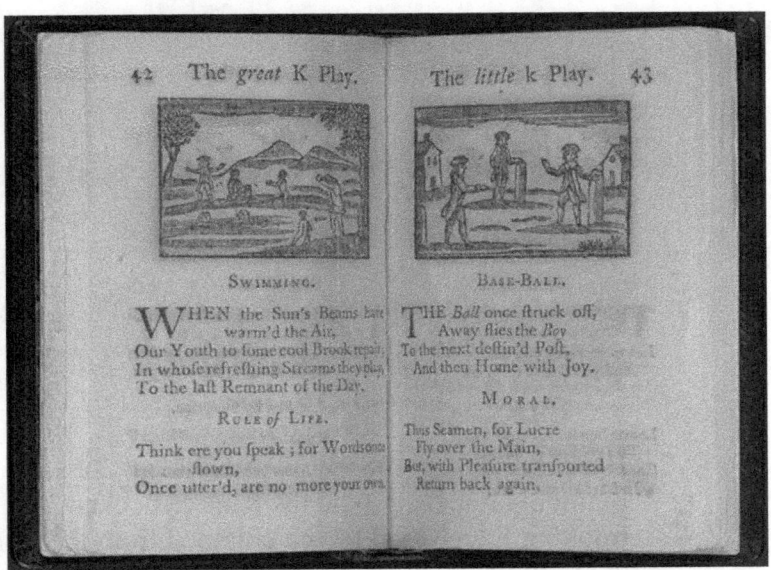

Refer to the righthand excerpt from Newbery's *A Pretty Little Pocket Book* (First American Edition. Worcester, Massachusetts: Isaiah Thomas, 1787). Note the three stations in the illustration. Photo credit to the Rare Book and Special Collections Division, Library of Congress (005.00.00). https://www.loc.gov/exhibitions/baseball-americana/about-this-exhibition/origins-and-early-days/baseballs-roots/a-little-pretty-pocket-book.

"Base Ball Team – 1858". The depicted clubs are commonly believed to be the Knickerbockers and Brooklyn Excelsiors. Image obtained from the Miriam and Ira D. Wallach Division of Art, Prints and Photographs: Photography Collection, The New York Public Library. https://digitalcollections.nypl.org/items/510d47da-667e-a3d9-e040-e00a18064a99.

2: Early Rules

"This invigorating exercise and manly pastime may now be justly termed the American Game of Ball, for though of English origin, it has been so modified and improved of late years in this country, as almost to deprive it of any of its original features beyond the mere groundwork of the game."[28]

- Hall of Fame sportswriter and "Father of Baseball" Henry Chadwick

Starting from Scratch

Humor me for a moment and compartmentalize everything you know about replay reviews, infield flies, double switches, three-batter minimums, designated hitters, strike zones, and fair and foul rules. In fact, go ahead and temporarily discard everything you know from Major League Baseball's nearly 200 pages of rules (you're welcome).

Attempting to reconcile today's Official Rules of Major League Baseball to the game's mid-19th century version is an exercise in extreme futility, not unlike when I tried to teach myself cricket while watching Australia host England in the 2013-2014 Ashes Cup with nothing but baseball knowledge to guide me. After wondering where the other two bases were and failing to accept that a batter (known as a batsman) can score by hitting the ball backwards, I gave up and decided to start fresh and learn the rules anew.

To that effect, this chapter will provide a high-level crash course on the key rules of the original game, dating back to the mid-19th century when rules were first codified. But like any game played far and wide, the variations in rules are vast. In fact, the Vintage Base Ball Association lists dozens of rulebooks prevalent in the 19th century including the New York Knickerbockers' first attempt in 1845 and the National Association of Base Ball Players' 1857 Rules and Regulations, the first to be widely adopted. While volumes could be devoted to the variations and commonalities amongst early base ball rulebooks and their followers, this chapter will focus on arguably the most prevalent version, which often remains the template for today's vintage clubs: *1860 Beadle's Dime Base-Ball Player.*

The Father of Baseball

Written by English-American sportswriter Henry Chadwick, who is commonly known as the "Father of Baseball" for cultivating widespread interest in the game through his half-century of media coverage, Beadle's Dime Base-Ball Player quickly became the standard for the game's rules given its widespread distribution out of New York and Chadwick's celebrity.

Born in Exeter, England in 1824, Chadwick grew up playing cricket and rounders before immigrating to New York in 1837. While an avid cricketer, Chadwick soon realized his talents lie in covering the game versus playing it. In 1843, Chadwick became a cricket reporter for Brooklyn's *Long Island Star*. While at the *New York Times* in 1856, Chadwick stumbled upon a base ball game between the local Gotham and Eagle clubs. Instantly enamored by this intriguing yet fledgling game, Chadwick wrote:

"Americans do not care to dawdle over a sleep-inspiring game, all through the heat of a June or July day. What they do they want to do in a hurry. In baseball all is lightning; every action is as swift as a seabird's flight."[29]

Seemingly overnight, Chadwick became the voice of the game, reaching national audiences through his coverage in the New York Clipper and Sunday Mercury. Credited with the first official box score, including usage of the iconic "K" to denote a strikeout, and formalized tracking of player statistics like batting average and earned runs, Chadwick emerged as base ball's definitive authority, which made him the logical choice to author the game's preeminent rulebook in 1860.

The Vintage Rules

Although published annually until 1881, the inaugural 1860 Beadle's Dime Base-Ball Player, remains the template for many of today's vintage clubs due its historical significance, comprehensiveness and clarity, which led the National Association of Base Ball Players to adopt it as their official rulebook on March 14, 1860.

As *1860 Beadle's Dime Base-Ball Player* is over 40 pages and covers more than just rules, including historical background, strategic recommendations and even club governance templates, the following sections are simply intended to summarize and provide commentary on some of the key rule holdovers and differences that continue to separate vintage leagues from their modern counterparts.

Similarities

While baseball's predominant rulebook has ballooned from roughly 40 pages in 1860 to nearly 200 today, many of the core aspects have remained. To begin, clubs fielded nine players including a pitcher, catcher, infielders and outfielders, and were opposed by a single striker (hitter). The bases, also stuffed canvas bags, except the circular iron home plate and pitcher's point, were arranged in a diamond formation. Matches were officiated by an umpire, although the 19th century version was often dressed in a long coat and top hat, and were played over nine innings, each with three outs per side. In the event of poor weather or darkness, a match required at least five complete innings.

In addition to similarities in club composition, game format, field layout and some of the equipment, various aspects of gameplay have largely remained consistent. Perhaps most notably, base stealing and sliding were critical aspects of the early game. And while matches were played on open fields without fences, fair and foul rules were enforced (albeit quite differently), base running outs were registered via tags or force-outs, and multiple base hits including home runs were common.

Yet while the modern game has retained many fundamental aspects of its predecessors, an unfamiliar observer at one of today's vintage games will instantly recognize just how drastically the game has changed.

The Field

While observing a vintage game today, one will notice (unless played in a modern ballpark for a special event) the general lack of common modern fixtures including outfield walls, dirt base paths, light fixtures, dugouts, bullpens, bleachers and backstops. Perhaps even more staggering, vintage fields were significantly larger. In his 1860 rulebook, Chadwick provides comprehensive specifications for a suitable field including dimensions, markings, measurements, and even grass and dirt quality, which he cautioned should be level and not gravelly around the bases to limit injuries. Chadwick goes on to specify the ideal field size as 600 feet long by 400 feet wide (240,000 square feet), but acknowledges that smaller fields can suffice. To put that in perspective, the MLB's largest park, Colorado's Coors Field, has under 120,000 square feet of fair territory, or less than half of Chadwick's prescribed dimensions.

Despite the larger field, Chadwick's infield dimensions include bases that are 90 feet apart arranged in the same diamond pattern as today. In lieu of a mound, as overhand pitching was still prohibited in 1860, pitchers stood at a white circular iron plate 45 feet from the similar home plate, as opposed to the 60 feet 6 inches distance today. And while foul poles were occasionally used, Chadwick recommended they be placed at least 100 feet on a line from first and third (at least 190 feet from home). Unlike modern foul poles that sit atop outfield walls, often well in excess of 300 feet from home, Chadwick's 1860 usage of "foul ball posts" were solely for helping the umpire judge fair and foul balls landing in the outfield, as fielders could retrieve balls, regardless of how far they were hit, to attempt to catch the runner, who could only achieve a home run by running the bases before the fielders could return the ball, thus preventing frequent and unsportsmanlike slow home run trots common in today's professional game.

Equipment

While new observers immediately notice the full-length wool uniforms as the main difference from modern baseball's double-knit, polyester, short-sleeved jerseys and vests adorned with numbers (introduced professionally in 1916) and names (1960), nearly every aspect of equipment, or lack thereof, has adapted in some form. Most notably, vintage ballists rarely use gloves as they were not widely adopted until the late 19th century. While a modern professional catcher without a glove is akin to a football player without a helmet, 1860's-style vintage pitchers deliver the ball via slow, underhand deliveries, which also explains why batting helmets and catcher protective equipment were not part of the 1860's game.

Like today, hitters swung round wooden bats subject to limits on width (2.5 inches across vs. today's 2.61 inches MLB limit). However, vintage bats were not restricted in length or weight, unlike MLB's 42-inch limit and two-pound minimum, respectively. While not mandated in his 1860 rulebook, Chadwick does recommend that:

"Bats are from thirty to forty inches in length, and from two to three pounds in weight being most desirable. The description of wood most in use is ash, but maple, white and pitch pine, and also hickory bats are in common use, weight for the size governing the selection."[30]

While ash remains the material of choice by today's major leaguers, the modern bat has a thinner handle, which can lead to both greater power and opportunity for breakage. In fact, today's vintage players may use the same thicker-handled bat for upwards of 10 or 15 seasons.[31] To put this into perspective, a bat broke every 2.74 games during the 2014 MLB season.[32] In addition to swinging a sturdier, thicker and heavier bat, vintage ballists are no strangers to calluses, as batting gloves were not part of the 19th century game.

Lastly, the 1860's version of the ball differs significantly from its modern successor. For starters, the vintage ball has crisscrossing stitches (known commonly as a "lemon peel" design due to its resemblance of a scored fruit) versus the modern pattern, where the seams run parallel at points for better grip. Further, the vintage ball, at roughly six ounces in weight and ten inches in circumference, is considerably larger than today's MLB ball, which weighs roughly five ounces with a nine-inch circumference. Essentially, the 1860's ball fell midway between a modern baseball and softball.[33] In addition to different stitching and sizes, vintage balls also have different compositions. Today, baseballs have a lighter-weight cork center (conducive to traveling farther) wrapped in wool and polyester or cotton yarn and covered in cowhide. Conversely, vintage balls have a wound-rubber center wrapped in yarn and covered with sheepskin or leather.

Pitching

The 1860's vintage game employs underhand, pendulum-style, slow pitching consistent with the original Knickerbocker Club in the 1840's. While overhand pitches were prohibited until the 1880's, Chadwick's 1860 rulebook did not restrict spin or velocity even acknowledging the emergence of faster pitching styles:

"In the choice of a bat, select a light one (not much under two pounds), as it can by wielded better, and in match games it is desirable that the player be able to strike quick enough to meet the rapid pitching that has recently come in vogue."

As Chadwick's 1860 rules predate the strike zone, which was not formalized until the 1880's, pitchers were simply obligated to "deliver the ball as near as possible over home base, and for the striker, and sufficiently high to prevent its bounding before it passes the base".

The notion of obligating the pitcher to deliver a hittable pitch seems counterintuitive in today's professional game. While strike zones and walks remain as a deterrent to erratic pitching and to help level the playing field for the statistically disadvantaged batter, they hardly promote hittable pitching as evidenced by the 2022 MLB league batting average of .243, which tied for fifth-lowest in history. Oftentimes, modern pitchers embrace the "chase pitch", a ball intentionally thrown out of the strike zone in hopes the hitter takes the bait, or even the occasional "brushback", a pitch thrown near the batter as a means of intimidation or to discourage crowding the plate. And while modern rules and conditions often favor the pitcher, Chadwick's 1860 rules seemed to favor the hitter and fielders by encouraging batted balls in play, which can both accelerate pace and keep fans and players engaged.

Given the underhand, slow pitch style, 1860's-style pitchers stand 45 feet from the plate on flat ground. To accommodate faster, overhand-throwing professionals, the pitching mound was introduced and moved back to 60' 6" from home plate in 1893.

Chadwick's 1860 rules also prohibit the pitcher from "jerking" (touching the body during the forward motion of the arm), stepping over the line or failing to finish an initiated delivery. The latter rule was likely intended to protect base runners, who were permitted to lead off or steal (although today's vintage leagues have varying dispositions on stealing and sliding given their safety risks and ungentlemanly connotation). Any of the aforementioned pitcher offenses could be declared balks, resulting in the runners advancing a base as remains the case today.

While leadoffs, stolen bases and pickoff plays were permitted in early base ball, they were less prevalent, unlike today's all too common "game within the game" between the pitcher and base runner that can result in dozens of fruitless and time-consuming pickoff plays that extend the game and agitate fans.

Despite the varying styles and rules that differentiate the vintage and modern professional pitcher, Chadwick extolls the virtues of a good pitcher that continue to resonate in today's game:

"He should be a good player at all points, but it is especially requisite that he should be an excellent fielder and a swift and accurate thrower".

Hitting

While more akin to their modern counterparts than pitchers, 1860's batters, or "strikers" as they were commonly known, played a noticeably different game. Although disadvantaged by the aforementioned equipment differences, which included heavier balls and bats, and a lack of helmets and gloves, strikers were aided by the underhand pitching and balk rules that encouraged the delivery of hittable balls. Additionally, the lack of a formal strike zone allowed strikers some discretion on pitch selection, although they could (at the umpire's judgment) receive strikes by refusing to swing at good balls. In fact, Chadwick outlines his expectations for proper striker etiquette in in *1860 Beadle's Dime Base-Ball Player*:

"Batsman strikes at the first good ball pitched to him, and this is decidedly the fairest and best method to be adopted, as it is the most likely to lead to a successful result, and keeps the game lively and interesting. It is exceedingly annoying to the spectators, and creates a bad impression of the merits of the game on those not familiar with it, to see good balls repeatedly sent to the Batsman without being hit, or the ball passed to and from the pitcher and catcher, while the Batsman stands still, awaiting the movements of the player on the first base. No good players resort to this style

of play, except in very rare instances, and it would therefore be desirable to avoid it as much as possible."

While intended as a recommendation, as the punishment for taking good pitches (a strike call made at the discretion of the umpire) was light and selectively enforced, Chadwick's support of first-pitch hitting in the interest of competitive advantage and spectator engagement runs contrary to the modern professional "a walk is as good as a hit" mentality that stresses on-base percentages and pitch counts thanks in part to continued advancement and adoption of data analytics. However, as Chadwick's work predates modern analytics by over a century, his comments on maintaining the pace of play to retain fan interest seem especially prescient. In fact, the inverse correlation between modern professional baseball game duration and viewership is irrefutable. For example, World Series viewership peaked at 44.2 million in 1978, where the average game that season lasted roughly 2 hours and 30 minutes, before continually declining to a record low of 9.9 million viewers in 2020, where the average game lasted nearly 40 minutes longer.

Unlike today's professional game, where lineups average nearly nine strikeouts per game, strikeouts in the vintage game were and continue to be rare, requiring three swinging strikes with the last caught by the catcher (in the air or off a single bounce) or an umpire judgment for refusal to swing at hittable pitches. Similar to today's game, a swinging third strike not handled by the catcher is a live ball requiring a throw to first to retire the runner (with some exceptions in the modern rules).

And while the pitching limitations helped minimize strikeouts, other vintage rules were less advantageous, most notably the following from Chadwick's *1860 Beadle's Dime Base-Ball Player:*

"SEC. 11. The striker is out if a foul ball is caught, either before touching the ground, or upon the first bound."
"SEC. 13. Or, if a fair ball is struck, and the ball is caught either without having touched the ground, or upon the first bound."

The single-bounce or bound catch rule, while logical and prudent given the lack of fielding gloves, presents a significant challenge for the striker, who is more likely to reach base via grounders or line drives through the outfield gaps. Yet, as savvy competitors do in all sports, vintage strikers, both then and now, have adapted to the rules through updated strategies and new techniques, including the popular "daisy cutter", a sharply hit grounder that Chadwick himself admits is "very difficult to field, and consequently, shows good batting."[34]

Alongside the bound catch rule, the vintage fair-foul rules offer the most dramatic contrast from the modern game, which Chadwick articulates in Section 8:

"If the ball, from a stroke of the bat, is caught behind the range of home and the first base, or home and the third base, without having touched the ground, or first touches the ground behind those bases, it shall be termed foul, and must be so declared by the umpire, unasked. If the ball first touches the ground, or is caught without having touched the ground, either upon, or in front of the range of those bases, it shall be considered fair."

To understand how advantageous this rule is for the hitter, one can simply imagine the ramifications if all of MLB's failed bunt attempts, where balls either roll in and out of fair territory prior to passing first or third or even balls chopped into home plate, were called fair. In addition to a proliferation of infield singles and skyrocketing batting averages, such fair-foul rules would lead to high-risk, encroaching defensive alignments seen only in the likes of cricket.

While the 1860 fair-foul rules are often observed in today's vintage leagues due to their historical accuracy, and many opportunistic strikers have perfected chop swings and spinners that are nearly impossible to defend, the rules were short-lived as they were amended in 1877 to require grounders to initially hit and stay in fair territory until passing first and third base. The downfall of the original fair-foul rules is likely due to a combination of common exploiters, like four-time .400+ hitter and three-time batting champion "The Great and Only" Ross Barnes of the Boston Red Stockings, fan backlash and officiating challenges. As baseball historian Peter Morris noted "spectators perceived the play to be unsporting and often became openly hostile". He added that "the impetus to abolish the fair-foul was the fact that it was very difficult for umpires to determine whether a ball was hit into the ground first hit fair or foul".[35]

Base Running

Like today, Chadwick's 1860 rulebook places minimal restrictions on the running game. To begin, runners were allowed to steal bases, advance on errors and passed balls, and even slide, most commonly while leading with the hands. Simply put, runners were only limited from advancing on foul balls or fly outs. Runners were required to stay within three feet of the base paths and were protected from infielder attempts to obstruct their lanes. Additionally, runners were not called out after being struck by a batted or thrown ball unless done intentionally to disrupt the play. Also, like today, runners could not register an ace (run) after reaching home if the striker on the play is called for the final out, regardless of whether the other runner arrived home first.

In addition to the lack of base coaches, which debuted in the 1880's, one of the key baserunning rule differences between the vintage and modern games is the first base overrun, which Chadwick alludes to in the following:

"SEC. 15. Any player running the bases is out, if at any time he is touched by the ball while in play in the hands of an adversary, without some part of his person being on a base."

While the literal interpretation of the above would support that a runner who surpasses first after a sprint can be tagged out before returning to the base, the topic remains debated amongst today's vintage clubs and is often deferred to the umpire's judgment or predetermined ground rules amongst clubs.

Another critical difference is the concept of tagging up after flyouts, which Chadwick summarizes as follows:

"SEC. 16. No ace nor base can be made upon a foul ball, nor when a fair ball has been caught without having touched the ground; and the ball shall, in the former instance, be considered dead, and not in play until it shall first have been settled in the hands of the pitcher; in either case the players running bases shall return to them, and may be put out in so returning in the same manner as the striker when running to the first base."

Foul balls, regardless of whether they are caught on a fly, bounce or not at all, cannot result in the runner tagging up and advancing. Further, the runner is obligated to return to their original base or risk being called out if the ball beats them back, although the pitcher must have handled the ball during the play. On the other hand, fair balls that are caught on the fly require the runner to tag up before advancing. Conversely, a ball caught on the bounce, while considered an out for the striker, does not require the runners to tag up. While confusing and a leading cause of baserunning errors among vintage novices, the added complexities of the 1860's rules further emphasize strategy, situational awareness and vigilance that has been overshadowed by the modern game's emphasis on raw speed.

Despite the relative lack of restrictions on the running game, present day vintage clubs, like their 1860's counterparts, have adopted varying interpretations. For starters, sliding is often restricted in today's vintage leagues due to safety and injury concerns. Additionally, base stealing, excluding advancing on errors or passed balls, is often debated among vintage clubs given its deceptive nature and ungentlemanly connotations.

Defense

Beyond the bound catch and lack of gloves, vintage base ball defense varies significantly from the modern game both in rules and strategy. And while the majority of these differences were covered in the prior sections, one of the most notable differences is Chadwick's "no ringers" rule outlined in Section 27:

In playing all matches, nine players from each club shall constitute a full field, and they must have been regular members of the club which they represent, and of no other club, for thirty days prior to the match. No change or substitution shall be made after the game has been commenced, unless for reason of illness or injury. Position of players and choice of innings shall be determined by captains previously appointed for that purpose by the respective clubs.

While the aforementioned rule was likely Chadwick's attempt to promote fair play and curb widespread abuse during his time, the rule is largely omitted from today's vintage leagues due its impracticality and exclusivity, which could hinder the growth and momentum of the ongoing vintage base ball revival. In fact, many of today's vintage clubs not only allow in-game substitutions, but also courtesy runners, who can replace a player on the bases without either player losing eligibility.

Another key vintage rule difference is the lack of an infield fly rule, which was not adopted until 1895, and often became a strategic decision for infielders, who could intentionally drop a ball and make a double play by either catching it on a single bounce and tagging the lead runner or even letting it drop twice and quickly turning two via force-out.

Prohibition of Gambling and Monetary Compensation

Like today, Chadwick's 1860 rules (Section 30) prohibit anyone "engaged in a match, either as umpire, scorer or player, (from being) either directly or indirectly interested in any bet upon the game." While noble and in the best interest of the game, Chadwick's denunciation of gambling was and remains somewhat naïve given the ever-present specter of gambling scandals that have plagued the game throughout its history including the 1877 Louisville Grays and 1919 Black Sox scandals (both covered in Chapter 4), where a combined dozen players received lifetime bans based on match-fixing allegations, and even the ongoing clemency debates over Pete Rose's transgressions while managing the Reds in the 1980's.

Chadwick's denunciation of money in the game is well-documented. In addition to Section 30's gambling prohibition, Section 36 states:

"No person who shall be in arrears to any other club, or who shall at any time receive compensation for his services as a player, shall be competent to play in any match."

Similar to his aforementioned fair-foul and no ringers rules, Chadwick's restrictions against paying players were short-lived due to their impracticality and rampant noncompliance. Most notably, the first openly all-professional team, the Cincinnati Red Stockings, debuted in 1869 (covered in Chapter 3), and the rest is history.

Disciplinary Measures

The final pages of *1860 Beadle's Dime Base-Ball Player* offer a constitution template to govern new clubs. The boilerplate standardizes virtually every aspect of the club including governance model, voting rules, meeting cadences, membership fees, and even fines. And while the template leaves it up to the clubs to specify such amounts, fines are to be levied in "cents" and, as Chadwick advises, "should be light, being thereby easier of collection, and fully as effective as if of great amount."

As an aside, and with all due respect to the "Father of Baseball", Chadwick's assertion that a fine's impact is independent of its amount would seemingly ring hollow in today's "hit them in the pocket, where it hurts" mindset. After all, why else were the Houston Astros fined an unprecedented $5 million for their 2017 sign-stealing scandal, which was somewhat offset by the $2 million they received from the St. Louis Cardinals after a hacking scandal involving former team executive Christopher Correa? (Both covered in Chapter 5).

While the extent of fines to levy is ambiguous, Chadwick clearly outlines the triggering events in Article IV:

"SEC. 1. Any member who shall use profane language, either at a meeting of the club, or during field exercise, shall be fined _____cents.
SEC. 2. Any member disputing the decision of the Umpire during field exercise, shall be fined_____cents.
SEC. 3. Any member refusing obedience to the Captain during field exercise, and while he has lawful authority, shall pay a fine of _____cents.
SEC. 4. Any member who shall absent himself from a business meeting without a sufficient excuse, shall be fined_____cents.
SEC. 5. Any member, either at a meeting for business, or field exercise, not coming to order when called upon to do so by the President or Captain, shall be fined _____cents.
SEC. 6. Any member refusing to pay the fines and dues imposed by these By-Laws, or who shall absent himself from field exercise for the space of three months, may be suspended or expelled by a vote of_____of the members present at a regular meeting.
SEC. 7. Any member under suspension, is subject to dues and cannot either vote or participate in field exercise."[36]

To say that modern professional baseball has drifted from these principles over the years is an understatement akin to saying that Ty Cobb, with over 4,000 hits and a career .366 average, was a pretty good hitter. Further, the immateriality of the fines coupled with the pervasiveness of these infractions today evokes idioms beginning with "If I had a nickel for every time…" While some of the aforementioned infractions remain discouraged in modern professional baseball, like Section 4's unexcused absence policy or Sections 6 and 7's prohibition of activities until fines are paid and/or suspensions served, others have reversed course entirely.

To begin, Section 1's prohibition of foul language not only during games but also team meetings seems unenforceable to say the least in today's era of closed-door meetings and clubhouse cell phone bans. With the rampant use of profanity in today's game, as evidenced by the countless infractions caught on live broadcasts through boom mics and mic'd up segments with players (see White Sox Closer Liam Hendriks at the 2021 All-Star Game), and not to ignore the unsavory language permeating in clubhouses (see Cardinals rookie Randy Arozarena's leaked cell phone recording of manager Mike Shildt's expletive-laced congratulatory speech after their 2019 NLDS triumph in Atlanta), the likelihood of such restrictions passing a collective bargaining agreement is infinitesimal.

Further, Section 2's automatic fines for contesting umpire decisions run contrary to today's replay review rules, which actually encourage teams to challenge at least one ruling per game and rewards them with another if successful. While replay reviews have rectified copious errors in umpire judgment and arguably would have prevented notable misses, like Tigers pitcher Armando Galarraga's near-perfect game at Comerica Park in 2010, they've slowed the game down considerably. In fact, according to Baseball Reference, since manager replay challenges were implemented in 2014, the average length of a nine-inning major league game has exceeded three hours each year, except 2015's 2:56 mark. To put things in perspective, MLB had never averaged more than three hours per nine in their history prior to 2014. And while the pace of the game has gradually slowed, especially since 1942's lightning season (1:45 per nine), and replay reviews are just one of many contributing factors (e.g., television timeouts, increased substitutions and mound visits, pickoff plays, increasing foul ball and pitch take rates, etc.), the correlation between replay reviews and game duration is undeniable. In fact, 2021's record high of three hours and ten minutes per nine represents over a 10% increase from the last full decade without manger-initiated replay reviews (2000's).

Lastly, Section 3 and 5's empowerment of team captains and punitive stance against dissension seem inconceivable in today's professional game, where increasing media coverage and visibility inside the dugouts and clubhouses have underscored the abundance of power struggle and conflict within clubs. In fact, a 2020 *Stadium Reviews* piece titled "Best MLB Teammate Fights" cites over 20 high-profile intrasquad incidents, mostly in the past two decades, ranging from dugout arguments that escalated to shoving matches to full combat resulting in season-ending injuries, as we saw in 2019 with Pirates teammates Kyle Crick and Felipe Vazquez. The cause of the argument? Crick's refusal to turn off the music at his locker. While both players were fined, they were not levied at Chadwick's recommended rates ($2,500 for Crick, $10,000 for Vazquez).[37]

Restoring Order

While presentists may dismiss Chadwick's 1860 rulebook, especially the etiquette and decency rules, as archaic, unenforceable and even unsustainable as evidence by the modern game's continued adaptation, idealists, like those behind the ongoing vintage base ball revival, have championed them as a means to restore the original game's order and emphasis on sportsmanship, camaraderie and recreation. And while the nature and extent of contrast between the modern and vintage games is clear, the root causes are far more complex, several of which are explored in the following chapters.

Rule Changes in the 1800's

While the *1860 Beadle's Dime Base-Ball Player* rules were widely adopted at the time and remain the standard for many of today's vintage clubs, the frequent rule changes and the diversity of eras portrayed by vintage clubs can present challenges for ballists, umpires and spectators alike. The following table excerpt, re-printed with permission from *Baseball Almanac,*[38] provides a chronological summary of key rule changes throughout the 19th century.

Year	Changes Made to Official Knickerbocker Rules[1]
1857	The game used to end after the inning in which a team reached 21 runs.
	Now it is a 9-inning contest and the higher scoring team wins.
	No base can be made on a foul ball.
1858	Called strikes are introduced.
	A batter is out on a batted ball, fair or foul, if caught on the fly or after one bounce.
1862	Pitcher's box introduced 12 feet by 3 feet.
1863	Bat size is regulated.
	Called balls and bases on balls introduced
	Pitcher's box is now 12 feet by 4 feet.
	is no longer allowed to take a step during his delivery and he with both feet on the ground at the same time.
	Home base and pitcher's box must be marked.
1862	Each base runner must touch each base in making the circuit.
1864	Out on a fair bound is removed and the "fly catch" of fair balls is adopted.
1866	Pitcher's box narrowed to six feet wide.
1867	Pitcher is now permitted to move around inside their box.
1868	Bat length limited to 42 inches.
	Pitcher allowed to lift feet when delivering the ball.
	Pitcher's box is now made into a 6-foot square.
1870	The batter-runner may overrun first base.
1871	The batter is officially given the privilege of calling for a low or high pitch (in practice since 1864).
1872	Ball size and weight are made smaller, to dimensions currently in use today.
1873	Batter's box introduced.
	Any player, umpire, or scorer who gambles on a game he takes part in shall be expelled from his club and the National Association.
1877	Canvas bases 15 inches square were introduced.
	Home plate was placed in the angle formed by the intersection of the first and third base lines.

[1] In the *Baseball Almanac* version, the table header changes from "Changes made to Official Knickerbocker Rules" to "Changes Made to Official National League Rules" before the row beginning with 1877.

Year	Changes Made to Official Knickerbocker Rules[1]
	Player reserve clause was written into the contracts for the first time.
	The base runner was out if hit by a batted ball.
	The hitter was exempted from a time at bat if he walked.
1878	The number of "called balls" became 9 and all balls were either strikes, balls or fouls.
1879	Player reserve clause was for the first time put into a contract.
	The pitcher had to face a batsman before pitching to him.
	Base on balls was reduced to 7 "called balls."
	Batter no longer got a fourth strike.
1880	Front of pitcher's box moved to 50 feet from the center of home plate.
	The catcher had to catch the pitch on the fly in order to register an out on a third strike.
	Pitchers now allowed to throw sidearm.
1882	The "foul bound catch" was abolished and the pitcher could deliver a ball from above his waist.
1883	Championships were to be decided on a percentage basis.
	Six "called balls" became a base on balls.
1884	All restrictions on the delivery of a pitcher were removed.
	A granulated substance may be applied up to 18" from the bottom of the bat.
	Chest protectors worn by catchers and umpires came into use.
1885	Home base could be made of marble or whitened rubber.
	One portion of the bat could be flat (one side).
	The pitcher's box was changed to 4 feet by 7 feet.
1886	Stolen bases became an official statistic.
	The pitcher's box was reduced to 4 feet by 5 1/2 feet.
	Calling for high and low pitches was abolished.
	Choice of innings given to home team captain.
	Five balls became a base on balls.
1887	Four "called strikes" were adopted for this season only.
	Bases on balls were recorded as hits for this season only.
	The batter was awarded first base when hit by a pitch.
	Home plate was to be made of rubber only - dropping the marble type and was to be 12 inches square.

Year	Changes Made to Official Knickerbocker Rules[1]
	Pitcher must keep back foot on the rear line of the pitcher's box (55.5 feet from middle of home plate).
	Strike zone established between shoulders and knees.
	Coaches were recognized by the rules for the first time ever.
1888	A batsman was credited with a base hit when a runner was hit by his batted ball.
	Batter awarded a hit when a runner is out for being hit by batted ball.
	The base on balls exemption from a time at bat was restored.
	A sacrifice hit was statistically recognized.
1889	Four balls became a base on balls.
	One predesignated substitute may be used at the end of any complete inning.
1890	Two substitutes may be used and may enter at any time.
1891	Substitutions were permitted at any point in the game.
	Large padded mitts were allowed for catchers.
	The pitching box was eliminated and a rubber slab 12 inches by 4 inches was substituted.
1893	The pitcher was required to place his rear foot against the slab.
	The slab was moved from 50 feet to 60 feet 6 inches from rear of home plate.
1893	The rule allowing a flat side to a bat was rescinded.
	The requirement that the bat be round and wholly of hard wood was substituted.
	Foul bunts were classified as strikes.
1894	Sacrifice hits limited to bunts and not counted as at bats.
	The rule exempting a batter from a time at bat on a sacrifice was instituted.
	A held foul tip was classified as a strike.
	Bats were permitted to be 2 3/4 inches in diameter and not to exceed 42 inches.
1895	Infield-fly rule was adopted.
	Pitching slab was enlarged to 24 inches by 6 inches.
	Size of gloves limited except for catchers and first basemen.
1899	Batter awarded first on catcher's interference.
1900	Plate changed from square to five-sided figure.

View from the circular home plate at Columbus' Muffin Meadow, home of the Ohio Village Muffins and Diamonds vintage base ball clubs, during the 2022 Ohio Cup on Labor Day Weekend. Photo courtesy of Don Andersen of the Ohio Village Muffins.

Panoramic view of picturesque Silver Park in Upstate New York's Genesee Country Village and Museum taken in 2021. Photo courtesy of the Akron Black Stockings.

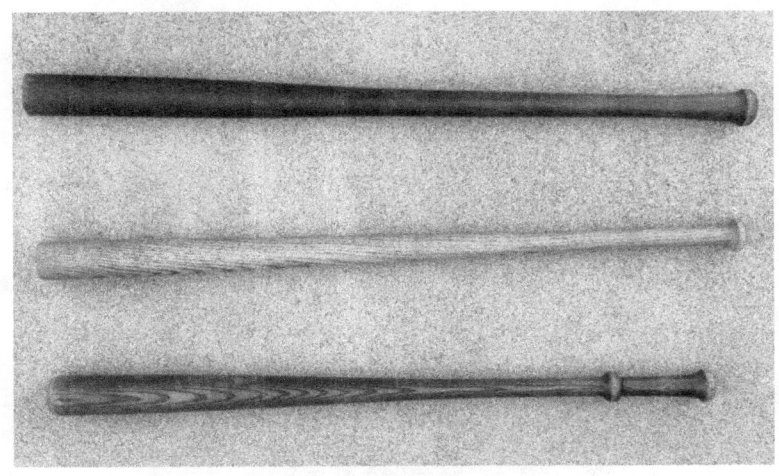

Ash replica bats used by vintage ballist Don "Big Bat" Andersen. The bats represent various eras including the top bat (c. 1860) and the bottom split-grip "Lajoie" bat (c. 1900). Photo courtesy of Don Andersen.

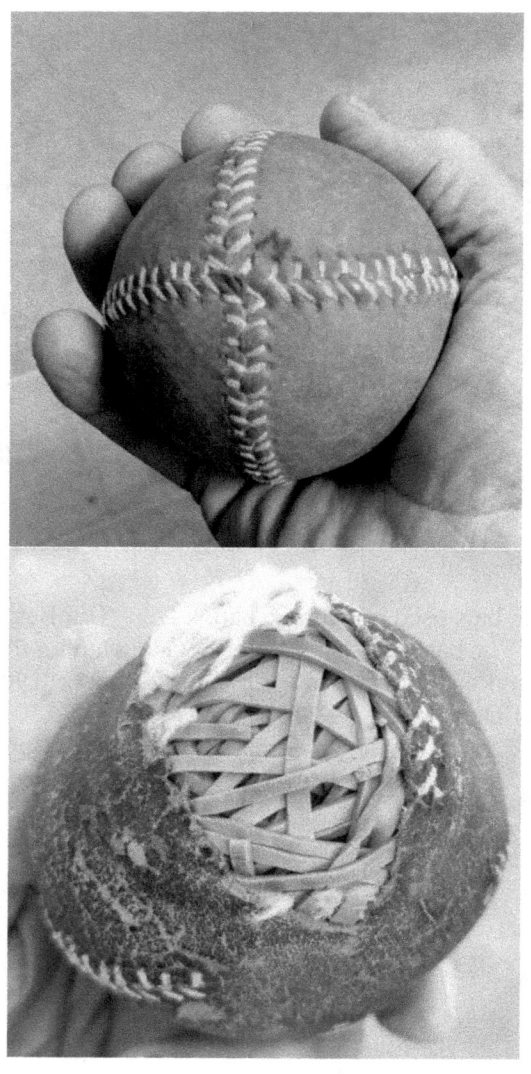

Replica balls modeled after the 1858 New York style. Note the perpendicular "lemon peel" stitching and the wound-rubber core. Photos courtesy of Don Andersen.

3: Gaining Momentum

Modern baseball had been born in the brain of an American soldier. It received its baptism in the bloody days of our Nation's direst danger. It had its early evolution when soldiers, North and South, were striving to forget their foes by cultivating, through this grand game, fraternal friendship with comrades in arms.[39]
 - Hall of Fame executive, pitching great and sporting goods magnate Albert Goodwill Spalding.

Surviving the War (1861-1865)
While virtually every aspect of American life was profoundly disrupted by the Civil War, the upstart game of base ball managed to endure. Regardless of whether the relatively new game's survival through those perilous years was attributable to its newfound popularity and prominence as a national game or its simplicity and portability that allowed civilians and soldiers on both sides a much-needed release from the daily terrors of war, the game not only managed to survive but also grow during that time, thanks largely to its widespread dissemination and popularity within both armies.

Prior to the April 12, 1861 battle in South Carolina's Charleston Harbor that effectively began the Civil War, the once fledgling "New York Game" was now flourishing, thanks to the Knickerbocker Base Ball Club's publication of standardized rules in 1845 and 1854, expansive and innovative media coverage aided by Henry Chadwick's statistics-driven accounts, and the growth of the game's flagship league the National Association of Base Ball Players. At just its third official convention, held in New York in March 1860, the membership had grown from the original 16 clubs (all from the New York area) to approximately 60 including two from south of the Mason-Dixon Line (Baltimore and Washington). Beyond the member clubs, the game's reach had expanded west of the Mississippi after St. Louis' Morning Stars defeated the cross-town Cyclone Club 49-24 on July 9, 1860.

Despite the game's impressive momentum heading into 1861, it would inevitably stall as the country's focus shifted to wartime efforts. For starters, roughly three million or ten percent of the country's population was deployed to fight, including 2.1

million for the Union and 900,000 for the Confederacy (not counting the millions of others that worked jobs supporting wartime industries), with roughly 750,000 deaths or 2.5% of the country's population.[40] To add to the tragedy, various clubs in divided states like St. Louis' Cyclone Base Ball Club (covered in Chapter 9) would see former teammates on opposite ends of the battlefield.

While the game's governing entity, the National Association of Base Ball Players, did not cease operations or league play, membership and participation declined precipitously. In fact, the March 1860 convention featured approximately 60 clubs, before dropping to 34 in December 1861, all of which were from New York and New Jersey.[41] Furthermore, after nearly doubling the number of league games played from 597 in 1859 to 1024 in 1860, the number dropped to 428 in 1861 and bottomed out at 257 the following year before rebounding to 1,260 games in 1865 (as a full season began after Lee's surrender in April).[42]

The league's championship had also become diluted. Despite adding a final series format in 1860, where the prior season's champion would have to be defeated in a three-game series by a challenger (commonly the team with the best record but also required acceptance from the reigning champion) to relinquish the title, the format was rife with controversy as many early member clubs did not play league games and those that did played varying numbers. For instance, in the abbreviated 1862 campaign, the Eckford Club of Brooklyn played a nearly full slate of 13 games (as top clubs played roughly 20 games in seasons immediately prior to and after the war before totals regularly exceeded 50 by the end of the decade) before challenging the reigning champion Brooklyn Atlantics, who had played only a couple of games due to wartime roster attrition. Despite their depleted roster and lack of practice, the Atlantics proved why they were the three-time defending champions. In a series billed as the "Silver Ball Match" by its creator and NABBP Rules Committee Chairman Henry Chadwick, the Eckfords won a contested opener 20-14 on Friday, July 11th in front of over 3,000 at Brooklyn's Union Skating and Base Ball Grounds, where attendance proceeds were donated to the US Sanitary Commission benefiting sick and wounded soldiers. The following Friday, the Atlantics retaliated with a 39-5 blowout in front of roughly 8,000. The series then took a two-month hiatus while Eckford's ace Joe Sprague returned from a tour with the Union Army. Naturally, the anticipation and media coverage for the decisive rubber match mounted as a record crowd of approximately 10,000 returned to the Union Grounds for the September 18th finale. And while the Atlantics jumped out to a 2-0 lead after the top half of the second, the Eckfords responded with five in the bottom half and cruised to an 8-3 triumph.[43]

And while prominent clubs like the Eckfords and Atlantics and the celebrated Silver Ball matches helped the National Association of Base Ball Players remain relevant during the war, base ball's future ultimately hinged on the Union and Confederate armies. Even though many of the fighting men and (sadly) boys were at least familiar with base ball or its precursors, the game assumed a far more prominent role in their daily lives during and after the conflict. Understandably, the game was appealing to both officers and infantrymen alike. For starters, the game's simple rules, adaptability and minimal equipment made it portable and widely accessible. Further, the early game's recreational and childish nature provided soldiers with essential distractions and relief from the terrors of war, the rigor and monotony of camp and, in some cases like Salisbury, NC and Sandusky, OH, the hardships of being a prisoner of war.

From an officer's perspective, the game promoted fitness, teamwork, strategy and camaraderie and boosted morale across the ranks. In fact, some officers played alongside their direct reports, temporarily abandoning the chain of command in a game that was egalitarian by nature. This sentiment was captured in various soldier's journals like Private Alpheris B. Parker of the 10th Massachusetts, who wrote:

"The parade ground has been a busy place for a week or so past, ball-playing having become a mania in camp. Officers and men forget, for a time, the differences in rank and indulge in the invigorating sport with a schoolboy's ardor."[44]

While the majority of games among soldiers were largely recreational and tracked only in isolated diaries, several high-profile, publicized games were played on both sides, most notably the 1862 Christmas Day match in Union-occupied Hilton Head Island, South Carolina between New York's 165th Volunteer

Infantry and a picked nine from New York's 47th and 48th Infantries. The 165th club was known as the "Second Duryee's (or "Duryea's") Zouaves", a combination of the French military term for Berber soldiers recruited from Algeria (Zouaves) and Abram Duryeé, the commander of New York's 5th Infantry, the original Zouave regiment. While neither "Zouave" regiment was of Berber heritage, their distinctive uniforms featured red balloon pants, ornate cloth jackets and tasseled fez hats. While little is known of the contest, including its score, due to the lack of detailed written accounts, prevailing accounts cite as many as 40,000 civilians, Union soldiers and Confederate prisoners attended the contest.[45]

Meanwhile, the Confederate Army played the game for the same reasons, including the 24th Alabama Regiment, who scrimmaged in the days leading up to Sherman's advance. And as baseball was played so widely and frequently throughout the war, certain contests were even interrupted by combat, including the 1863 surprise attack of the 176th New York Infantry's scrimmage in Alexandria, Texas, which Union Sergeant George H. Putnam described:

"Suddenly there came a scattering of fire of which the three outfielders caught the brunt; the center field was hit and was captured, the left and right field managed to get back into our lines. The attack...was repelled without serious difficulty, but we had lost not only our center field, but...the only baseball in Alexandria, Texas."[46]

Fortunately, 1865 ushered in the first signs of truce beginning with Lincoln's Hampton Roads Peace Conference with Confederate Vice President Alexander Stephens. While the January 29th truce was brief, as talks ended unresolved on February 3rd, and limited to isolated conflicts like the ongoing siege of Petersburg, Virginia, soldiers briefly made peace with some even finding common bonds with their adversaries. In a testament to the game's healing power, a February 6, 1865 Cincinnati Enquirer article cites the following soldier's letter from the Union Army of the Potomac:

"For five hours after the truce was declared along our lines in front of the 9th Corps, thousands of our boys threw down their

arms and engaged in ball playing with the rebel soldiers. The utmost good feeling prevailed."

And while the initial truce was short-lived, it provided invaluable hope for a forthcoming resolution, which came shortly thereafter on April 9, 1865. One week after the fall of the Confederate capital in Richmond, Robert E. Lee surrendered to Ulysses S. Grant in Appomattox Court House, Virginia, bringing the bloodiest period in American history to a merciful close. In the spirit of peace, healing and new beginnings, some members of Grant's Army of the Potomac and Lee's Army of Northern Virginia played base ball around the proceedings.[47]

Postwar Fervor (1865-1870)
While Lee's April 1865 surrender began an era of peace (although intermittent skirmishes continued until President Johnson formally declared the conflict over in August 1866)[48] and new beginnings, the internal struggle remained in the more than two million returning soldiers. In addition to struggling with numerous physical injuries and post-traumatic stress disorder, which would not be formally diagnosed and treated until the 20th century, many civil war veterans struggled to find and retain employment and transition to the relatively monotonous lifestyle of a peacetime civilian. Hall of Fame executive, pitching great, sporting goods magnate and baseball historian Albert Spalding summarized this sentiment in his 1911 baseball history book *America's National Game:*

"No human mind may measure the blessings conferred by the game of Base Ball on the soldiers of our Civil War... It calmed the restless spirits of men who, after four years of bitter strife, found themselves at once in a monotonous era, with nothing at all to do."

Naturally, many veterans filled this void through base ball as they did during the war. Having either learned the game during their service or fondly remembering it for its therapeutic qualities, base ball had evolved from inconsequential to an essential part of many soldiers' lives. As a microcosm of the game's postwar boom, the National Association of Base Ball Players quickly emerged from its wartime struggles at the 1866

Winter Convention. Down from their prewar numbers around 60 clubs, the Association's convention attendance had dwindled to around 30 (almost entirely in New York) by the end of the war. Yet after an abundance of invitations (that included a pre-meeting social hour) were sent to clubs across the country, the 1866 Convention (held in December 1865) welcomed more than 60 new clubs from ten different states, spanning as far west as Kansas and south as Tennessee. With a membership approaching 100 clubs, little doubt remained that the once "New York Game" was now the national game, or at least in the northern states.

By 1867, membership doubled to over 200 clubs across nearly 20 states including Oregon (Portland's Pioneer Base Ball Club). Despite the surge in member clubs, only three were from former seceding states (Tennessee and Virginia). Furthermore, Virginia's lone member was Richmond's Union Club, comprised largely of transplanted northerners unabashed in their political views. In either an ill-conceived attempt to gain traction with southern clubs or a blatant exposure of their lingering grudges, the Union Club publicly challenged the neighboring Richmond Base Ball Club to a league-sanctioned match in September of 1866. Predictably, Richmond declined within a week, publishing the following response:

"I am instructed to state that the Richmond Baseball Club does not desire, and will not play the Union Baseball Club a single game. We are not or do we expect to be members of the National Baseball Convention. Our reason: We are Southerners. Hoping this may be satisfactory, I am J.V. Bidgood, Secretary, Richmond Baseball Club."[49]

Naturally, the Richmond Club's rejection garnered national attention and provoked greater debate. Northern papers like New York's *Sunday Mercury* decried the rejection as "an insult to the whole baseball fraternity" and further asserted that "politics or sectionalism have been kept out of our national game" and that interested southern clubs would be "met with a very cordial reception."[50]

Despite the NABBP's lack of southern clubs in 1866 and abundance of outspoken critics like in Richmond, base ball flourished in the South. With virtually no organized clubs prior to the war, at least 30 organized clubs (in addition to hundreds of recreational clubs) formed in the South by 1866.⁵¹ And while tensions between the NABBP and southern clubs had eased over the past year due to continued outreach, including a planned (but ultimately canceled) exhibition tour of the South by the reigning champion Brooklyn Atlantics, and the election of the Association's first president from south of the Mason-Dixon line in Washington, D.C.'s Arthur Gorman, their newfound alliance was lukewarm at best. In a watershed moment that altered the course of baseball history, the December 11, 1867 NABBP Convention resolved, with minimal resistance, to exclude all clubs of color from membership, including Philadelphia's Pythian Club, who had lobbied unsuccessfully in prior years. The resolution was lauded by southern clubs and even rules commissioner Henry Chadwick, who noted:

"The game has taken strong root in popular estimation, and we trust, ere many years have elapsed, to learn of our anticipations in regard to Southern ball players being fully realized; and these are that the South will one day furnish the most expert and brilliant ball players the country has yet seen."⁵²

While the resolution eased tensions with the southern clubs and rapidly expanded the NABBP's membership and geographic reach, it also established a standard of inequality that officially stood for nearly 80 years until broken by Jackie Robinson on April 15, 1947. Even then, the game remained plagued by racial tensions for decades thereafter.

To manage the rapid growth, the annual convention switched from individual clubs to state delegations by the December 1868 convention. And with the growth in membership came competitive parity. Since the league began formally naming a champion in 1859, only two clubs, both of which in Brooklyn, had claimed the title over those first eight seasons: the Atlantics (6) and Eckfords (2). Yet as more clubs entered the mix after the war, competition elevated significantly. In 1867, the Union Club of Morrisania (South Bronx) or the "Unions" challenged and prevailed against the defending champion Atlantics in a classic series that was not without its share of controversy. Again, the league's championship format was not a simple playoff between the regular season's top clubs, but rather a boxing-style format where the defending champion had the liberty of accepting or rejecting challenges, which were played in a best-of-three series featuring home-and-home contests with the rubber match (if needed) often at a neutral site. While the challenger was often the club with the best regular season record, this was far from the case in 1867. In fact, Philadelphia's Athletic Club dominated the regular season with a record 44-3 (.936), which far exceeded the Unions' win total (21) and percentage (.724). As the only true powerhouse outside of the New York area, the Athletics were a regional all-star team led by second baseman, former Brooklyn Eckford's great, and future owner of the Philadelphia Phillies Al Reach, who was lured for a $25 weekly salary in what is widely regarded as the formal beginning of professional baseball.[53] Yet the Atlantics did not avoid the surging Athletics, or at least not entirely. In fact, the clubs had played each other rather civilly since 1863 until tensions simmered in 1865 over a scheduling mishap and contentious series sweep by the Atlantics. After losing another series (2-1) to the Atlantics in 1866, which bled into 1867 due to a postponed rubber match over a lingering revenue-sharing dispute, the clubs met for a new series beginning on September 23, 1867 in Philadelphia, which began with a dominant 28-8 Athletics' victory. Perhaps out of fear of their opponent or vulnerabilities within their own club, the retreating Atlantics resorted to subterfuge in the rematch the following week in Brooklyn. Instead of their first nine, the Atlantics fielded a "muffin nine" of inept players. Refusing to partake in such a charade, the Athletics declined the match that led to a lengthy, bitter dispute that, despite receiving a majority opinion from the NABBP that the Atlantics had not fulfilled their obligation, ultimately went unresolved as the clubs would not play again that season and the championship series scrapped for a new one with the Unions who, in perhaps an act of poetic justice, dethroned the defending champions with a series-clinching 14-13 victory on October 10th. The Athletics were not to be pitied though, as they went on to win the inaugural and undisputed championship of the National Association of Professional Base Ball Players in 1871.

    The Athletics' mistreatment inevitably led to public backlash and allegations the league colluded with the Atlantics to keep the title in New York. Although unproven, the allegation has merit if only for the fact that only one club outside of the New York area won the title in the league's existence: the 1870 Chicago White Stockings (now the Cubs, covered in Chapter 4).

And while the lack of champions from outside New York and the suspicious circumstances around the 1867 season challenged the league's integrity and championship format, the Cincinnati Red Stockings' legendary 1869 campaign effectively provided the coup de grace for the embattled National Association of Base Ball Players.

The 1869 Cincinnati Red Stockings

Given the competitive parity of modern professional sports, the concept of a perfect season, one without defeats or draws, is utterly unrealistic. While remotely conceivable in American football because of fewer games per season and the one-time precedent set by the 1972 Miami Dolphins, who went 17-0-0 (season and playoffs), the perfect season in other major professional sports, most notably baseball, is unfathomable. In fact, Major League Baseball's winningest season is credited to the 1906 Chicago Cubs, who won 116 regular season games (thanks to their four Hall of Famers in player-manager Frank Chance, second baseman Johnny Evers, shortstop Joe Tinker and pitcher Mordecai Brown) but still lost 36 (.763-win percentage) plus the 1906 World Series to the cross-town White Sox. It would be nearly a century before that win total was matched, this time by the 2001 Seattle Mariners who went 116-46 but failed to reach the World Series.

Dominant as both clubs were, their regular seasons were by no means perfect. Even in professional baseball's formative years in the early 1870's, where seasons rarely exceeded 60 games, top teams seldomly registered single-digit let alone nonexistent loss totals. For a professional baseball team to go undefeated, one might suggest cheating as a requirement. But the unblemished 57-0 professional campaign (64-0 in all competitions) of the 1869 Cincinnati Red Stockings was not only innovative and brilliantly orchestrated, it was also, thanks to an amendment at the December 9, 1868 NABBP Convention, completely legal.

While the practice of paying individual players was hardly novel at the time, as noted through prominent examples like the Philadelphia Athletics luring second baseman Al Reach from the Brooklyn Eckfords for $25 a week in 1865, the practice was technically forbidden by the league thanks to the idealism of founding member and rules commissioner Henry Chadwick. But even Chadwick realized by 1868 that professionalism was inevitable. In a compelling speech to the delegation, George Sands of the Cincinnati Buckeyes advocated for professionalism:

"Professional base ball playing, although discountenanced by our National Base Ball Constitution, has been gradually gaining strength and influence, until now it seems necessary for us to recognize it, and enact laws for its government. Since we have failed to suppress it, we ought now legislate, to control its management."[54]

The resolution passed with minimal resistance with the only caveat that professional players be formally designated as such. While the moment's gravity may not have been immediately felt, the landmark shift is described by baseball historian Mark Pestana as:

"Perhaps the most fateful words in the history of the game. For better or worse, all that the game is now, and all it probably ever will be, had its seed in that speech."[55]

And while the legalization of professionalism escalated an ongoing arms race between at least a dozen of the league's leading clubs with sufficient financial resources like Brooklyn's Atlantics, Philadelphia's Athletics and Washington's Nationals, few anticipated an all-professional squad right out of the gates like 1869's Cincinnati Red Stockings.

The Red Stockings were informally established in 1866 after Harry Wright, a star cricketer and former Knickerbocker player, moved to Cincinnati and joined the vaunted Union Cricket Club, where he met club organizer and affluent local attorney Aaron Champion. While intending to advance his cricket career, Wright, with successful persuasion from Champion and assurances from other star cricketers to join him, decided to switch to base ball. And while initially founded as an amateur club, the Red Stockings were immediately competitive. Despite a 2-2 maiden campaign, the Red Stockings had already generated a buzz with a surprise 53-21 win over the more established crosstown Buckeyes. After joining the NABBP in 1867 and playing a full, albeit regional schedule, the Red Stockings put up gaudy run totals including a 109-15 victory over Newport,

Kentucky's Holt Club and a 77-17 thrashing of Louisville's Olympic Club. Despite their remarkable 16-1 campaign, their relatively soft schedule and lone defeat, a 53-10 schooling from the powerhouse Washington Nationals, left club manager and pitcher Harry Wright and executive Aaron Champion yearning to rival the dominant eastern clubs. Wright and Champion were not alone in this sentiment as a report in the *Cincinnati Commercial* referred to the loss as a:

"Waterloo defeat...showed to the officers that unless the club was strengthened, Cincinnati would never reap honors in first-class ball contests and being without money the prospect was gloomy."[56]

While technically still banned by the NABBP and decried by countless fans, the paying of players had become commonplace by 1868, not only among the top eastern clubs, but even in Cincinnati. With the neighboring Buckeyes signing at least seven professionals prior to the season, the Red Stockings would essentially have to either capitulate or join the arms race. Choosing the latter, Champion and Wright embarked on an aggressive roster build that included the luring of left fielder John Hatfield from the New York Mutuals for $1,500 per year plus a clerk position at club sponsor Boatmen's Fire and Marine Insurance Company. The pair continued their offseason shopping spree bringing in second baseman and pitcher Asa "Count" Brainard from the very same Washington Nationals that humbled them last season for a $1,400 salary and position at law firm Tilden, Moulton and Tilden. In a similar arrangement, the club added third baseman Fred Waterman from the Brooklyn Excelsiors, although this time with a shipping clerk position at the Water Street Commission House, where he likely "never shipped a pound of freight".[57] And if the prior season's two-game sweep of the rival Buckeyes wasn't enough, Wright added insult to their injury by poaching first baseman Charlie Gould.

Adorned with brilliant new white uniforms featuring knickers, their signature red stockings and a red, Old English "C" on their jerseys, the 1868 club started strong by winning their first five, including a 28-10 triumph over the semi-professional Cincinnati Buckeyes. Never satisfied, the Red Stockings added depth mid-season through the acquisition of Civil War veteran and catcher Doug Allison from Philadelphia's Geary Club. The improved Red Stockings strengthened their schedule and ventured out of the region challenging legendary clubs like the Philadelphia Athletics (20-13 and 15-12 losses), Brooklyn Atlantics (40-19 and 31-12 losses), defending champion Union of Morrisania (12-8 loss and 13-12 win), New York Mutuals (29-28 win) and the Washington Nationals (16-10 win). All in all, the Red Stockings finished the 1868 campaign with a 36-7 record and the reputation as the best of the "western" clubs. And unlike the prior year campaign, the Red Stockings proved they could, albeit inconsistently, defeat the top eastern clubs. Yet to achieve this level of consistency, the Red Stockings would have to go all in on their professional strategy.

With the financial backing from area businesses and elevated ticket prices that reached as high as $1 (as opposed to the 10 or 25 cents charged in prior seasons), the 1869 Red Stockings were not only able to fund a record annual payroll of over $9,000 but also complete a national tour that reached as far as California. The incentives of a lucrative salary and the opportunity to the travel the country while playing against the best made it easy for Harry Wright and Aaron Champion to build an all-professional roster. And despite the expulsion of left fielder John Hatfield, who had signed to play with both the Red Stockings and his former club the Mutuals, the club retained its core nucleus of Harry Wright, Asa Brainard, Charlie Gould, Doug Allison and Fred Waterman. Wright didn't have to go far for his first big acquisition when he tapped his brother and former Washington National and Morrisania Union George Wright to play shortstop. Motivated by more than just brotherly love, the younger Wright, who had garnered the reputation as the country's best shortstop and hitter, played for a team-leading $1,400 salary. The investment was worth every penny as the younger Wright slugged 49 home runs and hit .633 during the torrid 1869 campaign.[58]

To fill the remaining gaps, the elder Wright used a combination of poaching and keen scouting. As last season asserted the Red Stockings as the dominant club in the West, let alone Cincinnati, Wright was able to lure more former Cincinnati Buckeyes including second baseman Charlie Sweasy and outfielders Andy Leonard and Dick Hurley. To complete the game's first all-professional roster, Wright picked up 19-year-old, unknown right fielder Cal McVey, who went on to hit .346 in his decorated professional career.

With a loaded albeit expensive roster, expectations for the 1869 Red Stockings were at an all-time high. Despite the enormous pressure that accompanied their exorbitant salaries and national media coverage, the unflappable Red Stockings would not disappoint, not even once, on their way to a perfect 57-0 campaign (or 64-0 with exhibitions). And with few exceptions, including the 4-2 walk-off over the defending champion Mutuals in New York and the forfeit victory over Troy's (NY) Haymakers after their president pulled the club off the field over a disputed foul-catch ruling in the sixth, the Red Stockings dominated their opponents, most notably their beleaguered neighbor Buckeyes, who they defeated 103-8 and 71-15.

1869 Cincinnati Red Stockings Schedule/Results[59] – Final Record 57-0 (excludes exhibitions)

Date	Score	Opponent
4-May	45-9	Great Western of Cincinnati BBC
10-May	86-8	Kekionga of Fort Wayne
15-May	41-7	at Antioch College
22-May	41-7	at Kekionga of Fort Wayne
1-Jun	48-14	at Independent BBC
2-Jun	25-6	at Forest City of Cleveland
3-Jun	42-6	at Niagara of Buffalo
4-Jun	18-9	at Alert of Rochester BBC
7-Jun	38-31	at Union of Lansingburgh (Haymakers)
8-Jun	49-8	at National of Albany BBC
9-Jun	80-5	at Mutual Club of Springfield, MA
10-Jun	29-9	at Lowell BBC of Boston
11-Jun	40-12	at Tri-Mountain BBC of Boston
12-Jun	30-11	at Harvard College Crimson BBC
15-Jun	4-2	at Mutual of New York BBC
16-Jun	32-10	at Atlantic of Brooklyn BBC
17-Jun	24-5	at Eckford of Brooklyn BBC
18-Jun	20-4	at Irvington of New Jersey BBC
19-Jun	22-11	at Olympic Club of Philadelphia
21-Jun	27-18	at Athletic of Philadelphia BBC
22-Jun	45-30	at Keystone of Philadelphia BBC
24-Jun	30-8**	at Pastime BBC of Baltimore
25-Jun	30-13**	at Maryland of Baltimore

Date	Score	Opponent
28-Jun	16-5	at Olympic of Washington BBC
3-Jul	25-14	Olympic of Washington BBC
5-Jul	32-10	Olympic of Washington BBC
10-Jul	34-13	at Forest City of Rockford
13-Jul	19-7	Olympic of Washington BBC
22-Jul	71-15	Buckeye of Cincinnati BBC
24-Jul	15-14	Forest City of Rockford
30-Jul	85-7	at Cream City of Milwaukee
31-Jul	53-32	at Forest City of Rockford
2-Aug	28-7	at Forest City of Rockford
4-Aug	37-9	Central City Club of Syracuse (NY)
5-Aug	36-22	Central City Club of Syracuse
6-Aug	43-20**	Forest City of Cleveland
11-Aug	40-0	at Riverside of Portsmouth BBC
16-Aug	45-18	Eckford of Brooklyn BBC
23-Aug	35-3	Southern BBC of New Orleans
26-Aug	17-17*	Union of Lansingburgh (Haymakers)
31-Aug	103-8	Buckeye of Cincinnati
2-Sep	32-19	Alerts of Rochester (NY)
9-Sep	54-2	Olympic of Pittsburgh BBC
15-Sep	70-9	at Union Club of St. Louis
16-Sep	31-14	Empire Club of St. Louis
25-Sep	35-4	at Eagle of San Francisco BBC
27-Sep	58-4	at Eagle of San Francisco BBC
29-Sep	66-4	at Pacific BBC

Date	Score	Opponent
30-Sep	54-5	at Pacific BBC
1-Oct	76-5	at Atlantic BBC
11-Oct	65-1	at Omaha BBC
12-Oct	56-3	at Otoes (NE) BBC
13-Oct	51-7	at Occidental BBC
15-Oct	63-4	at Marion (IN) BBC
18-Oct	17-12	Athletic of Philadelphia BBC
3-Nov	59-8	at Kentucky of Louisville BBC
6-Nov	17-8	Mutual of New York

*Ruled a forfeit victory for the Red Stockings
**While consensus wins, the score and/or opponent varies between Baseball Reference and 1870 Beadle's Dime Base-Ball Player's reports. See endnotes for details.

Despite their flawless record, which included 29 wins against professional clubs, and staggering margins of victory, the 1869 Red Stockings would not take home the NABBP championship. Even after the Red Stockings vanquished the defending champion New York Mutuals (4-2) and powerhouse Brooklyn Atlantics (32-10), the trophy remained in New York with the Atlantics as the Red Stockings did not compete in a best-of-three challenger series, nor did they have the time or interest while on their over 10,000-mile coast-to-coast tour witnessed by roughly 200,000 fans. Further exposing the flaws of the league's championship format, NABBP rules commissioner Henry Chadwick himself declared the 1869 Red Stockings the "champion club of the United States."[60]

Trophy or not, the Cincinnati Red Stockings were the unequivocal champions of base ball after the 1869 season. And with the starting roster intact for the 1870 campaign, a Red Stockings' dynasty appeared imminent, especially after the club began the campaign with 24 straight wins. Unfortunately, the nascent dynasty sat atop a house of cards that unexpectedly toppled on June 14, 1870 in front of more than 12,000 at

Brooklyn's Capitoline Grounds. After finishing nine innings tied at 5, Atlantics captain Bob Ferguson offered the customary draw, which the emboldened Red Stockings captain Harry Wright unexpectedly declined. After a scoreless tenth, the Red Stockings tallied two runs in the eleventh expecting to close it out in the bottom half. However, an exhausted Asa Brainard struggled to retire hitters and outfielder Cal McVey fought off a frenzied crowd after a gap shot rolled into their section. After the Atlantics tied the game with only one out, center fielder George Hall hit an apparent double-play ball to superstar shortstop George Wright, whose throw missed second baseman Charlie Sweasy (the error was credited to Sweasy) allowing the winning run to cross home. Gracious in defeat, the suddenly mortal Red Stockings quickly departed the grounds and the pandemonium that ensued. Club president Aaron Champion described the setback in a telegram back to Cincinnati:

"The finest game ever played. Our boys did nobly, but fortune was against us. Eleven innings played. Though beaten, not disgraced."[61]

Despite their 24-1 record, the club's celebrity quickly diminished as fan interest and ticket sales rapidly declined. To make matters worse, the Red Stockings went on to lose five more games (including another to the Atlantics in October) over a grueling 67-6-1 campaign that would have been considered a resounding success by any other club. With skyrocketing costs and a product that lost its initial luster, the Red Stockings ownership agreed to fold at the end of the season.

While this Red Stockings dream team only lasted two seasons, their legacy endures. The players quickly found new clubs, including outfielder and manager Harry Wright, who was hired to build a new professional club in Boston, which he also named the Red Stockings. And why not? The club had a familiar feel as Harry brought along his brother George, and teammates Cal McVey (catcher), Charlie Gould (first baseman) and (in 1872) Andy Leonard (left field). While his trusty ace Asa Brainard signed with the Washington Olympics, Wright replaced him with future Hall of Famer and sporting goods magnate Albert Goodwill Spalding.

In the newly formed National Association of Professional Base Ball Players, which superseded the NABBP after the 1870 season to provide an all-professional league with more straightforward championship criteria (pennant went to the team with the best record), the Boston Red Stockings captured four straight league pennants from 1872-1875 thanks largely to Spalding's versatility (204 wins and 2.21 ERA as a pitcher plus a .323 batting average with 259 RBI as a hitter in five seasons with Boston). Shortstop George Wright also played an integral role with 483 hits (.350 average) and 194 RBI from 1871-1875. George went on to play a total of ten seasons with Boston and two with Providence, where he captained the Grays to a pennant in 1879 over his brother's Boston club. With seven pennants, 866 hits, a .301 average and 326 RBI to his name, Wright was elected to the Hall of Fame in 1937.

And while Harry Wright played full-time through the 1874 season (age 39) and amassed over 200 hits in the National Association, his true calling was as a manager. In his 23 seasons at the helm (11 with Boston, 2 with Providence and 10 with Philadelphia), Harry won 1,225 games (.581) and six league titles. Regarded by many as the "Father of Professional Baseball" Harry Wright joined his brother posthumously in Cooperstown in 1953.

Another Cincinnati franchise (Reds) would resurface with former Red Stockings first baseman Charlie Gould as manager but with a completely different roster in the National League's inaugural 1876 season, where they finished dead last at 9-56. After resuming (barely) winning records in 1878 and 1879 under manager and Red Stockings alum Cal McVey, the Reds were expelled from the National League in 1880 over president W.H. Kennett's refusal to sign a leaguewide pledge banning alcohol sales and Sunday games. After a brief hiatus, the third (and current) version of the Red Stockings joined other clubs from Philadelphia (Athletics), Louisville (Eclipse), Pittsburgh (Alleghenys), St. Louis (Brown Stockings) and Baltimore (Orioles) in the American Association, or "Beer and Whiskey League" for its more lenient policies, where they won the inaugural pennant in 1882.

Even though the 1869 Red Stockings are remembered for their unprecedented dominance, payroll and star-studded roster, their true legacy is as the team that forever changed baseball by ushering in the inevitable era of professionalism in such a grandiose manner, that it not only proved its viability but also enamored the fanbase. And while their successful "experiment" in 1869 spawned fan interest and immense wealth for club owners and players that has helped shape today's roughly $11 billion Major League Baseball empire, the Red Stockings also put a sudden and irreversible end to the simpler Pioneer Era and its noble values of amateurism and equality championed by the Knickerbockers. As explored in the following chapters, this irreversible shift to professionalism has not been without drawbacks, some of which continue to divide the game's stakeholders and stoke the fires of debate as to how the game should be played and administered.

Union prisoners at Salisbury, N.C. / drawn from nature by Act. Major Otto Boetticher; lith. of Sarony, Major & Knapp, 449 Broadway, N. York. Photo credit to Library of Congress Prints and Photographs Division Washington, D.C. 20540 USA https://www.loc.gov/item/94508290

The American national game of base ball. Grand match for the championship (c. 1866 at the Elysian Fields, Hoboken, N.J. / lith. of Currier & Ives. [New York: Currier & Ives] Photograph. Retrieved from the Library of Congress, www.loc.gov/item/90708565

The Cincinnati Red Stockings' First Nine and their iconic uniform. Rendering by Tuchfarber, Walkley & Moellman c. July 31, 1869. Photo credit to the Library of Congress' Popular Graphic Art Print Filing Series.
https://www.loc.gov/resource/pga.04207

Part II: Passed by the Pro's – Commercialization, Corruption and Adaptation

4: Meteoric Rise, Commercialization and Scandal

"The idea staggered me. I remembered, of course, that the World Series had been fixed in 1919, but if I had thought of it at all I would have thought of it as something that merely happened, the end of an inevitable chain. It never occurred to me that one man could start to play with the faith of fifty million people — with the singlemindedness of a burglar blowing a safe."[62]
- Fictional Narrator Nick Carraway in F. Scott Fitzgerald's 1925 novel *The Great Gatsby*

The End of the Amateur Era

After the National Association of Base Ball Players' (NABBP) legalization of player compensation and the Cincinnati Red Stockings' ensuing 57-0 campaign in 1869, the proverbial gauntlet had been thrown and professional clubs, upstart and blue bloods alike, quickly followed suit. While intended to accommodate the influx of professional clubs, the NABBP's establishment of separate divisions for professionals and amateurs further widened the rift. And as the 1870 season's controversial finish proved, the rift was irreparable.

Throughout the NABBP's brief yet turbulent history, the league title had remained with New York area clubs, including at least seven with the vaunted Brooklyn Atlantics. And while these claims were occasionally disputed by out-of-town challengers, as noted in Chapter 3's discussion of the 1867 Philadelphia Athletics and 1869 Cincinnati Red Stockings, the league title never officially left New York, that is until the league's final season in 1870.

Inspired by the Red Stockings' success, a group of Chicago investors pooled together a reported $18,000 payroll[63] (roughly double the Red Stockings' prior season mark) to poach top talents from established clubs including former Troy Haymakers infielder/catcher Bill Craver and Philadelphia

Athletics' infielder/outfielder (and later St. Louis Brown Stockings manager) Ned Cuthbert, to form the Chicago White Stockings (now the Cubs). Despite winning their first 31 contests, the early season was overshadowed by a couple of lowlights, including a July home-and-home sweep by the 1868 champion New York Mutuals punctuated by a 9-0 home defeat, after which the *New York Herald* coined the term "Chicagoed" as a synonym for shutout. [64] Undeterred, the resilient White Stockings rebounded with impressive victories over the reigning champion Atlantics, a revenge road triumph against the Mutuals and a home-and-home sweep of their inspiration and suddenly fallible Cincinnati Red Stockings. Meanwhile, the Mutuals completed a series victory over the Atlantics in September to temporarily capture the league crown. Instead of resorting to scheduling subterfuge, as many of the league's prior champions had done, the emboldened Mutuals ventured to the Windy City in November with their title on the line.

In a controversial match befitting of the perpetually embattled league's tenure, the tightly contested game headed into the ninth with Chicago leading 7-5. Despite mounting adversity and pressure, the veteran Mutuals capitalized on a host of errors and followed with six straight hits to take a commanding 13-7 lead. With the match seemingly over, the White Stockings received some unexpected help from hometown umpire Tom Foley, who ironically had been selected by the Mutuals from a local umpiring pool. After being assessed three consecutive walks, where the White Stockings essentially refused to swing, Mutuals pitcher Rynie Wolters quickly unraveled. After a string of hits and fielding errors tightened the score to 13-12, the White Stockings again resorted to offense-by-umpire, allowing over a dozen deliveries without offering. The flabbergasted Mutuals had seen enough as captain Charles Mills called his men off the field, making way for the jubilant crowd of more than 7,000. While the score had still been 13-12 in favor of the visitors, umpire Tom Foley nullified the chaotic and technically incomplete ninth inning and awarded Chicago the 7-5 victory, a decision panned by the *New York Clipper*:

"No one would be more delighted than I to see the Chicagos the champions, but were I asked my unbiased opinion as to how the

Mutuals came to lose the game they had so handsomely in hand, I should reply, "Out umpired."

Even one of the "Fathers of Baseball" and NABBP Rules Commissioner Henry Chadwick was at a loss when he remarked in his *Clipper* editorial:

"Who are the Champions for 1870? If we have been asked the question once this week, we have been asked fifty times, and from the position of things we find it a rather tough question to solve."[65]

Despite any ill will between clubs, they were united in their distaste of the NABBP, including its arbitrary championship format and the comingling of professionals and amateurs. Just four months later in March 1871, both clubs joined seven other top clubs from the Northeast and Midwest, including Philadelphia's Athletics, Boston's Red Stockings, Washington's Olympics, Troy's Haymakers, Cleveland's Forest Citys, Fort Wayne's Kekiongas and Rockford's Forest Citys to form the first all-professional league (National Association of Professional Base Ball Players or "National Association") beginning a trend that endures to this day.

While the National Association's charter clubs and subsequent additions, including Brooklyn's Atlantics and Eckfords, shared common interests in professionalism and a revised championship format that awarded the pennant to the club with the best regular season record, there was little else beyond an annual convention to sustain this loose alliance. With minimal restrictions on scheduling or membership, the league navigated inconsistency and turnover with fledgling clubs quickly coming and going. Additionally, the lack of a governing body prevented the upkeep and enforcement of league rules. Meanwhile on the field, the competitive disparity was obvious, as evidenced by Boston's four straight pennants under the leadership of former Cincinnati Red Stockings greats Harry and George Wright. On February 2, 1876, the National Association's top clubs, including Boston, Chicago, Philadelphia, New York (Mutuals), St. Louis (Brown Stockings) and Hartford (Dark Blues), split off from the National Association to form the National League of Professional Club, better known today as the National League. Unlike its unorganized predecessor, the NL implemented a central league office led initially by Morgan Bulkeley and subsequently by Chicago White Stockings president William Hulbert, who had full authority to control membership and discipline clubs for non-compliance with league rules. But the six National Association defecting clubs were not alone in their maiden NL campaign. Rather, they invited large market independent clubs including the Cincinnati Reds, a short-lived reboot unrelated to the current version, and the Louisville Grays, who would greatly test the mettle of the league's policies and enforcement mechanisms the following season.

Louisville Grays Scandal (1877)

With sports betting not only legal in an increasing number of states, but also ubiquitous thanks to endless prop bets and one-click wagering, one cannot simply evaluate baseball's gambling history through a modern lense and essentially condone it, especially those transgressions that happened over a century ago in very different social, political and economic climates as was the case in 1877 Louisville. Despite being a booming industrial city of over 100,000 with global acclaim for its bourbon, Louisville was in the heart of the American Bible Belt during what many historians considered to be the third edition of the Great Awakening, a series of Christian revival movements led by preachers and civic leaders advocating a return to piety and departure from vices, especially alcohol and gambling. One of gambling's most outspoken critics in the early 19th century was Pennsylvania justice Jacob Rush (brother of Declaration of Independence signer and Surgeon General Dr. Benjamin Rush) who noted:

"[Gambling] tyrannises [sic] the people beyond their control, reducing them to poverty and wretchedness. The mind is deeply contaminated, and sentiments, the most hostile to its final peace and happiness, are harbored and indulged."[66]

And while gambling had rapidly spread throughout the fanbase and was a catalyst for the game's sudden popularity, players and clubs had largely avoided gambling-related controversy up to this point, which was likely due to a combination of the National League and its predecessors' vehement stances against it and the lack of adequate detection, penalization and publication of past incidents.

Founded in 1876 by local businessman and *Louisville Courier-Journal* owner Walter Newman Haldeman, the Grays were built to compete for the pennant at the onset with a roster of poached national stars like New York Mutuals second baseman Joseph Gerhardt, Chicago White Stockings pitcher and infielder Jim Devlin and Philadelphia (Athletics and Whites) and New York Mutuals outfielder and pitcher George Bechtel. Despite a talented and experienced roster, the Grays struggled against the more established and cohesive clubs in their maiden campaign, settling for a 30-36-3 record and fifth-place finish (22 back of the champion Philadelphia Athletics). In addition to a disappointing season, the Grays barely averted scandal after George Bechtel was expelled amidst match-fixing allegations that not only included throwing games himself, but also inviting teammates to join. While the move was initially perceived as a sign of the club's ethical commitment, skepticism resumed after the club's controversial offseason signing of the aforementioned Bill Craver, a former Bechtel teammate with the Philadelphia Whites, instigator of the Troy Haymakers' notorious 1869 skirmish with the Cincinnati Red Stockings, and 1870 Chicago White Stockings' castoff for "insubordination and gambling."[67]

Despite the disappointing and controversial initial campaign, the club entered the 1877 season as a pennant contender, thanks largely to Jim Devlin's breakout prior season (30 wins, 1.56 ERA and 122 strikeouts as a pitcher, plus a .315 average as a hitter) and the offseason acquisition of Philadelphia Athletics star outfielder George Hall. The Grays appeared to have lived up to the hype after assuming a commanding four-game lead in mid-August on the heels of winning 15 of their last 18. However, their fortune quickly reversed on a brutal northeastern road trip where the Grays dropped seven of eight (including one tie) to Hartford and eventual league champion Boston. Yet concerns were not directed at the number of losses on that disastrous trip, but rather how those games were lost. In addition to a sudden power outage, where the club averaged less than two runs and were shut out twice during that trip (they had only been shut out once in their first 42 games), the team's defensive stalwarts including Devlin, Craver and Hall were suddenly erratic. Additionally, after a painful underarm boil sidelined third baseman Bill Hague, George Hall successfully lobbied to replace him with fellow Englishman Al Nichols. The decision was later questioned by club management and the media given Nichols' prior history as a .179 hitter with the Mutuals. The suspicions were clearly warranted as Nichols continued his light-hitting (4 of 19) and committed an astounding five errors in his brutal six-game stint with the Grays.

Even though the Grays were far away from their home fans and media during that dreadful stretch, their suddenly poor play did not go unnoticed. Internally, the suspicions began with a series of anonymous telegrams sent to club president Charles E. Chase during the trip, including one urging him to "watch (his) men" and another accurately predicting his club's loss to Hartford later that day.[68] In addition to the telegrams, Chase was also suspicious of the high volume sent to recent addition Al Nichols. His fears were affirmed when Nichols refused to talk or turn over his telegrams (although he later acquiesced), resulting in his immediate release. Meanwhile, John Haldeman, *Louisville Courier-Journal* baseball writer and son of club president Walter Haldeman, commenced an investigation amid fears of match-fixing, even articulating his suspicions in the *Courier-Journal*:

"I had followed the club so closely during the season, and was so well acquainted with its inner workings, what it could and what it could not accomplish, that I knew that 'funny business' had been going on during its last Eastern trip."[69]

Despite the ominous specter of scandal, the club resumed its winning ways by going 8-5 in the final stretch to finish at 35-25-1 and second in the league, 7 games back of Boston. Days after the season ended, the club's investigation bore fruit when Chase obtained two telegrams from Brooklyn bookmaker P.A. Williams intended for Nichols. And while the cryptic telegrams were inconclusive, they gave Chase predication to question his targets including Devlin, Hall and (due to his prior history) Craver. While Devlin and Craver vehemently denied the allegations, George Hall offered the following partial confession:

"I know I have done wrong (fixing exhibitions in connection with his brother-in-law Frank Powell), but as God is my judge, I have

never thrown a league game. If I tell you all I know about this business, will you promise to let me down easy?"[70]

Hall later followed with a broader confession that also implicated Nichols in fixing multiple exhibitions. Hall's confession prompted club president Charles Chase to demand the telegrams of all team members, a request that was honored except by Craver, who was in the midst of a salary dispute. A review of the alleged conspirators' telegrams obtained from Western Union not only corroborated Hall's confession but also proved Devlin's involvement, including receipt of $100 payments from a New York gambler for fixing exhibitions in Cincinnati and Indianapolis.

Following the investigation on October 30, 1877, the three confirmed (George Hall, Al Nichols, Jim Devlin) and one alleged (Bill Craver) conspirators were expelled from the Grays. Further, in an attempt to quell the nationwide shock and reassert order as league president, William Hulbert punished all four with lifetime bans. And while the Grays organization was not directly punished, the club opted to permanently fold before the 1878 season. And despite the swift and highly publicized justice the four former players received, the scourge of match-fixing in professional baseball was only just beginning.

Expansion of Professional Leagues (c. 1882-1915)

Despite the negative publicity from the Louisville Grays Scandal, business was booming for the nascent National League, with top clubs like the Chicago White Stockings drawing nearly 60,000 fans over the following season (at around 50 cents per ticket). And with the subsequent entry of other major market clubs with large venues like Detroit's Wolverines (1881) and New York's Gothams/Giants (1883), attendance figures skyrocketed with several leading clubs like Boston and Chicago eclipsing over 100,000 fans annually by the early 1880's, and single game attendance records exceeding 20,000 (New York in 1886).[71]

As expected in any capitalist society, healthy attendance figures were not nearly enough for some club owners. Doubling down on his commitment to morality after the Grays Scandal, League President William Hulbert outlawed Sunday baseball and beer sales following the 1880 season. While the reforms were largely embraced by club presidents, Cincinnati Reds' president W.H. Kennett provided the lone dissenting vote, due to the club's lucrative history in both, effectively removing his club from the league. While Kennett may have been the only active National League president opposed to the prohibition of beer sales and Sunday games, he was certainly not alone in his sentiment. Just over a year later on November 2, 1881, *Cincinnati Enquirer* sports editor O.P. Caylor and former club president Justus Thorner had resurrected the Reds franchise and met in Cincinnati with likeminded clubs including the Philadelphia Athletics, Louisville Eclipse, Pittsburgh Alleghenys, St. Louis Brown Stockings and Brooklyn Atlantics (replaced by Baltimore's Orioles prior to the start) and formed the American Association the following season. And while the rules and constitution were largely consistent with the rival National League, beer sales and Sunday baseball were legal and tickets were priced at 25 cents (half of the National League price) to make the game more accessible to working class fans. Because of these loose standards and party atmosphere in the ballparks, the American Association quickly garnered the nickname "The Beer and Whiskey League." And while considered rivals, the National League and American Association engaged in an informal precursor to the modern World Series, where both champions met in postseason series from 1884 to 1890, which were dominated by the National League clubs, with the lone exception of the St. Louis Browns' 1886 4-2 series victory over the Chicago White Stockings.

While not nearly as well-attended as the rival National League, largely due to the lack of teams in major markets beyond Philadelphia, the American Association's initial success and viability as a competitor to the National League inspired yet another league in the oft forgotten Union Association of 1884. Unfortunately, the third "major" league was doomed from the start thanks largely to extreme competitive disparity, as evidenced by the champion St. Louis Maroons' 21-game lead over second-place Cincinnati, and widespread insolvency that saw four clubs fold and one relocate during the lone season. Similarly in 1890, the Players' League was formed by union members/players from the National League and American Association that were engaged in pay disputes, exacerbated by recent salary caps and the NL's reserve clause, which essentially bound players to their clubs unless traded or released. Despite the league's high-caliber talent and presence in major markets like New York, Boston and Chicago, it suffered a similar fate as the Union Association and folded after a single season due to insolvency.

Even though the Players' League was not a serious threat as a standalone entity, its depletion of talent from other leagues proved costly, especially for the struggling American Association, which had already seen three clubs defect to the National League by 1890 (Pittsburgh, Cincinnati and Brooklyn) as they were permitted to continue Sunday baseball and beer sales. After the 1891 season, the American Association formally shuttered and leading clubs like the St. Louis Browns (Cardinals), Baltimore Orioles, Louisville Colonels and Washington Senators joined the twelve-team National League in 1892, which remained the only major league for nearly a decade.

Despite its restoration as a monopoly, the National League experienced mixed results in the 1890's. With dwindling attendance and a relative lack of competitive parity amongst the smaller-market clubs, most notably the Cleveland Spiders' 20-134 disaster in 1899, the National League owners voted to cull the league's membership down to eight teams in advance of the 1900 season by releasing perennial bottom-feeders Cleveland, Washington and Louisville. Surprisingly, the Baltimore Orioles were also ousted, despite winning three consecutive pennants from 1894-1896, in a move that seemed purely commercial. Meanwhile, Ban Johnson, a former Cincinnati journalist and now president of the upstart Western League, which had been a minor league affiliate of the NL, recognized the opportunity to not only regain market share by placing clubs in jilted former markets including Baltimore (Orioles), Washington (Senators), Cleveland (Blues), Milwaukee (Brewers) and Detroit (Tigers), but also to compete directly with the NL, including placing second major league teams in top markets like Chicago (White Sox), Philadelphia (Athletics) and Boston (Americans). By 1901, the newly established American League rejected the National Agreement and established themselves as the second major league. But unlike prior NL rivals like the Union Association and Players' League, the American League remains to this day. And despite their initial protest, the National League accepted their counterparts (albeit under the enduring moniker of the "Junior Circuit") as the other major league by 1903 under an amended National Agreement and instituted the first edition of the modern

World Series, a thrilling 5-3 series victory by the Junior Circuit's Boston Americans over Honus Wagner's Pittsburgh Pirates thanks to brilliant pitching from Bill Dinneen and the immortal Cy Young.

Black Sox Scandal (1919)

As expected, the inaugural modern World Series in 1903 was a commercial success with over 100,000 fans attending. And despite a brief hiatus in 1904, where the National League Champion New York Giants boycotted the series out of refusal to play their cross-town rival Highlanders, who ironically lost the AL Pennant to Boston on the last day but the Giants' position was irreversible by then, the World Series continually grew in popularity and established itself as the country's premier sporting event. Unlike its prior iteration between the National League and defunct American Association from 1884-1890, the modern World Series was far more competitive and balanced with the American League taking six of the first ten series with the championship won by seven different clubs during that span. And while competitive parity existed, at least within baseball's upper echelon, certain clubs asserted their dominance early including the American League's Philadelphia Athletics, who claimed five pennants and three World Series by 1914, and the Babe Ruth-led Boston Red Sox, who claimed three titles in four years from 1915-1918. But not far behind these juggernauts were Chicago's Southsider White Sox, who captured both the 1906 (from the cross-town Cubs) and 1917 World Series.

Despite a disappointing 57-67 sixth-place campaign in 1918, where star "Shoeless" Joe Jackson left the club to work in a military shipyard in accordance with the government's "work or fight rule", expectations for the White Sox were at an all-time high, especially after club owner Charles Comiskey welcomed back his players returning from the wartime efforts:

"Our war madness of six months ago has subsided to a great degree and we have learned...to take a new view of the man...The government said work or fight...the players obeyed the highest order. There's nothing more to be said."[72]

The optimism was clearly warranted as the White Sox held the American League lead from the April 23rd opening day all the way until June 23rd after a 3-2 loss to Cleveland. But the resilient White Sox reclaimed the lead for good after a doubleheader sweep of the Philadelphia Athletics on July 9th, and finished the season at 88-52, 3.5 games ahead of second-place Cleveland. While Jackson's .351 average and 96 RBI stole the headlines, the White Sox enjoyed contributions across the board including righthander Eddie Cicotte's league-leading 29 wins and Eddie Collins' 33 steals. Additionally, the White Sox led the league in hits (1,343), average (.287), runs (668) and steals (150).

Despite the dominant season and impressive accolades, the 1919 White Sox had yet to face their toughest opponent in the Cincinnati Reds. Led by league batting champ (.321 average) and eventual Hall of Famer Edd Roush and lefty Dutch Reuther (1.82 ERA), the Reds cruised to their first National League pennant with a 96-44 campaign, which was a staggering nine games clear of the runner-up Giants. Despite their superior record, the Reds entered the World Series as the overwhelming underdog.

This seemingly lopsided matchup presented a unique opportunity for bookmakers, including Joseph "Sport" Sullivan given his notorious gambling and bribery history, including a rejected bribery attempt of Cy Young in 1904, a 1906 public official bribery allegation, and a 1907 arrest for gambling at a Boston Braves game, [73] and close relationships with various White Sox players including good friend and first baseman C. Arnold "Chick" Gandil. With a relatively mediocre salary of $3,5000 (fifth among American League first basemen), Gandil is believed to have been receptive to Sullivan's proposition to fix the upcoming World Series, especially after the rumored payout of $100,000 (over $1.6 million today), which was allegedly bankrolled by New York mob boss Arnold "The Brain" Rothstein.[74] Realizing the need for several other co-conspirators to pull off the scheme and the likelihood of interest given the gargantuan payout, Gandil allegedly approached various teammates including pitchers Eddie Cicotte and Claude "Lefty" Williams, shortstop Charles "Swede" Risberg, third baseman George "Buck" Weaver, outfielder Oscar "Happy" Felsch and reserve infielder Fred McMullin. Star outfielder Shoeless Joe Jackson was also propositioned, providing an enticing opportunity to supplement his $6,000 annual salary.

While closely kept amongst the alleged conspirators leading up to the best-of-nine series, suspicions quickly arose after an erratic 9-1 opening defeat on October 1st in Cincinnati, where over 30,000 fans saw and 0-for-4 performance from Jackson, an error from Chick Gandil, and a dreadful six-run, 3.2-inning outing from ace Eddie Cicotte that included a hit batsman on just his second pitch in what many believe was a signal affirming the fix. While fans and media were dumbfounded by the lackluster performance, Cicotte chalked it up to just a bad day:

"I didn't put a thing on the ball (during Game 1). You could have read the trademark on it, the way I lobbed it over the plate. A baby could have hit 'em."[75]

While the host Reds again triumphed, Game 2's 4-2 contest appeared far more competitive with the White Sox outhitting the Reds 10-4 and managing just one error to the Reds' three. And while Lefty Williams' eight-inning, four earned run stat line did not raise eyebrows, his three walks in the fourth that led to three runs certainly did. Yet suspicions were at least temporarily put to rest when the White Sox blanked the Reds 3-0 back in Chicago on the arm of non-conspirator Dickie Kerr. But the good feelings were short-lived when the Reds returned the favor the following night with a 2-0 triumph, aided by two fielding blunders in the fifth by the otherwise unhittable Eddie Cicotte. All hope was nearly lost after another shutout defeat (5-0) in Chicago to draw the Sox to brink of elimination. Despair had even reached the Sox clubhouse when non-conspiring manager Kid Gleason remarked:

"We aren't hitting. I don't know what's the matter, but I do know that something's wrong with my gang. The bunch I had fighting in August for the pennant would have trimmed this Cincinnati bunch without a struggle. The bunch I have now couldn't beat a high school team."[76]

While the alleged conspirators were doing their part on the field, they appeared to have second thoughts after receiving only a portion of the promised payouts, which were believed to total around $20,000 per loss.[77] Their apprehension was evident when the series returned to Cincinnati, where the Sox took Game 6 by a margin of 5-4, thanks to a ten-inning outing from unlikely hero Dickie Kerr, and Game 7 by a score of 4-1, thanks to a complete game from Eddie Cicotte.

With the outcome of the series now in doubt at 4-3, it is widely believed that the bankrolling gangsters took action by threatening the players and their families. With the message received, the alleged conspirators resumed their losing ways with a 10-5 series-ending defeat in Chicago. In the series' most suspicious sequence, starter Lefty Williams yielded four runs while registering just one out before being pulled. The offense showed little fight in the first seven frames beyond a Shoeless Joe Jackson homer in the third. Apparently unphased by their prior threats, Gandil and Jackson combined for another 3 RBI in the eighth, but the comeback fell well short and the Reds claimed their first World Series title.

The aftermath included a series of criminal conspiracy trials prosecuted by newly elected State Attorney Robert E. Crowe in 1921, beginning with a judge's dismissal in March due to lingering questions on the transcripts of Cicotte, Jackson and Williams' prior grand jury testimonies. After regrouping, Crowe re-indicted the accused conspirators in a trial that ran from July 18th-August 2nd, 1921. The accused included the eight White Sox players and a laundry list of gambler and informant accomplices that included the at-large "Sport" Sullivan, former Cincinnati Red Hal Chase, and boxing champion Abe Attell. After weeks of arguments between the state and some of the nation's best defense attorneys, the jury ruled in less than three hours in favor of the defendants, much to the delight of the partisan crowd. The ensuing celebration, which included post-trial photos and a meal among defendants and jurors, only raised further suspicions on the fairness of the trial. Unmoved by the legal proceedings, newly appointed Baseball Commissioner Kenesaw Mountain Landis swiftly moved to ban all eight accused players for life, which not only ended their major league playing careers but also kept Shoeless Joe Jackson from the Hall of Fame.

Jackson's case is perhaps the most complicated. Jackson's performance during the series, which included a .375 overall batting average and .545 average in their three victories, and subsequent recanting of his signed admission (that he accepted $5,000) on the grounds he was misled by attorneys into signing a confession he could not read due to his illiteracy, only adds to the lingering mystery and the ongoing debate as to whether the league's punishments were justified.[78]

The Golden Era (1920-1960)

Similar to the aftermath of the Louisville Grays, the public outrage from 1919's Black Sox Scandal was not nearly enough to derail the momentum of America's beloved pastime. In fact, the game was on the brink of four decades of unprecedented prosperity in a period widely known as the Golden Era (or Golden Age). When considering the volumes of literature and film devoted to this period, one can easily understand why the period is so widely romanticized. Whether it's the abundance of unforgettable moments, including Babe Ruth's accurately called shot during the 1932 World Series, Jackie Robinson breaking the color barrier on April 15, 1947, and Willie May's over-the-shoulder catch during the 1954 World Series, iconic teams, including 1927's 110-win "Murderers' Row" Yankees, and St. Louis' Hall of Famer and championship-laden "Gashouse Gang" of the 1930's, and immortal players like Ruth, Gehrig, Williams, Robinson and Mays, the Golden Era has no shortage of star power or Hollywood storylines. And thanks to rapidly expanding media coverage made possible by technological advancements in radio, television and film, fans were not only granted unprecedented access to the game at the time but also to robust and well-preserved records for later generations to relive. And while the period was not without its share of challenges including the Great Depression of the 1930's, where attendance plunged by as much as 40%,[79] and the Second World War, where over 500 players were deployed including two (Elmer Gedeon and Harry O'Neill) who did not return home,[80] the resilient game not only withstood these challenges but re-emerged even more popular and profitable, a trend that continues today. But as the past 60 years have proven, the game's growth and survival have hinged on its continued adaptation to meet the everchanging needs of its broadening stakeholder base. And while this continued adaption has ensured the game's ongoing commercial success, it has not been without its drawbacks and detractors as noted in the following chapter.

5: Free Agency, Tanking and Analytics, Oh My!

"Baseball has always been a reflection of life. Like life, it adjusts. It survives everything."[81]

- Hall of Fame Outfielder Willie Stargell

Not Your Ancestors' Game

Up to this point, the book's focus has been on the key people, clubs and formative moments in baseball's early years. However, the narrative is not complete without an understanding of the various watershed moments and eras, particularly over the last 50 years, that have irreversibly shaped the game's identity, fragmented the fanbase and, as detailed in Part III, motivated some to resurrect the early game. As attempting to comprehensively summarize over a century's worth of baseball history, in a single chapter nonetheless, is a hopeless endeavor, this chapter is limited to brief summaries and analyses of a small yet impactful subset of events that have, for better or worse, accelerated modern baseball's adaptation and deviation from its roots.

It should also be noted that this chapter is by no means a critique of modern professional baseball. In fact, many of today's vintage base ball revivalists, including the clubs featured in Part III, embrace baseball in all forms, with some going as far as playing exhibitions at major league parks. Truth be told, I was a St. Louis Cardinals season ticket holder for an entire decade and only discontinued after starting a family. And who knows? Maybe I will again someday. Regardless, the point is that while many of the topics covered herein like analytics and competitive balancing are certainly polarizing, as evidenced by the ubiquitous debates and "hot takes" heard throughout stadiums, barbershops and radio airwaves, fan interest is far from a zero-sum game between the early and modern editions. Rather, a compelling argument can be made that to truly love the game is to also love its journey from a humble niche to global empire.

Flood v. Kuhn (1972) and Free Agency

While a boon for players and a bane for owners, free agency represents arguably the most seismic shift in baseball (and professional sports) history. Beyond the obvious economic implications, where a roughly half-billion-dollar industry in 1972 morphed into an $11 billion empire today, free agency has impacted virtually every aspect of the game ranging from labor relations and collective bargaining to the fan experience. And while impossible to definitively argue whether free agency and its historical administration have been "good for the game", we can all agree that it has and will remain a polarizing issue amongst the game's stakeholders. Even the United States Supreme Court struggled with the decision, as evidenced by the 5-3 margin in their 1972 decision in favor of MLB Commissioner Bowie Kuhn against former St. Louis Cardinals outfielder Curt Flood:

"Without re-examination of the underlying issues, the [judgment] below [is] affirmed on the authority of Federal Baseball Club of Baltimore v. National League of Professional Baseball Clubs, supra, so far as that decision determines that Congress had no intention of including the business of baseball within the scope of the federal antitrust laws. 346 U.S., at 357.
And what the Court said in Federal Baseball in 1922 and what it said in Toolson (v. New York Yankees) in 1953, we say again here in 1972: the remedy, if any is indicated, is for congressional, and not judicial, action. The judgment of the Court of Appeals is affirmed. Judgment affirmed."[82]

As background, Curt Flood was a superstar outfielder whose decorated career included seven Gold Gloves, three All-Star selections, two world championships ('64 and '67 with St. Louis), and a career WAR of 41.9. Following the 1969 season, the 32-year-old and 12-year veteran may have been in the "twilight" of his career but still incredibly productive as evidenced his .285 batting average and Gold Glove the prior season. Nonetheless, Cardinals ownership and General Manager Bing Devine sought to maximize their return on veteran talents including Flood, catcher Tim McCarver, outfielder Byron Browne and pitcher Joe Hoerner by sending them to the hapless Philadelphia Phillies, who finished the prior season 37 games back of the NL East Champion Mets, for slugging infielder Dick Allen, second baseman Cookie Rojas and pitcher Jerry Johnson.

A blindsided yet resilient Flood refused his assignment even though mandatory under the league's reserve clause, which essentially bound players to their clubs unless traded or released, and notified league commissioner Bowie Kuhn via the following letter on December 24, 1969:

"After twelve years in the Major Leagues, I do not feel that I am a piece of property to be bought and sold irrespective of my wishes. I believe that any system which produces that result violates my basic rights as a citizen and is inconsistent with the laws of the United States and of the several states.
It Is my desire to play baseball in 1970, and I am capable of playing. I have received a contract offer from the Philadelphia Club, but I believe I have the right to consider offers from other clubs before making any decisions. I, therefore, request that you make known to all the Major League Clubs my feelings in this matter, and advise them of my availability for the 1970 season."[83]

As one can infer, Flood's request was denied by the league, resulting in a multi-year legal battle that culminated in the Court's 5-3 ruling in favor of Bowie Kuhn and Major League Baseball on the grounds of a legal precedent established a half-century prior (1922's *Federal Baseball Club of Baltimore v. National League of Professional Baseball Clubs)* that exempted Major League Baseball from the Sherman Antitrust Act and related labor laws governing nearly all other forms of interstate business.

In addition to enduring an exhausting and costly legal battle punctuated by a gutting outcome, Flood sat out the 1970 season, foregoing a $100,000 salary from the Phillies. And while he briefly resurfaced in 1971 with the Washington Senators, cumulative wear and tear, distraction of the ongoing legal battle, and an overall decline in physical conditioning and on-field production (batting 7 for 35 or .200) led Flood to retire just 13 games into the season.

Despite the league's victory in court, their control rapidly dissipated thanks to growing support from the public and player's union. After a series of watershed rulings in the mid-70's from independent arbitrator Peter Seitz that released pitchers Jim

"Catfish" Hunter (Oakland), Andy Messersmith (Dodgers) and Dave McNally (Montreal) from their clubs, free agency was inevitable. Not surprisingly, league commissioner Bowie Kuhn fired Seitz shortly thereafter. To prevent the floodgates from fully opening, the league and player's union negotiated a compromise in advance of the 1976 season that limited clubs to six years of player control prior to free agency, a rule that remains in place and hotly contested to this day.

And while Flood, then retired and plagued by a myriad of legal, financial and health woes, would tragically not get to enjoy the fruits of his own labor, he looked back upon his eventual victory with pride during a 1981 interview with *Ebony*:

"I certainly don't begrudge the players getting that money. They're finally getting a fair share of the incredible amount of money they're making for the baseball teams."

As another silver lining, Bill Clinton signed the Curt Flood Act in 1998, which ended MLB's exemption from federal antitrust laws, just one year after Flood's death. And while the league's administration of free agency will always provoke debate, especially with the player's union (as evidenced by the nine labor stoppages since 1972) and amongst fans, the importance of Flood's accomplishment is irrefutable, a sentiment perhaps best-articulated by Pulitzer Prize-winning author George Will:

"(Flood) lost the 1970 season and lost in the Supreme Court, but he had lit a fuse... Six years later – too late to benefit him – his cause prevailed. The national pastime is clearly better because of that. But more important, so is the nation, because it has learned one more lesson about the foolishness of fearing freedom."[84]

Technology, Moneyball and the Analytics Overdrive

While popularized by Michael Lewis' 2003 bestseller *Moneyball: The Art of Winning an Unfair Game* and the resulting 2011 film starring Brad Pitt, the concept of data-driven analysis and decision-making was hardly novel at the time. In fact, statistical analysis in baseball is as at least as old as Henry Chadwick's first published box scores in the *New York Clipper* and *Sunday Mercury* in 1859. Notable later applications include legendary Brooklyn Dodgers' General Manager Branch Rickey's hiring of statistician Allan Roth in 1947 to evaluate talent, and Hall of Fame Orioles' Manager Earl Weaver's usage of index cards with opposing hitter statistics and tendencies to coach his pitchers from the late '60's to the mid-80's.

While used intermittently throughout the game's history, data analytics would become industry standard after renowned analyst Bill James coined his signature philosophy Sabermetrics in 1980, which he defined as the "the search of objective knowledge about baseball."[85] While concise, the definition is also polarizing, particularly between modern baseball proponents and advocates of the earlier, simpler versions, where decisions were often made based on instincts, hunches, eye tests, gut reactions and other visceral clichés. And even though statistics are the official language and currency of today's game, the modern analytics proponent's tendency to assert their approach's superiority with (you guessed it) more data can feel like a self-fulfilling prophecy. But instead of fighting fire with fire and analyzing historical success rates of managerial decisions with lower probabilities (aka "gambles"), one can simply recall classic examples where such gambles paid off like Hall of Fame Dodgers Manager Tommy Lasorda's decision to pinch hit Kirk Gibson, who was battling two leg injuries and a stomach virus to boot, while down a run with two outs in the bottom of the ninth of Game 1 of the 1988 World Series against AL saves leader Dennis Eckersley nonetheless. As we all know, Lasorda's gamble paid off with Gibson's two-run walk-off homer, which set the tone for the Dodgers' eventual 4-1 series victory.

To use another high-stakes yet more contemporary example, where data analytics had already permeated the game's DNA, the St. Louis Cardinals' 2014 playoff run to the NLCS featured multiple improbable yet ultimately effective managerial decisions. Most notably, Manager Mike Matheny's decision to keep in lefthanded batter Matt Adams while trailing 2-0 in the bottom of the seventh during Game 4 of the Division Series despite hitting and slugging under .200 and .300 against lefties respectively, let alone against his current adversary and imminent Cy Young and MVP awardee Clayton Kershaw, would have likely been press and social media fodder if it had not resulted in a three-run homer that ultimately clinched the series. Perhaps emboldened by the successful gamble, Matheny continued to roll the dice. In the Game 2 NLCS victory against the eventual world champion Giants, Matheny's improbable gambles included a Yadier Molina sacrifice bunt with no outs and runners on first and second (despite a 0.1 or 7% higher run expectancy if swinging away)86 that led to a Randal Grichuk RBI single, and leveraging righthanded reliever Seth Maness instead of lefty Marco Gonzales to retire Pablo Sandoval in the top of the ninth, despite his torrid .317 average against righties and sub-Mendoza .199 against lefties.[87]

To clarify, the Lasorda and Matheny examples are not intended to disparage the modern game's analytics-first approach, where roster constructions, daily lineups, in-game substitutions and even defensive alignment (i.e., when to shift) decisions are driven or at least influenced by statistical analyses, including historical and simulation, but rather to point out that statistics and predictive analytics are not foolproof, nor will they (hopefully) ever be. And if they were, would there even be a need for human managers and umpires? While the former scenario seems more akin to science fiction, the latter has become a partial-reality in certain independent and minor leagues. In fact, the prevailing and ironically named technology "TrackMan" debuted at the independent Atlantic League's 2019 All-Star Game. After a successful pilot, robot umpires, which are large 3-D Doppler radar dishes typically mounted on stadium roofs behind home plate that automatically measure strike zones for each batter, track pitch locations, and provide an auditory signal to the human umpire behind home plate, were not only retained in the Atlantic League, but also expanded to a selection of major league affiliates including a handful of spring training and Triple-A parks. Despite being just one level from the majors and receiving support from the MLB Umpires Association, skeptics can relax for the time being as (at the time of publication) there were no imminent plans to implement in MLB parks as noted by Chief Operations and Strategy Officer Chris Marinak:

"It's hard to handicap if, when or how it might be employed at the major league level, because it is a pretty substantial difference from the way the game is called today."[88]

Despite Major League Baseball's continued investment, the debate over technology and data's role will likely go unresolved amongst fans as opposing viewpoints will always harken back to the philosophical question of "whether it's good for the game". And as this question is inherently subjective, often evoking emotional responses, the very data and technology that are capable of answering so many other important questions, like whether that pitch was a strike or whether to bring in the slumping lefty reliever because he has excellent splits against a particular hitter, are seemingly of little use.

Stealing More than Bases: Hacking and Sign Stealing Scandals

Like the game itself, baseball's scandals have evolved over time and become increasingly more sophisticated, complex and technologically-dependent. As discussed in Chapter 4, the majority of baseball's most publicized scandals in the 19th and early 20th centuries involved some variation of gambling and match-fixing including the Louisville Grays, Hal Chase, and the Black Sox Scandal. And while these early forms of scandal have not disappeared entirely, as evidenced by more contemporary editions like Pete Rose betting Reds games while managing the club in the 1980's, they have largely been replaced with newer methods in what has essentially become a game of cops and robbers not only between the league and players, but also at times with regulators, as was the case with the FBI and DOJ's 2015 probe into the St. Louis Cardinals' alleged involvement in a 2013-2014 incident known simply as "Hackgate."

For background, Jeff Lunhow, an Ivy League and McKinsey alum, worked for the Cardinals from 2003-2011, where he quickly climbed the ranks and led amateur scouting and the farm system. During his impressive tenure, Lunhow accelerated the organization's analytics program, expanded scouting and development in the Dominican Republic and Venezuela, and elevated the club's Baseball America Farm System Rankings from dead last in 2005 to as high as 8th (2009) while with the organization and first shortly thereafter (2013). Not surprisingly, competitors quickly took note and Lunhow was named General Manager of the struggling Houston Astros, fresh off a 56-106 nightmare campaign. The rebuild certainly did not occur overnight as the Astros went on to average more than 103 losses over Lunhow's first three seasons, which garnered Houston their second and third consecutive top draft picks which, unlike 2012's selection of superstar shortstop Carlos Correa, did not pan out as neither selection (Mark Appel in 2013 and Brady Aiken in 2014) played an inning for the Astros. Nonetheless, Lunhow's system began paying dividends in 2015 with a Wild Card birth and near defeat of eventual world champion Kansas City in a five-game division series.

Meanwhile, Lunhow's former employer was under FBI and DOJ investigation for the alleged hacking of his proprietary scouting and intelligence database, aptly nicknamed "Ground Control". The motivations behind the incident stemmed from allegations that Lunhow had taken intelligence from the Cardinals' proprietary system, aptly nicknamed "Redbird", with him to Houston. In a low-tech attack involving reuse of Lunhow's prior passwords while with the Cardinals, data was not only extracted, but ten months of transaction diligence were leaked to a public website (Anonbin) in 2014, thus triggering the investigation.[89] Just over two years after the leak, federal judges sentenced former Cardinals' scouting director and Lunhow's successor Christopher Correa to nearly four years in prison and $279,038 in restitution for his admission to five counts of unauthorized access of a protected computer from 2013 to at least 2014.[90] While no other individuals were prosecuted and Cardinals ownership denounced Correa's actions as "roguish behavior", Major League Baseball hammered the Cardinals with a $2 million fine and forfeiture of their top two 2017 draft picks, all of which went to Houston. And while the two inherited picks of pitcher Corbin Martin (since traded to Arizona) and infielder J.J. Matijevic (in Astros organization) have not (at least yet) come back to haunt the Cardinals, Lunhow's Astros went on to win the 2017 World Series and 2019 AL Pennant.

But Lunhow and the Astros' characterization as victims soon changed when Major League Baseball fined the club $5 million and required them to vacate their first and second round picks in both 2020 and 2021 after their investigation found the organization guilty of an elaborate sign-stealing scheme in 2017 and 2018, a punishment decried by opposing players since no Astros players were directly punished. The scandal led to Lunhow and Manager A.J. Hinch's terminations in January 2020 and the organization's continued antagonization by opposing players and fans. The scheme, nicknamed "Codebreaker", featured a combination of technology, including stadium cameras and dugout monitors to identify upcoming pitch types, and manual techniques like clapping or banging trash cans in the dugout as pre-delivery signals. The latter tactics occasionally drew suspicion from opposing players like White Sox reliever Danny Farquhar in September 2017:

"There was a banging from the dugout, almost like a bat hitting the bat rack every time a change-up signal got put down. After the third one, I stepped off. I was throwing some really good change-ups and they were getting fouled off. After the third bang, I stepped off."[91]

Farquhar's suspicions were later reaffirmed by the league's 2019 investigation, which stemmed from former Astros pitcher Mike Fiers' interview with the Athletic:

"I just want the game to be cleaned up a little bit because there are guys who are losing their jobs because they're going in there not knowing. Young guys getting hit around in the first couple of innings starting a game, and then they get sent down. It's [B.S.] on that end. It's ruining jobs for younger guys. The guys who know are more prepared. But most people don't. That's why I told my team. We had a lot of young guys with Detroit [in 2018] trying to make a name and establish themselves. I wanted to help them out and say, 'Hey, this stuff really does go on. Just be prepared.'"[92]

But the Astros were not the only club associated with sign-stealing scandals. In fact, the Boston Red Sox were accused in at least two separate schemes, one in 2017 involving the usage of stadium cameras to intercept pitching signs and relay them to Apple Watches in the dugout, and another during their 2018 championship season, while under the watch of new manager and former Astros bench coach Alex Cora, involving video-replay rooms (not formally monitored by the league until the 2018 postseason) to study and relay pitching signs, which prompted another league investigation that ultimately cost the Red Sox a 2020 second-round pick.

While each of the aforementioned scandals are certainly disconcerting, especially to fans, they are hardly shocking when considered in the context of famed criminologist Donald R. Cressey's iconic Fraud Triangle, which consists of three components: opportunity, rationalization and incentive/pressure. With respect to opportunity, each of the aforementioned scandals were enabled by technology (e.g., concealed cameras, computers) and a perceived lack of monitoring as evidenced by minimal prior convictions. Second, fraud rationalization is commonly aided by the natural human impulse to commit wrongdoings when others are doing the same. In the hypercompetitive arms race that is modern professional baseball, the temptation to emulate other clubs, even in wrongdoings, is presumably much higher than most industries. Furthermore, fraud rationalization is exacerbated when the perpetrator feels they too have been wronged and that their subsequent misdeeds are justifiable retribution. In the case of Hackgate, Chris Correa's allegation that Jeff Lunhow carried proprietary Cardinals' intelligence with him to Houston likely provided rationalization for the ensuing breach. And in the case of sign-stealing, a transgression as old as baseball itself, the penalized clubs likely felt their own signs were also vulnerable, as evidenced by the proliferation of sign-stealing countermeasures (e.g., concealing, rotating or comingling real and false signs, speaking into gloves during mound visits, etc.). And lastly, with respect to the third fraud triangle component of pressure/incentive, at risk of stating the obvious, Major League Baseball is a high-stakes pressure-cooker with vast incentives for successful organizations, including the upstart Astros and blue blood Red Sox and Cardinals.

Tanking and Competitive Balancing Incentives

The concept of deliberately losing games or "tanking" is arguably as old as sport itself and the most publicized instances in baseball history have widely been associated with gambling. Even the most casual fans are well-versed on Shoeless Joe Jackson and the 1919 Black Sox Scandal and Reds Manager Pete Rose betting on his club's games in the 1980's, and have likely debated the fairness of those resulting lifetime bans. Yet until recently, tanking in baseball was mostly associated with individual players. And while struggling clubs have been incentivized to lose games since the inaugural Major League Player Draft in 1965 which, unlike other major professional sports that allow draft orders to be reconfigured via trades or (in basketball) lotteries, has always ordered picks conversely with the prior season's standings, organization-wide tanking had been intermittent and isolated to few clubs. While speculative, the root causes for the historical lack of tanking in baseball (at least until recently) are less likely due to morality and obligation to fans than they are to bottom-line risk and the strategy's lack of consistent success.

For every rags-to-riches example extolling the virtues of tanking, there are far more, albeit less-publicized, examples to the contrary. In an attempt to quantify this phenomenon, Erik Larsen of *The Lefty Catcher* completed a statistical deep-dive into frequency and success rates of tanking in the MLB from 2011-2021. While the ability to accurately and quantitatively evaluate tanking success rates would require unequivocal proof or admissions from the participating clubs, the analysis considered multiple factors including the statistical correlation between significant payroll reductions and winning percentages across the league over that span. Without getting into the mechanics, the assessment noted at least twelve MLB clubs that could potentially be considered to have "tanked" for multiple seasons over the past decade. Of those twelve, three have won World Series (Cubs in 2016, Astros in 2017 and Braves in 2021), but one (Cubs) has arguably begun another rebuild and the remaining nine have collectively mustered just five division series births (all defeats) since beginning their rebuilds.

Another historical deterrent to tanking in baseball has been the improbable nature of the draft and player development in the minor leagues. For the NBA, NHL and NFL, drafts are not only smaller, both with respect to the candidate pool and the number of rounds, which range from two to seven as opposed to MLB's 20 (lowered from 50 in 2011), but the payback period at the highest level is much shorter, especially in football and basketball where most draft picks are assigned to their organization's highest club immediately as opposed to spending years in the minors. Dodgers president and part-owner Stan Kasten articulated this sentiment for his time as the Washington Nationals' president from 2006-2010:

"We got lucky with those two (top overall picks Stephen Strasburg in 2009 and Bryce Harper in 2010). Getting the front office and the scouting and player developments systems in place — that was the key. Without that, those two players wouldn't have mattered as much. This isn't the NBA. In the NBA, you draft LeBron

[James] and you go to the [NBA] Finals every year. In baseball, you need 25 [big league] players and 200 more in the minor leagues just to get a foundation in place."[93]

To further understand Kasten's point on getting lucky with his top draft selections, one can simply analyze the career Wins Above Replacement (WAR) of the top draft picks over the past couple decades. For instance, the 2000 and 2001 drafts began with the selection of transformational talents in first baseman Adrian Gonzalez (43.5 WAR) and catcher Joe Mauer (55.2), but were followed by top picks Bryan Bullington (-0.2), Delmon Young (3.2) and Matt Bush (2.5) until the Diamondbacks struck it rich with Justin Upton (32.3) in 2005. And while one can presume that continued improvements in data gathering, technology and analytics have taken some of the guesswork out of talent evaluation, as evidenced by the unprecedented run of superstar top selections from 2009-2012 (Stephen Strasburg, Bryce Harper, Gerrit Cole, and Carlos Correa) that have combined for around 150 WAR,[94] the system is hardly foolproof as evidenced by the Astros' beleaguered top picks in 2013 and 2014 (pitchers Mark Appel and Brady Aiken) that never pitched for Houston's big club.

Despite its lack of consistent success, unpredictability of top draft picks and the often-immense financial risks, including foregone ticket and merchandise sales and poor television viewership, tanking not only continues but many would argue that it has become pervasive, as evidenced by the aforementioned accounts that as many as twelve clubs (40% of the league) have attempted it over the past decade. While attributable to a multitude of reasons, which are often bespoke to individual clubs and almost never disclosed publicly, one can reasonably speculate the underlying motives. For starters, many of the clubs, particularly those in smaller markets with limited payroll flexibility, simply cannot retain top talent due to expiration of player control and inability to match competing free agent offers from deeper-pocketed clubs. For instance, Oakland's 2022 opening payroll of roughly $33 million [95] not only paled in comparison to the league leading Dodgers' roughly $300 million, plus over $30 million in luxury taxes, for exceeding the league's $230 million threshold,[96] but also some individual 2022 salaries like Mets pitcher Max Scherzer ($43.3 million), Rangers shortstop Corey Seager ($37.5 million), and Angels third baseman Anthony Rendon ($37.5 million). Second, perpetually downtrodden clubs already dealing with poor attendance and viewership may feel they have little to lose by tanking. Moreover, such clubs may be encouraged by examples of others in previously similar positions that were able to reverse their fortunes through successful rebuilds. Lastly, the lack of penalties coupled with competitive balancing incentives, which not only include higher draft picks but also (as of 2011) a significantly higher spending limit to sign draft picks, can be quite appealing to clubs contemplating a rebuild. For example, in the 2021 MLB Draft, in addition to receiving the top pick (thanks to their 19-41 record in 2020) the Pittsburgh Pirates were allocated over $14 million to sign their draft picks (with over $6 million going to top pick Henry Davis), which far exceeded the defending champion Dodgers' $4.6 million. Given the signing risk of elite talents, particularly high school prospects, this signing bonus disparity provides a compelling incentive for tanking clubs.

While fans will continue to oppose tanking by not showing up or tuning in, the practice will likely continue without significant rule changes. Even though other sports have had success with anti-tanking measures, most notably European soccer's relegation system that demotes bottom-feeders into less competitive and lucrative divisions, they hardly seem feasible in baseball given MLB's continued revenue growth aided by long-term television contracts with individual clubs and healthy ticket sales in major markets with large, modern stadiums (not to mention the logistical nightmare of reconfiguring farm systems and affiliations after each season's wave of club promotions and relegations). Yet fans are not alone in their opposition to tanking. Even one of professional baseball's most powerful forces, "Super-Agent" Scott Boras decries the practice:

"A team can say, 'We don't particularly want to win for a three- or four-year period, because we can go get draft picks. That is not a reason to come to the ballpark. That's not major league-standard baseball. It's something different now (implying at least twelve clubs were tanking leading up to the 2018 season) ...*We [should] never want to reward non-competitiveness. It's a cancer. It damages the brand of baseball."*[97]

Yearning for the Simpler Times

Even though the aforementioned analyses covered an infinitesimal fraction of the people, clubs and events over the past century that have molded America's Pastime, they are a microcosm for the greater movement to rekindle the game in its purest form, where rosters were consistent, decisions were only made in hearts and minds, there were no incentives to lose (apart from the occasional bribery scandal) and computers were mere fantasy. Despite the reality that these old-fashioned scenarios will never resurface in today's ever-evolving professional baseball landscape, their proponents have not abandoned hope. And while baseball has seemingly always been blessed with outstanding historians, hence the abundance of stellar accounts chronicling its nearly two centuries of history, living vicariously through text, audio and film is not nearly enough for some. Rather, as the various accounts in the following chapters will note, a small yet passionate and growing community of historians, nostalgists, purists and dreamers continue to gather in the nondescript corners of city parks and country fields on blazing summer and picturesque autumn weekends to celebrate the game in its most elemental form. Whether it's the period uniforms, old-fashioned nicknames and vernacular or the 19th century rulebooks, nearly every detail is painstakingly preserved out of love of the game and reverence of its past. And while today's roughly 400 vintage clubs pale in comparison to MLB's $11 billion dollar empire, the vintage revival's burgeoning success, which includes over 100% growth over the past decade,[98] provides hope for those longing for the earlier game.

Part III: Alive and Well – Vintage Base Ball's Revival

6: Back to Basics: Reemergence of Vintage Base Ball

"This is baseball in its purest form. It's a window back into our youth, but also into America's past. It's a real counterpoint to the commercialism of modern-day baseball, where the focus is on marketing and skybox seats."[99]
  - Former Glen Head (Long Island) Zig Zags Captain Dan "the Man" Moskowitz

A Long Hiatus

While not attributable to a specific year or even decade, as noted in subsequent chapters featuring clubs that play by rules ranging from 1858 to 1898, the term "vintage base ball" is associated with recreating the 19th century game, most commonly during the 1860's. In fact, the Vintage Base Ball Association's mission is to "preserve, perpetuate, and promote the game of base ball as it was played during its formative years in the nineteenth century and other historic eras." However, as noted in Part II, baseball's rapid evolution over the 20th century, largely aided by accelerating professionalism and commercialization, irreversibly shaped the game and, in a sense, estranged it from its roots. And while the modern professional game's skyrocketing revenues ($10.7 billion leaguewide in 2019) and sustained growth (2019 marked MLB's 17th consecutive year of record growth)[100] are indicative that most baseball fans continue to embrace the dynamic game, the stories of the vintage clubs and ballists in the following chapters remind us of the growing community looking to rekindle the game in its purest form.

While one can argue that the desire to anchor the game to its roots is not a recent phenomenon, as evidenced by isolated accounts of historical exhibitions in Elmira, NY (an 1887 match between the Unions and Alerts that featured 1866 rules), Cooperstown (a 1939 schoolyard-style town ball game commemorating the centennial of the Doubleday Myth), and

Amherst, MA (a 1959 centennial reenactment of the first collegiate game played between Amherst and Williams Colleges under the 1859 Massachusetts town ball rules), organized vintage base ball clubs, seasons, leagues and tournaments were not commonplace until the 1990's.[101] And while difficult to pinpoint each of the underlying causes that led to this century-long hiatus, one can attribute this gap to key factors including the sustained growth and prominence of professional baseball, abundance and popularity of recreational outlets like slow pitch softball, and the early challenges encountered by vintage clubs.

Early Years: Old Bethpage Village Restoration (Long Island, New York) and Ohio Village (Columbus, Ohio) (c. 1979-1991)

Much like the game's formative years in the mid-19th century, the earliest days of vintage base ball's revival were modest and experimental. Despite the aforementioned one-off exhibitions, which were more akin to Civil War reenactments than authentic, competitive matches, the first organized vintage base ball programs would not emerge until the 1980's. Commonly regarded as the birthplace of the vintage base ball revival, Old Bethpage Village Restoration (OBVR) is around 200 acres of living history museum nearly 40 miles east of Manhattan in Long Island's Nassau County. Founded in 1970, OBVR features more than 60 historic structures (e.g., homes, barns, shops, church, school) from the 17th through 19th centuries staffed with in character curators. As base ball had been a core component of the American experience for soldiers and civilians alike in the mid-19th century, former museum director Ken Balcom, along with Civil War reenactor Terry Hunt, organized the museum's first historical base ball game in 1979 in the style of an 1860's soldiers' match. The well-received pilot led to additional matches the following season and the formation of two clubs: the Hempstead Eurekas, comprised of OBVR museum workers, and the Mineola Washingtons, a converted softball team. Both clubs, whose names and uniforms were modeled after actual 1860's clubs, competed in as many as four matches each summer under similar period rules, including bound catches and prohibition of gloves, although many rules were loosely interpreted in the early years as the clubs continued to research and adjust to the intricacies of the early game.[102]

While the OBVR vintage base ball program slowly gained momentum in the early 1980's, the movement simultaneously took shape in the Midwest beginning in Columbus' Ohio Village. Similar to the OBVR, Ohio Village is a living history museum featuring curated exhibits intended to educate visitors on daily life in the 19th century. Additionally, both museums belong to the Association of Living History, Farm and Agricultural Museums (ALHFAM), which hosts annual conventions for members to share ideas and hold presentations, including the OBVR's presentation on their nascent vintage base ball program. Following a trip to Cooperstown, Dr. Amos Loveday, chief curator of the Ohio Historical Society, implemented a vintage base ball program to expand Ohio Village's research and educational scope to include 19th century social customs and pastimes in addition to daily work life.[103] Facing potential cutbacks, museum employee and schoolmarm reenactor Vicky Branson, volunteered to lead the research and manage the inaugural club named the Ohio Village Muffins, an 1860's vintage club whimsically named after the period term for unskilled players. And like the first OBVR clubs, the inaugural Muffins roster in 1981 primarily consisted of museum workers.

Despite the makeshift roster at the onset, the program soon grew organically as one longtime Muffin notes:

"Recruiting players was not a problem, ads were placed in local publications including college newspapers, which produced many new volunteers. It should be noted that playing ability has never been a requirement to join the Muffins since the goal of the organization is historical interpretation rather than competition. We also got our wives involved wearing vintage clothing acting as sideline interpreters. We played in Ohio Village at the time, a reproduction of an 1860's town on the grounds of the Ohio Historical Society. In fact, the first Muffin Team in 1981 was made up of the village shopkeepers as the Society wanted to show the public one of the leisure activities of the period. It became popular enough to get a team of volunteers to relieve the shopkeepers. The biggest challenge was there were no other vintage teams, so they had to recruit teams. I just found the roster of the 1991 organization and by then, we had 29 players, 8 tallykeepers and umpires and 21 interpreters. Six of those players are still involved with the program."[104]

As the only vintage club within roughly 600 miles, the Muffins resorted to creative means to fill their schedules, often engaging other historical reenactors including fellow living history museum employees from Columbus' Slate Run Farm and the cast of Chillicothe's production of *Tecumseh*. But more commonly, the Muffins engaged area softball teams provided the matches were played under 1860's rules.[105] By playing these exhibitions, the Muffins were not only able to fill their schedules but also promote interest in the vintage game and, as a result, recruit new members. One such recruit is none other than Don "Big Bat" Andersen, who joined the Muffins after his church softball team competed against them in 1986. Now in his 80's, Andersen remains active with the Muffins and vividly recalls his introduction:

"The Muffins were looking for opponents since there were no other vintage teams in Ohio or the Midwest. Teams never turn down an opportunity to play a game, so we accepted the invitation. I am a Brooklyn boy who grew up playing stickball in the streets. At that time, the Muffins were using an IncrediBall (Easton's soft-stich, foam ball often used by some vintage clubs in lieu of more authentic and expensive lemon peel balls) and some narrower bats that brought back memories of years' past. Plus, you could make an out by catching the ball on one bound. That was the original hook. Two weeks later, they invited us back to play a game that Sports Illustrated was going to use to do a feature on them (Joel Schwartz's 4/27/1987 piece "Playing Baseball the Old-Fashioned Way"). That set the hook! I joined them in 1987 and have been with them ever since."[106]

The 1987 *Sports Illustrated* article represented just one of many successful publicity pieces that elevated the Muffins' profile and broadened national awareness of the overall vintage base ball revival as Andersen notes:

"After the Sports Illustrated article ran things started moving for the Muffins. We were invited to be on Good Morning America in 1988 the week of the MLB All Star Game. Invitations to fairs and centennials started to roll in. The Grandaddy of All Vintage Base Ball Events (the Ohio Cup, hosted by the Muffins at Ohio Village) started as a four-team competitive event on the Memorial Day

weekend in 1992. Over the next few years, based on early results, we decided to move it to Labor Day weekend and change it to a festival format and schedule teams to play others they haven't had a chance to meet. It was well-received and has grown to an event with over 30 teams (typically from six or seven states) and a waiting list of teams wanting to come. It's a weekend of vintage camaraderie. You can now find tournaments all around the country. Publications the Muffins have been featured include a second Sports Illustrated (1994), Southwest Airlines' (Spirit) Magazine (1993), Wall Street Journal (1992) and numerous newspapers and Sunday supplements."[107]

In addition to successful print campaigns, the Muffins were able to continually thrive through sponsorships, including Ohio-based Marathon Petroleum Corporation and National City Bank, showcase events, including the aforementioned Ohio Cup and exhibitions at Major League parks like Cincinnati, Pittsburgh and Cleveland, and, while of secondary importance to the club's focus on historical authenticity, on-field success, including a 17-3-1 campaign in 1986.[108]

Despite the Muffins' sustained success, vintage base ball's momentum had stalled back in Long Island. While the OBVR maintained a steady annual cadence of four contests (one each month from June to September) between the aforementioned Hempstead Eurekas and Mineola Washingtons throughout the 1980's, stakeholder interest gradually waned as noted by former Hempstead Eurekas captain, nearly 40-year vintage base ball veteran and umpire extraordinaire Gary "Reverend" Monti:

"Though it was the first of its kind anywhere, it was a sleepy little program and its vintage rules were spotty at best in their accuracy. By 1991, the program was down to one game a year, which was a shame and made it hardly worth doing."[109]

Rebirth (c. 1992-1997)

Undeterred by the OBVR program's regression, Monti remained optimistic about vintage base ball's future. Pointing to a renewed national interest in baseball history, aided largely by recent television and box office successes like *Eight Men Out* (1988), *Field of Dreams* (1989) and Ken Burns' *The Civil War*

(1990), Monti established another vintage base ball program in nearby Westbury:

"I knew it was a good idea and wasn't ready to let go. At the time, I was the president of the Westbury Historical Society. I concocted an idea to have the society sponsor an 1887 base ball team called the "Westburys" (an actual team of the time), and also put together a second team to play in communities. I made contact with the people heading up the Freeport Centennial Committee because I heard that, as part of their commemorations, they were recreating a period baseball team, The Freeport Athletics" (again, an actual team of the period). I made arrangements with them to play community games. I chose 1887 (overhand pitching) because I didn't want to directly compete with the 1860's program at Old Bethpage. It wasn't a matter of conflict of interest because, by this time, I left the County museums and moved to the Brooklyn Museum; it was a courtesy, though not much of one. We played that summer season about six times and it was great fun. At the end of the season, I got a call from the Asst. Supervisor at Old Bethpage (Ken Balcom), who suggested that I bring my 1887 base ball to the village."[110]

Monti's new clubs and Balcom's leadership resuscitated the once-fledgling OBVR program. By 1993, the OBVR played roughly 20 games per season amongst clubs in its 1866 and 1887 leagues, up from just one game in 1991.

While 1994 continues to live in infamy amongst many baseball fans, thanks to a bitter 232-day work stoppage that abruptly ended the season and the hopes and dreams of the 74-40 Expos and their long-suffering fans, it's seen as miracle amongst the vintage base ball community. As if in a zero-sum game, disenchanted professional baseball fans gravitated to the vintage game seemingly overnight as Monti notes:

"In 1994 something amazing happened. Major League Baseball went on strike, which angered all baseball fans, a result of which we were inundated with the media using us as a positive juxtaposition against the pros. Our player recruitment skyrocketed, that summer we had four 1866 teams and six 1887 teams, so we played 60 games that season. Prior to 1994, the media who came to us did "fluff" pieces. The print media wasn't

too bad but the TV stations would send their "hilarious" morning guy or sometimes the weather guy to play in a game and act goofy. We did not mind this so much because any publicity was good for the program. In 1994, during the strike, an old school sportswriter from Newsday did a piece on us. He got what we were trying to do and wrote a wonderful multi-page story. This led to a photo journalist who published his piece in the American Airlines in-flight magazine (American Way) which was read by the sportswriter for the Boston Globe, who in 1997 did a major story on us that appeared on the front of the sports page on the first day of that year's World Series. The Smithsonian article (Doug Stewart's 1998 piece "Baseball – as it was meant to be played") followed that. At one time or another we were in every major newspaper and on multiple TV shows, notably ESPN and all three networks."[111]

Despite the OBVR program's newfound popularity, the clubs continued to research customs and rules to attain greater alignment and historical authenticity. Fortunately and unexpectedly, help came in 1994 via an immensely knowledgeable spectator, as over 30-year vintage base ball veteran Ed "Pigtail" Elmore notes:

"I was told that the rules they used were not completely accurate, as no one at that time had (fully) done the research…Sometime during that year, a man named Al ("Old Dutch") Dieckmann stopped by to watch the games. After the games, he came over to tell us that we were doing some things wrong according to the real rules of those years. It was evident right away that he knew what he was talking about. Before long, we began having some get-togethers with Al to discuss the rules. He pointed out to us that what the 1892 teams were playing was most closely to the rules of 1887, and that there were other things wrong with the 1866 game. Within a year or two the number of teams started to grow, as more and more players started appearing. One source of players came from the fact that we didn't have exact team rosters, and we often invited spectators to suit up and play. Within a couple of years under Al's leadership, we had two "leagues", an 1887 league with six teams and an 1866 league with four teams, a total of ten teams playing out of OBVR."[112]

Despite the success of the New York and Ohio programs and the emergence of isolated clubs across the country, vintage base ball programs essentially operated in vacuums until the mid-90's. Without the constant interconnectedness of the internet and the marketing muscle of social media, early vintage revival clubs had to resort to word-of-mouth and grassroots methods to not only spread the game but maintain consistent standards on rules and historical authenticity. For example, the OBVR gladly hosted clubs from as far as Colorado to teach and grow the vintage game. Similarly, the Ohio Historical Society, now known as the Ohio History Connection, began hosting public informational sessions each winter. These sessions, along with their supplementary materials, were not only well-received throughout Ohio, but also nationally, as evidenced by the influx of information requests received. To better address this widespread and growing need, Doug Smith, then manager of the Ohio Village Muffins and Ohio Historical Society employee, contacted clubs across the country (and even Canada) and held an introductory meeting during the Ohio Cup in September of 1995 to gauge interest for a centralized association to oversee the vintage game. And on February 11, 1996, which aptly marked the 150th anniversary year of the first official base ball game, delegates from 13 clubs across five states officially formed the Vintage Base Ball Association (VBBA) under the following purpose, mission and objectives:

"The purposes of the Association shall be to help preserve, perpetuate, and promote the history and heritage of the game of base ball as it was played during its formative years and other historic eras, in order that these may contribute to the present and future of baseball to inspire and inform future generations. This worthy objective shall be accomplished by the following activities and endeavors:
1. *Presenting the game of base ball as it was actually played in accordance with the rules, equipment, uniforms, field specifications, customs, practices, language, and behavioral norms of the period.*
2. *Supporting the formation and strengthening of vintage base ball clubs by sharing vintage base ball information, setting standards of historical accuracy and participation, and providing a means to recognize and communicate with other vintage base ball clubs.*

3. *Encouraging research and disseminating information in order to re-create the game in keeping with the highest levels of accuracy and authenticity.*
4. *Educating the public regarding the character, history, and growth of the game with attention to the historical context in which it originated and developed."*[113]

Using the template of base ball's first central governing body, the National Association of Base Ball Players organized by the Knickerbockers in 1858, the VBBA ratified bylaws (https://www.vbba.org/bylaws) with provisions for annual conventions, member voting and governing committees, including a Rules and Customs Committee to continually research historical customs, uniforms, equipment and conventions as well as interpret rules and share such findings with member clubs to promote consistency and historical authenticity. Now over a quarter-century later, the VBBA remains the guiding light for the vintage base ball community, keeping hundreds of geographically dispersed clubs united under common standards and informed through recurring communications and events.

Traveling Era (c. 1998-present)

The continued success of the VBBA and the vintage game's flagship programs in New York and Ohio led to a steady increase in new clubs and tournaments in the late-90's. However, instead of resting on their laurels, leading vintage programs, much like their 19th century barnstorming forefathers, took their shows on the road as Gary Monti explains:

"It was at this time that we created a traveling team (Brooklyn Atlantics in '97 and the New York Mutuals in '99) *to take on the road to demonstrate the game. The team went up and down the east coast and west to Ohio and Minnesota. Teams there were created soon after. There were about 45 teams in 1998, now there are close to 400. We were being taken seriously, which was good because we were serious about what we were doing. Occasionally, we would still get the local TV idiot to do his thing as a player but we made sure he would go home with some bruises* (from barehanded fielding). *We didn't much like fluff pieces anymore. That bring us to 2004 when Conan O'Brien came. He*

did the goofiest bit that has ever been done on us. We didn't mind at all because it was so good."[114]

And while the OBVR's traveling clubs have been instrumental in the vintage game's outreach and growth, travel has presented its share of challenges as Brooklyn Atlantics co-founder Ed "Pigtail" Elmore explains:

"The Atlantics played in New York, New Jersey, Connecticut, Massachusetts, Pennsylvania, Maryland, Delaware, Ohio, Michigan, North Carolina, West Virginia, and twice in Canada. One innovation in the vintage game that the Atlantics started was that since we traveled many hours to play, we convinced the other teams to play doubleheaders, one of each team's representative year, giving spectators the chance to see how the game changed between years. However, the 1864 game soon became the chosen year to play for many teams on the east coast (probably because it is the most fun to play, in my opinion), which took away from sometimes getting to showcase two different eras."[115]

Meanwhile, the Ohio Village Muffins had also hit the road, traveling to matches at distant, yet iconic locations like Hoboken's Elysian Fields in 1996 to commemorate the 150th anniversary of base ball's first organized game; Sandusky, Ohio and Salisbury, North Carolina to re-create the Civil War POW matches; Cooperstown's Doubleday Field for a town ball match with the local Leatherstockings; Dyersville, Iowa's Field of Dreams; Pittsburgh's Three Rivers Stadium; and even Denver for their "Best of the West" vintage showcase.

While not of the same historical significance as many of the aforementioned venues, one trip and its catalyst events particularly stand out to Muffin veteran Don "Big Bat" Andersen:

On Father's Day in 1991 we were playing a game in our (Ohio) Village. A woman brought her husband down as a Father's Day gift. As part of our role, we always talk to folks during our off-the-field time. He was fascinated with it and as the game went along a player was injured and that team needed a replacement. We asked him if he would like to try his hand at the game and he jumped right in. After the game, I gave him my card in case he had any interest. That Fall, I got a call at work and the woman on the line asks if I could hold for Mr. Burr. I said sure not knowing who I was going to talk to. It turns out to be the man who we asked to play on Father's Day and he was the President of Atlas Steel Products in Chagrin Falls, OH. He was forming a team called the Forest Citys and wanted us to play at a big Memorial Day weekend and be in a parade they have, which we did. We did it again in 1993 and, while we were chatting, the opening of the new Cleveland Indians Stadium (Jacobs Field) in 1994 came up. We said "Wouldn't it be great if we could play that day." Bo said "let me see what I can do about that." Turns out, he had friends on the Indians' board and they made it happen. That's how my wife and I celebrated our 30th Anniversary at Jacobs Field."[116]

With the growth in traveling clubs also came an abundance of tournaments. In addition to the Ohio Cup, which has grown from a four-team local competition in 1992 to a more than 30 team national showcase today, notable annual tournaments have emerged across the country and are often played at storied venues like the Gettysburg National 19th Century Base Ball Festival, the Silver Ball Tournament in Upstate New York's Genesee Country Village and Museum, and Greenfield Village, Michigan's World Tournament of Historic Base Ball among many other national, regional and local competitions. And while these events range from ultracompetitive to no champions named, camaraderie and historical preservation remain the prevailing sentiments.

Preserving the Legacy

As noted previously and in subsequent chapters, while many clubs, especially the OBVR and Ohio Village programs, pride themselves on their painstaking efforts to authentically re-create as many details of the 19th century vintage base ball experience, occasional exceptions are made out of necessity. One such development, as Gary "Reverend" Monti points out, was the shortage and prohibitive costs (often exceeding $40 each) of authentic, hand-stitched leather base balls, especially during the rapid growth of vintage clubs in the late-90's. While many clubs had been compensating with modern substitutes like Easton's IncrediBall, these alternatives not only detracted from the historical aesthetic, but their slicker, synthetic grips often flummoxed gloveless fielders. [117] Borrowing a page from countless other consumer products, replica vintage base balls, including the perpendicular "lemon peel" stitching, were being mass-produced in China for roughly $10 each by 1999, a landmark shift that Monti cites as necessary to sustain the growth of vintage base ball.

Beyond maintaining an adequate supply of historically authentic yet affordable equipment, vintage clubs will continue to face challenges maintaining rosters, especially as many of the game's pioneers retire. While transitioning the vintage game to later generations is second nature to clubs like the Muffins, where parents often play alongside their children like Don "Big Bat" Andersen and his son Craig, who have been teammates for over 30 years, other clubs like Ed Elmore's Brooklyn Atlantics rely on robust succession planning:

"Our Atlantic team, as was true with most of the teams on the east coast, included players of a wide range of ages, from late-teens to sixties, with many in between. This mix has helped in keeping the team going, with new blood always being added. There also seems to be a slight drop-off with players in their late-twenties through thirties as they are having children of their own and need to attend to them, but many return later on, or even stay with the team on a part-time basis."[118]

And while Don "Big Bat" Andersen is "amazed at the growth of vintage base ball", which includes the addition of over 400 clubs since he joined the Muffins in 1987, he speaks with cautious optimism of the game's future and continued adherence to its founding principles of historical preservation, sportsmanship and camaraderie:

"To me, it seems to be progressing in much the same manner as the original game did, human nature being what it is, moving from friendly games between clubs to more competitive games between skilled ones, (and) *leagues being formed. There are hundreds of clubs out there now playing* (by) *rules from many different eras* (with) *lots of competition and not much interaction with the spectators with the exception of a few clubs...It appears to me it is going to become more commercialized."[119]*

The Ohio Village Muffins at the Battle of Pea Ridge Civil War Reenactment in Keokuk, Iowa (c. 1993). Photo courtesy of Don Andersen.

The Ohio Village Muffins and Forest Citys at Cleveland's Jacobs Field prior to the Indians' inaugural game there on April 4, 1994. Photo courtesy of Don Andersen.

Don "Big Bat" Andersen at the Society for American Baseball Research (SABR) 1998. "Old-Timer Exhibition" at San Francisco's 3Com (Candlestick) Park. Photo courtesy of Don Andersen.

7: Mountain Athletic Club (Fleischmanns, NY)

In this somewhat remote place, determined individuals and families who love the old ways are working to be sure of the past; the extent of their success will indeed predict the future of Fleischmanns and so many other communities whose histories, if properly understood and conveyed, are their principal assets.[120]
  - Official Historian of Major League Baseball John Thorn

Raised by Yeast
Unless you're a resident of Upstate New York or have vacationed in the region's breathtaking Catskill Mountains, chances are you're not familiar with the small village of Fleischmanns. While this close-knit community of roughly 300 is over a two-hour drive north of New York City, the idyllic settings, which include the adjacent Belleayre Mountain Ski Center and the New York State Forest Preserve Land, make Fleischmanns a festival, vacation home and tourist destination.

While officially incorporated in 1913, Fleischmanns was the consolidation of adjacent hamlets including the Fleischmann family's property to the east and Griffin Corners, which dates back to the 1830's, to the west. Initially a remote farming community, the completion of a railroad connection to New York City in the 1870's opened the floodgates to tourists looking for a respite from the big city bustle and summertime heat waves. In fact, some very wealthy tourists loved the area's friendly community and natural splendor so much that they built palatial estates, most notably yeast magnate and patriarch of the village's eventual namesake family Charles Fleischmann.

Born in 1835 in Moravian Silesia (modern day Czech Republic) of Hungarian ancestry, Fleischmann perfected his father's craft of yeast production, along with its byproducts of alcohol and vinegar, before moving to Cincinnati, Ohio in 1865. Disappointed with the quality of American bread, Charles, his brother Max and their business partner James Gaff founded the country's first commercial yeast producer as Gaff, Fleischmann & Company in 1868.

If the Fleischmann name still does not ring a bell, visit your local grocery store where you'll likely find those iconic little yellow packets of yeast, a tub of their margarine, or even bottles of their gin or vinegar. This family-owned business eventually morphed into a global food conglomerate (Standard Brands) before merging with Nabisco in 1981 in a $1.9 billion deal (around $6 billion in modern terms). Note that the Fleischmann's Yeast brand is now operated by St. Louis-based AB Mauri Food Inc., which remains a generous benefactor of today's Mountain Athletic Club and their various charitable causes.

Yet the company's success did not occur overnight. In fact, the struggling family business waited eight years for its big break, which came in the form of its Model Vienna Bakery exhibit at the 1876 World's Fair in Philadelphia, which attracted over ten million visitors. The bakery exhibit garnered immediate international acclaim for the quality of its bread and yeast. After rapidly ascending as the world's largest yeast producer, with 14 plants nationwide (including one that employed over 600 in the Upstate New York town of Peekskill) supported by a rail-based distribution system, and a major player in the vinegar and gin industries, the company relocated to New York, where the Fleischmann family invested in various philanthropic causes and civic projects, most notably their development of a sixty-acre resort community in Griffin Corners from 1883 until their departure in 1913.

Despite their immense wealth and success, the Fleischmann's were ostracized by New York's social elite because of their Jewish and immigrant heritage, and were even denied entry to certain luxury establishments.[121] Resolved to provide a more inclusive yet extravagant resort experience for the Jewish Community, the Fleischmann's spared no expense in making their vision a reality. After the Fleischmann's purchased 160 acres overlooking Griffin Corners and built a family compound that featured five mansions and various service buildings, other wealthy families followed suit like prominent New York City physician Dr. Alexander Skene, the namesake of the town library and childhood friend of Andrew Carnegie, who also invested in the village. The investments extended beyond residential properties as luxury hotels like the Grand and Regis sprouted up to accommodate the influx of visitors, who had their pick of activities including swimming pools, golf courses, deer parks and even a man-made lake for swimming, boating and fishing.

The Original Mountain Athletic Club

Despite the abundance of recreational options, Charles Fleischmann's sons Julius and Max were determined to bring the now-thriving American Pastime to the Catskills. After purchasing and clearing four acres on the west side of town along Bushkill Creek in 1895, the brothers constructed a baseball diamond surrounded by a bicycle track that would become the Mountain Athletic Club Grounds. Shortly thereafter, an "amateur" baseball club organized as the Mountain Athletic Club, but known colloquially as the M.A.C.'s or Mountain Tourists in homage to the area's multitude of visitors.

Given the Fleischmann brothers' immense wealth and fervor for the game, the M.A.C. Grounds and their distinguished list of visitors were so impressive that a July 12, 1900 *New York Sun* article noted:

"(The) diamond is at the base of the mountains and the field has been laid out with no sparing of expense. The grounds are inclosed [sic] with a wire-netting fence and there is a small grand stand, which is always devoted to the Messrs. Fleischmanns' guests. Guarantees, as much as $150 a game, are paid to the clubs to play there, irrespective of the small gate receipts. The players are quartered at a first-class hotel, and are serenaded by a band once a week."[122]

While billed as an amateur or semi-pro club due to their lack of affiliation with an established professional league, the M.A.C.'s roster proved the contrary. With seemingly infinite financial resources and considerable influence as the Mayor of Cincinnati and owner of the Reds, respectively, M.A.C. player-owners Julius and Max Fleischmann easily lured various collegiate, minor-league and professional players to their nascent and remote club.

One such player is believed to be the iconic shortstop Honus Wagner, a 1936 Hall of Fame inductee whose T206 baseball cards sold at auction for a staggering $6.6 and $7.25 million in 2021 and 2022, respectively, making them the highest-selling cards of all time.[123] While spending that kind of money on anything, let alone a baseball card, seems unfathomable, a closer look at Wagner's career and achievements may prove otherwise. In a 21-year professional career, including 18 with his hometown

Pittsburgh, Wagner amassed 3,420 hits (eighth of all time), 643 doubles (tenth), 1,732 RBI (24th), 723 stolen bases (tenth), a .328 average (41st) and 131.0 Wins Above Replacement (tenth). Beyond the gaudy numbers and career leader rankings, which have stood for over a century, Wagner's collection of hardware and accolades is equally impressive including National League titles in batting (eight), doubles (seven), stolen bases (five), RBI (four) and triples (three), along with one all-important World Championship (1909). While primarily a shortstop, Wagner played every position except catcher, even logging over eight innings and six strikeouts as a pitcher.[124] Nicknamed the "Flying Dutchman" for his speed and German heritage (an enduring corruption of the Germanic term "Deutsch"), Wagner's versatility was so exceptional that longtime opposing manager and Hall of Famer John McGraw of the New York Giants described him as "the nearest thing to a perfect player no matter where his manager chose to play him." McGraw would add that "(Wagner) is not only a marvelous mechanical player, but he has the quickest baseball brain I have ever observed" and that he would "take Wagner as (his) pick of the greatest".[125]

But even Hall of Famers have to cut their teeth somewhere. One of nine children to German immigrant parents, John Peter "Honus" Wagner was born in 1874 in the remote Pittsburgh suburb of Chartiers (now Carnegie). In between supporting his family with various jobs in coal mines and steel mills that began at age twelve, Wagner joined his four brothers on the diamond every chance he could. After dominating in various community leagues, Wagner joined his brother Al on the semi-pro circuit, beginning as a pitcher with Mansfield in the 1893 Allegheny League and the Carnegie Athletic Club the following season. Seeking higher competition and pay in 1895, Wagner followed his brother to the professional, albeit fledgling Inter-State League's Steubenville (Ohio) club for the mere sum of $35 per month. In fact, Al had to convince the owner to take on his younger brother by telling him:

"I've got a brother who is a peach. He's loafing now (was training to be a barber at his brother's shop), and maybe you could get him to play for you. If so, you won't go wrong. He's a great ballplayer."[126]

The elder Wagner's words were especially prescient as Honus not only homered in his professional regular season debut against Canton, but also threw out a runner at home from left field. Unfortunately, Honus' on-field success coincided with his various clubs' insolvencies, as he competed for at least five clubs in three states. Despite the lack of continuity, Wagner thrived wherever he played, accumulating a .360 average over the summer.[127]

While Honus eventually landed with a more stable club in 1896, joining the Atlantic League's Paterson (New Jersey) Silk Weavers, where he hit .337 over nearly two seasons before signing with the National League's Louisville Colonels for $1,500,[128] the exact locations and durations of his various stops on that turbulent and nomadic 1895 campaign remain unclear. One alleged stop is none other than Fleischmanns' Mountain Athletic Club. The basis for this hypothesis is in a photograph at the end of the chapter.

Current M.A.C. manager and historian Collin "Stumpy" Miller has gone to great lengths to authenticate the image and caption, including comparing to several other verified images and even contacting Bob Kelly, the nonagenarian son of the Fleischmanns postmaster that lent the photo to the newspaper in 1963. Yet, as noted in Miller's March 2020 M.A.C. site blog entry *Will the Real Honus Please Stand Up?* the mystery remains unsolved:

"The burden of proof for the Fleischmanns connection that hangs on this one team photo taken over 120 years ago still lingers on. But then again, baseball history is full of myths, legends, mystery and intrigue which is why among other sports, it is by far my favorite".

While the veracity of the Wagner account remains in question (although a June 8, 2019 Resolution from the Baseball Hall of Fame acknowledges him as a former member of the club's roster), the unprecedented depth of the early M.A.C. rosters is not. Beyond the obvious financial incentives afforded by the affluent owners, the M.A.C. was an appealing destination for top talent for a variety of reasons. For starters, the club was an instant powerhouse, overwhelming their outmatched opponents and amassing gaudy win-loss records like 1900's 56-4 campaign. In addition to playing in a brand new, professional-grade park that occasionally hosted upwards of 5,000 passionate fans a day (or roughly 2,000 more than National League Cincinnati's League Park), aspiring professionals had the opportunities to showcase their talents to the Fleischmann's, who held equity stakes in both the Reds and (secretly) Phillies [129], and to face off against professional clubs in occasional exhibitions like 1900's visit to Cincinnati.

After arriving in a luxury Pullman railcar, the visiting M.A.C.'s fielded a lineup that included Max Fleischmann, future MLB Hall of Famer Miller James Huggins (Reds and Cardinals second baseman and eventual longtime Yankees' manager), 1906 White Sox World Series hero George "Whitey" Rohe, and brief major leaguers Pete Cregan and Barney McFadden. In a complete team effort, the M.A.C.'s scattered 11 hits (vs. the Reds' five) and rallied behind dominant pitching from former professional (for one game) "Black Jack" Keenan to down the Reds 4-3.

As an unaffiliated club, the M.A.C.'s sought quality opponents from around the country, even if it bucked societal norms, like their 1897 and 1903 series against the Negro League powerhouses Cuban X-Giants and Cuban Giants, respectively. Nearly 50 years before Jackie Robinson broke Major League Baseball's color barrier, the M.A.C.'s graciously hosted their guests who, contrary to their moniker, were predominately African Americans based out of New Jersey. The 1897 edition was humbling for the M.A.C.'s, who dropped both games to the X-Giants by scores of 16-4 and 12-6. Longing for another quality opponent, the M.A.C.'s hosted the Cuban Giants from August 10-12, 1903. The Giants' loaded roster was headlined by second baseman Bill "Hipple" (later "Hippo") Galloway, the dual-sport phenom that helped break Canadian hockey and baseball color barriers just four years prior while with the Woodstock Hockey Club of the Central Ontario Hockey Association and baseball's Woodstock Bains of the Canadian League. Despite productive stints with both clubs, Galloway left Woodstock that same year amid racial tensions with baseball teammates. And while the M.A.C.'s were again gracious hosts in 1903, they were far more competitive this time. Aided by pitcher Abe Goldburg's nine stellar frames, where only Galloway crossed home, the M.A.C.'s claimed the series opener 3-1. But with Goldburg in center the following day, the M.A.C. pitching was far less dominant in a 6-

3 defeat. And while highly likely the clubs played a rubber match the following day, the outcome remains a mystery due to the lack of a verified scorecard. Nonetheless, over a century later, Galloway and his Cuban Giants remain a treasured piece of Fleischmanns' history, with scorecards from that 1903 series framed in the village's Museum of Memories and Galloway's picture adorned on the Wall of Fame scoreboard at the M.A.C. Grounds.

While a springboard for future Hall of Famers like the aforementioned Miller James Huggins and (maybe) Honus Wagner, World Series Champions George Rohe and his White Sox teammates Nick Altrock (83 major league wins and 2.67 ERA) and Doc White (five consecutive shutouts pitched in 1904), and other legends like Charley "Red" Dooin (caught 1,124 games for Phillies), the M.A.C. was also a twilight destination for past professionals like two-time major league home run champion James Wear "Bug" Holliday and former Giants and Pirates pitcher Tom Colcolough.

Despite the M.A.C.'s dominance, fan support and seemingly endless talent pipeline, the club's sustainability was inevitably tied to the deep pockets and interest level of its owners. While the M.A.C. was founded in 1895 as a hobby for the young heirs Julius (then 24) and Max (then 18), priorities quickly shifted from the club when Charles Fleischmann's 1897 death made Julius president of the family's yeast enterprise. As if the life of an executive was not busy enough, Julius' 1900 election as Mayor of Cincinnati and (with his brother Max) 1902 purchase of the Reds made their once beloved M.A.C. an afterthought. With Julius' demanding business and political interests, and Max's world travels and relocation to Santa Barbara, the Fleischmann's left the Catskills for good in 1913, thus pulling the plug on the Mountain Athletic Club. As a silver lining, Julius donated the beloved M.A.C. Grounds to the village with the caveat that it be properly maintained and free to the public, a gesture that was not only honored but reciprocated by local residents with the incorporation of the two hamlets (Griffin Corners and the Fleischmann's properties) as the Village of Fleischmanns.

Even with the pristine baseball diamond and continued tradition of recreational games, the Village of Fleischmanns underwent various hardships after their namesake family departed in 1913. After an initial tourism decline during World War I, continued advances in automobile and air travel created new options and gradually diverted tourists from the Catskills which, because of its remote location, was highly dependent on the rail route that eventually discontinued passenger service in the 1950's. To make matters worse, the abundance of commercial and residential air conditioning systems in the early 20th century (thanks to Syracuse, New York native Willis Carrier), lessened the need to escape the big city summer heat waves in favor of the cooler mountain air. As an unfortunate consequence of the gradual tourism, population and economic decline, several of the grand hotels and homes fell into disrepair, while others succumbed to fires, including over 100 hotels, motels, camps and homes between the mid-1940's and 70's.[130] And with the decline in visitors and lack of a passionate and wealthy ownership group, the Mountain Athletic Club remained nothing more than a fond memory for nearly a century.

Return of the M.A.C.

Long gone but not forgotten, the M.A.C. would make a glorious return to Fleischmanns and their original grounds in 2007 under the leadership of local distillery owner Todd "Moonshine" Pascarella and local politician Dave Morell. As an aside, both men went on to be mayor of Fleischmanns, with Morell serving from 2009-12 (including winning a contentious 2011 election by the slim margin of 37-35)[131] and Pascarella succeeding him.

What provoked this renewed enthusiasm after nearly a century? For starters, the vintage revival was in full swing, especially in the Northeast. In addition to prominent clubs like the Brooklyn Atlantics and New York Mutuals, which formed in 1997 and 1999, respectively, vintage base ball had even returned to the Catskills via the nearby Roxbury Nine, a reprisal of the area's 1890's-1900's clubs.

Like its neighbor less than 20 miles south in Fleischmanns, Roxbury, New York is a remote mountain town rich in history. As a member of the National Register of Historic Places, Roxbury is renowned for its historical celebrations, most notably the "Railride into Yesteryear". The festival includes train rides from neighboring towns and historical reenactments dating back to 1898 including market carts, flower girls, horse and carriage rides and, of course, vintage base ball. The latter of which caught the eye of M.A.C. co-founder Collin Miller. While Miller had been playing adult recreational baseball in his hometown 45 minutes from Fleischmanns, he was awestruck by the vintage game and hundreds of passionate fans that day in Roxbury. After learning about a potential opportunity in Fleischmanns from members of the Roxbury club, Miller befriended Todd Pascarella, learned even more about the town's rich baseball past and joined the other founders in making their dream a reality.

Another catalyst for Fleischmanns' baseball revival came in the form of MLB historian John Thorn's renowned 2004 essay *Mangled Forms,* which pays tribute to Fleischmanns citing his fond childhood memories vacationing there during its 1950's heyday and the village's rich baseball history:

"For years the onset of spring — which in our household meant the chance to play, watch, and chatter about baseball — was not assured until my sons and I drove up to Fleischmanns — gloves, bat and ball in the trunk — to cavort on the field along Wagner Avenue where we knew Honus Wagner, Ty Cobb and other major leaguers had once played (either as autumn hunting guests of the Fleischmann brothers or as ringers brought in for the semi-pro team they sponsored)."

To mark their long-awaited return on Saturday June 30th, 2007, the resurgent M.A.C.'s, comprised of Pascarella, Miller and other area residents like Grant "The Pounder" Cure and Jerrod "J-Rod" Hubbell, hosted the Roxbury Nine at the original M.A.C. Grounds. The match, which featured 1890's rules and uniforms, was a resounding success drawing over 500 fans.

As an interesting aside, the M.A.C.'s adhere to multiple sets of vintage rules to accommodate their opponents, who are often based on clubs predating the original M.A.C. In fact, the club frequently discloses the rule sets by game on their season schedules, which most commonly alternate between Chadwick-era 1864 rules and M.A.C. authentic 1895 rules, with the occasional doubleheader featuring both. Regardless, some of today's M.A.C.'s continue to play without gloves, even though they had become fairly common by the 1890's. In lieu of an itemized list of rule differences between the eras, I'll oversimplify by saying that the rules were materially similar but point out the most notable differences. For starters, pitchers were permitted to throw overhand beginning in 1884, creating a very different experience and strategy for batters. To accommodate for the faster deliveries, the pitcher's box was also moved back from the 45 feet of the 1860's underhand era to 60 feet, 6 inches (as is the case today). In addition to faster deliveries and varying arm slots, batters in 1895 games also have to worry about the strike zone, which was introduced around 1887, although they are advantaged by four-ball walks. Other more subtle differences in the 1890's game include the infield fly rule, freedom of substitutions (allowed only for illness or injuries in the 1860's) and changes to bat sizes (expanded legal diameter from 2.5 inches to 2.75 inches but instituted a maximum length of 42 inches).[132]

Despite the M.A.C.'s adaptability to different rulesets, they are most in their element while playing by the late 19th century "overhand rules". And while those rules are also embraced by their fellow clubs in Delaware County (Roxbury Nine, Bovina Dairymen and Delhi Polecats), they are seldom observed outside of the region. For this reason, M.A.C. manager Collin Miller takes great pride in preserving this era. As Miller points out, the late 19th century rules not only honor their namesake club, but also provide a competitive overhand baseball alternative for local adults, who were previously limited to slow pitch softball.[133]

Buoyed by their successful debut, the M.A.C.'s continued friendly competitions with nearby clubs, including a tripleheader at Cooperstown's Doubleday Field against Roxbury and Bovina, and expanded to play established clubs in New York, New Jersey and New England. Not only were the M.A.C.'s successful promoters and ambassadors of the vintage game, but they were also competitive from the onset. In fact, the upstart M.A.C.'s captured their first championship in just their third season, upsetting the host Roxbury Nine in the finals of the prestigious Harry M. Keator Cup, marking "the first and only time that Roxbury ever let this trophy slip out of their hands."[134]

Yet the M.A.C.'s achievements encompass far more than mere wins and trophies. For example, the M.A.C.'s attempted a world record for longest baseball marathon over the 2011 Memorial Day Weekend (note that this record is held by a group of over 50 friends in Alberta, Canada led by Dr. Brent Saik, who played for an astounding 83 hours and 13 minutes in August 2019). Inviting the public to join in on the fun by playing and donating to charity, the M.A.C.'s did not break world records but raised over $7,000 for the construction of the region's first accessible playground, which was to be constructed at Fleischmanns Park next to the M.A.C. Grounds. Unfortunately, that noble dream would have to wait.

Disaster and Resilience

On that fateful day of August 28, 2011, Fleischmanns and its beloved ballpark were ravaged by the devastating floods caused by Hurricane Irene. An event still regarded as one of the ten biggest natural disasters in New York history, Hurricane Irene made nine different landfalls across the Atlantic seaboard from the Bahamas all the way to Vermont, resulting in over 60 deaths and $15.8 billion in damage.[135] While the once Category 3 hurricane (characterized by devastating damage and winds up to 111-129 mph), was downgraded to a tropical storm by the time it reached New York and New Jersey, the torrential rains and tornadic activity wreaked unanticipated havoc over their inland paths, including Fleischmanns. Despite being nearly 100 miles from the ocean and 1,520 feet above sea level, Fleischmanns' proximity to the east branch of the Delaware river, which surged from over ten inches of rain and runoff over a couple of hours, and the already swollen lake and waterways from a wet August led to unprecedented flooding. Without the opportunity to evacuate or prepare, the village was taken by surprise with over two feet of water on its Main Street, causing millions of dollars in damage and the life of visiting 82-year-old Holocaust survivor Rozalia (Leah) Stern-Gluck.

Devastated but not broken, the resilient community bonded together and immediately went to work helping one another and repairing the damage, as noted by popular local Mexican restaurant La Cabana manager Rene Garcia:

"While they worked, the whole village of Fleischmanns, one of the most diverse communities in the Catskills, came together. The village has large populations of Mexican immigrants, vacationing Hasidic Jews from Brooklyn and a variety of other diverse communities. In the aftermath of the disaster, everyone in Fleischmanns looked past these differences. The Methodist Church was handing out free meals to anyone who came through the doors."[136]

While the outpouring of relief from various groups including the M.A.C. helped local residents and businesses like Garcia's restaurant, which reopened within a week, the village and its crown jewel ballpark would take years to recover.

By 2017, the M.A.C. Grounds had been restored, not to their original grandeur but as a serviceable grass field. And not to be forgotten, the dream of building Fleischmanns' first accessible playground, which began with that memorable 2011 baseball marathon fundraiser, finally became a reality.

Triumphant Return

With their home finally restored, club co-founder, manager and third baseman Collin Miller, who had recently moved back to the area from New Hampshire, rallied the community to restore their beloved M.A.C.'s for the Spring 2017 season. In a May 2021 interview with the Albany *Times Union*, Miller recalled why he loves the vintage game and his motivations for resuming the club:

"All of a sudden time stops and we're 12 years old again in some sand lot playing for the love of the game... I knew if I wanted to play, I was going to have to get the band back together and recruit players."[137]

Eager to return to the diamond, the rebooted M.A.C.'s hit the ground running in an abbreviated 2017 campaign. Continuing their momentum, the club received federal disaster relief funds and community support to install a new backstop as well as pitching and batting areas in the offseason. The M.A.C.'s would open their updated park in style, winning their 2018 season opener against the Connecticut Bulldogs (an homage to Yale's 1880's teams).

On June 8, 2019 the M.A.C.'s commemorated both the 150th anniversary of the Fleischmann's yeast company and the 148th birthday of club founder and town namesake Julius Fleischmann with the dedication of a manual scoreboard, which was hand-painted by the club's second basewoman and Broadway set painter Chrissy "Showtime" Skubish. The scoreboard is what Collin Miller calls on the M.A.C.'s site "a tribute to the thirteen major leaguers we know of that played for (or managed) the M.A.C. at the turn of the last century", which includes the aforementioned MLB Hall of Famer Miller James Huggins, Phillies ironman catcher Charlie "Red" Dooin, 1906 World Series hero George "Whitey" Rohe and even Fleischmanns' own Jay Kirke, who hit .301 in just 320 Major League games, but logged over 2,600 hits in the minors.[138]

This Founder's Day event was not without fanfare as nearly 1,000 revelers were treated to a pregame gala event at the Spillian, an arts and cultural center housed at the last of the original Fleischmann family mansions, featuring speeches from Miller and MLB Historian John Thorn, which included a resolution from the Baseball Hall of Fame recognizing the Fleischmann family for their contributions to the game and the historic M.A.C. Grounds, which would be added to the New York and National Register of Historic Places in 2020. Despite the disappointing 17-5 loss to local rival Bovina that followed, the celebration continued in true Fleischmanns' fashion with a bakeoff using their signature yeast. While unanimously enjoyed, Miller most fondly recalls the celebration and its significance to the still-healing community:

"It was a proud and cathartic moment for the ball club and the community at large. After all, the park grounds and ball field were ravaged by Hurricane Irene in 2011, suspending M.A.C. baseball indefinitely and leaving the Village dealing with restoration efforts several years later. Julius (Fleischmann) would be proud. I know I was..."[139]

Today's M.A.C.'s

Like the squads under the Fleischmann brothers' leadership 125 years ago, today's M.A.C. is stocked with talent. While most played at the high school level, others have professional resumes. In addition to the dominating Venezuelan lefty Winston "Winnie" Marquez, who logged over 140 innings and strikeouts in three seasons within the Twins' organization, the M.A.C. boasts pitcher/shortstop Nate Fish, who moved to neighboring Arkville prior to the 2021 season. In addition to starring on the University of Cincinnati's baseball team alongside former Red Sox great Kevin Youkilis, Fish had a successful international playing career with stops in Israel, Germany, Argentina, Puerto Rico and the Dominican Republic. And while Fish proves he still has it during occasional appearances with the

M.A.C., his true calling is now in the dugout. In addition to successful coaching stints in Europe, Cape Cod and the Dodgers' organization, Fish has coached with the Israel National Team, including at the 2017 World Baseball Classic, 2019 European Championships and 2020 Tokyo Olympics, where they defeated Mexico for their first Olympic baseball victory. In 2021, Fish was rewarded for his dedication by being named manager of the Israel National Team, which he promptly led to a 5-1 record and second-place finish at the European Championships (their only defeat was to the 24-time European Champion Netherlands squad headlined by longtime Washington National Roger Bernadina). Despite his decorated playing and coaching career in the modern game, Fish acknowledges the differences and challenges of vintage base ball noting:

"There's almost no such thing as a routine play...You just kind of throw your body on the grenade, kind of smother the ball."[140]

And while Fish brings celebrity, talent and unrivaled baseball acumen to the M.A.C., his teammates appreciate him most for his "easy-going attitude and generous spirit."[141]

Despite the M.A.C.'s talented roster and accolades, the club remains open to all who are interested regardless of background or playing ability. And the club's manager Collin Miller will not hesitate to remind his teammates to "dial it back" when competition briefly overshadows the club's greater purpose of serving the community through historical education, entertainment and philanthropy.[142]

Breakout Campaign

Amid frequent shutdowns and various challenges from the pandemic, the resilient M.A.C.'s persevered through an abbreviated 2020 campaign, where they fought to a 4-5 record in a slate that included seven matches with the neighboring Bovina Dairymen and a split with the Westfield (Massachusetts) Wheelmen. Despite the mixed results, the club remained highly competitive throughout, with their last two losses coming by a single run. Additionally, the club's offensive consistency, as evidenced by their averaging more than 11 runs per game, left them optimistic going into 2021's full campaign. But first they needed some new threads.

While today's M.A.C.'s pride themselves on "(connecting) generations to the National Pastime through authentic play according to the rules and customs of nineteenth-century base ball", as noted on the club's website, recreating history after 125 years is not without its share of challenges. For instance, since their 2007 revival, the M.A.C.'s have sported black and yellow uniforms as an homage to (possible) club alumnus Honus Wagner and his Pittsburgh Pirates. While the uniform design and lettering can be verified through review of historical photographs, the color scheme cannot as color photography was not widely available until after the original M.A.C.'s dissolution. However, prior to the 2021 season, club manager Collin Miller came across a May 11, 1897 article in the *Poughkeepsie Evening Enterprise* with a letter from Julius Fleischmann to his star catcher Granville Whitaker detailing the club's "beautiful new blue uniforms with maroon trimmings", which are commonly believed to be the inspiration for the 1900-1903 Reds while Fleischmann was the city's mayor and (beginning in 1902) team owner. In his endless pursuit of historical accuracy, Miller redesigned and ordered the blue and red-trimmed uniforms (the black and gold uniforms were retained as alternates) in time for the club's season debut May 15-16 at the Ommegang Historic Base Ball Festival in Cooperstown, New York.

The M.A.C.'s were clearly comfortable in their new threads winning all four matches in 1864 rules competition thanks largely to catcher and new father "Shoeless" Dave MacClintock's 15 hits (.789) and 48 total bases. The M.A.C.'s hard-fought sweep came against a difficult slate that included familiar foes the Providence Grays and Brooklyn Atlantics, as well as the Liberty Base Ball Club (CT) and Boston Union BBC.

After a successful weekend in Cooperstown, the confident M.A.C.'s returned home to dedicate the historical marker commemorating the M.A.C. Grounds' long-awaited addition to the New York and National Registers of Historic Places and host Providence, Rhode Island's Olneyville Cadets in an 1895 match. Despite falling behind 2-0 in the top half, the M.A.C.'s soon overwhelmed their shorthanded adversaries 23-6 aided by an offensive barrage highlighted by a three-for-five, four

RBI performance from new shortstop, Israel National Team manager and vintage game novice Nate Fish.

Two weeks later, the undefeated M.A.C.'s traveled south to the Fleischmann family's former home of Cincinnati for the National Showcase of Vintage Base Ball. But first, the club managed to visit the grave of early M.A.C. alumni and Baseball Hall of Famer Miller James Huggins before visiting the Reds Hall of Fame and taking in a game.

The following morning, the M.A.C. faced off against the Dayton (OH) Clodbusters. The undefeated M.A.C.'s got off to a sluggish start that Collin Miller attributed to the prior evening's "post-Reds game tailgate party and intense baseball strategy meeting that extended into the wee hours of the morning in the hotel parking lot."[143] After shaking off the cobwebs, the M.A.C.'s staged a valiant, late comeback that came up just short as the Clodbusters prevailed 13-11. Undeterred and no longer hungover, the M.A.C. went on to rally and win their remaining three matches to end the weekend on a high note.

Following their successful Cincinnati trip, the M.A.C. returned home for their first ever meeting with the newly formed Delhi Vintage Base Ball Club of 1886 (now known as the Delhi Polecats), a club located just 30 miles northwest of Fleischmanns and fellow member (along with the Bovina Dairymen) of the Delaware County Vintage Base Ball Association. After winning their initial duel in Fleischmanns, the M.A.C. played their neighbors four more times, dropping only one, a 17-8 setback (and Delhi's first ever victory) at the inaugural Delaware County Historical Association's Vintage Base Ball Round Robin (1864 rules).

Adding insult to injury, the M.A.C. lost again on that scorching, late-July day in the Delhi Hayfields, but this time to their longtime foes the Bovina Dairymen. Founded in 2008 in Bovina Center, New York (less than 20 miles northwest of Fleischmanns) and inspired by the town's 1890's teams, today's Dairymen are known for their distinctive uniforms of pressed white shirts and black trousers held up by suspenders, which resemble the common work uniform of 1890's dairy workers who played ball between shifts. Their rivalry with the M.A.C. is characterized on the Dairymen's website as a "classic frenemy situation", where "the two squads have played at least a thousand games against each other over the years, learning and playing tricks on each other since the misty times of baseball lore."[144] Except on that fateful July Saturday, the M.A.C. saved their tricks for themselves committing six errors over the first three innings. In a match characterized by hot temperatures, tempers and even hotter bats, the Dairymen edged their rivals 22-16 in their first of several encounters that season.

The M.A.C. would not have to wait long as they traveled to Bovina's aptly named Creamery Field the following Saturday for a rematch, which coincided with the town's Bicentennial Celebration. Unlike their first encounter, this match would be played under the 1895 "overhand pitch" rules, characterized by fewer runs and higher strikeouts. Unfortunately, this was not the case for the M.A.C. pitchers as they were blasted for 14 runs, and the offense could only muster three in this lopsided and third-straight defeat.

But the resilient M.A.C.'s would not capitulate on the young season. Two weeks later, the M.A.C.'s headed two hours north to Little Falls, New York for a doubleheader with the Dairymen and host Little Falls Alerts, a new club co-founded by M.A.C. catcher Andrew "Crutches" Krutz in homage of the town's 1886 club by the same name, which disbanded after a 12-15 maiden campaign due to the collective insolvency of the fledgling Central New York League and its member clubs.

In their first match of the day, a five-inning 1895 rules match against Bovina, the M.A.C.'s again fell behind their rivals early. But unlike the previous two encounters, the M.A.C.'s staged an impressive comeback on their way to an emphatic 13-6 victory, which not only halted the three-game slide but also marked their first victory over their rivals on the season. Demonstrating their versatility, the M.A.C. ended the day on a high note defeating the host Little Falls Alerts in a seven-inning hybrid match that featured the first four innings of 1864 rules (e.g., underhand pitching, single-bounce outs) followed by three under the 1886 overhand rules.

Building on their success in Little Falls, the M.A.C. continued to win their next three matches including a home 1864-style doubleheader sweep of the Mudville (MA) Base Ball Club and another win over neighboring Delhi.

After returning for their final game of the season at the M.A.C. Grounds with their perfect home record still intact, the M.A.C.'s sought revenge against the flummoxing Dairymen.

Determined to improve their pitching since yielding 14 runs in Bovina, the M.A.C. slotted their mid-season "acquisition" Venezuelan southpaw and former Twins' farmhand Winston "Winnie" Marquez, who was in town for a summer job. The fiercely competitive Dairymen countered with another southpaw in veteran Troy "Teabag" Tucker. To no one's surprise, pitching dominated the headlines as the pair of hard-throwers (with velocities reaching the 80's) combined for 30 strikeouts (18 from Marquez over eight innings of work). But after five-and-a-half innings of stalemate, the M.A.C.'s exploded with a six-run, two-out rally. The persistent Dairymen would not go away however, scoring six in the final three frames. Yet thanks to some late insurance runs, the M.A.C. would cement the 10-6 statement victory.

After a sweep of the Brooklyn Atlantics and Delhi at Bovina's inaugural Cowtown Scramble October 2-3, the M.A.C returned to Bovina's Creamery Field for a season-ending 1895 showdown with the Dairymen. The 150 in attendance were not disappointed as both sides left it all on the field in an epic, seesaw battle that featured more smoke from lefties Winston Marquez and Troy Tucker, clutch-hitting from both sides, and a broken finger for Dairymen captain Nicholas "Roughcut" Frandsen. With the Dairymen holding a seemingly comfortable 12-7 lead going into the eighth, the M.A.C. showed true grit by tallying four aces in the top half before holding the Dairymen scoreless. The momentum did not carry into the ninth as the M.A.C.'s fell just short in the 12-11 loss, which clinched the season series for the Dairymen 3-2.

Despite the season-ending setback, the M.A.C. finished their most successful campaign with an 18-5 record. And while the club can be proud of their recent success and enjoy a well-deserved break after a grueling season, they are always eager to return to work at their sacred M.A.C. Grounds as their leader Collin Miller notes:

"Although in one sense I'm glad the season is over (so I can tend to things on the home front), I know it'll be a long winter of yearning for more."[145]

August 20, 1899 photograph of the M.A.C. Grounds printed in the *New York World.* Courtesy of the Mountain Athletic Club.

The above photo was included in the March 14, 1963 version of the *Catskill Mountain News* with the following caption: "One of the most illustrious graduates of this Fleischmanns town baseball team of 1895 was John Peter (Honus) Wagner, who went on to stardom in major league baseball. Besides Wagner, who is in the top row left, there were Andy Cokley, Harry Stevens, manager, and Grandal Whitaker. In middle row are Frank Riley, Ed Winters, Julius Fleischmann, Max Fleischmann and Arthur S. Reynolds, who organized the team. Front row, Orson Hitt, Peter Cragin, Bill Doon and William Shuefelt. Pictured loaned to the News by John Kelly." Photo courtesy of the Mountain Athletic Club.

The M.A.C.'s traveled in style on their victorious 1900 trip to Cincinnati, where Julius Fleischmann (center) was the new mayor. Photo courtesy of the Mountain Athletic Club.

The M.A.C. Grounds after the September 2011 devastation of Hurricane Irene. It would take six years to eventually restore the grounds. Photo courtesy of Todd Pascarella.

M.A.C. co-founder Jerrod "J-Rod" Hubbell eyes a pitch at the June 8, 2019 Founder's Day match against the Bovina Dairymen. Photo courtesy of the Michelle Sidrane.

The M.A.C.'s in their authentic 1897 jerseys at the M.A.C. Grounds in 2021. Photo courtesy of the Mountain Athletic Club.

8: Akron Black Stockings (Akron, OH)

"I simply saw a need to remind people of what was important about the game of baseball — fun, entertainment, and gentlemanly competition. The success of the Akron Black Stockings has truly surpassed any dream that I had!"[146]

- Akron Black Stockings Founder Mark "Capt'n" Heppner

Akron: Where the Rubber Meets the Road

Lebron James and tires. While both have put this Northeastern Ohio city of roughly 200,000 on the map, one cannot ignore the many hidden gems the Rubber City has to offer. Less than an hour's drive south of Cleveland, the Akron area offers an impressive and diverse array of attractions.

Nature enthusiasts can visit nearby Cuyahoga Valley National Park, a nearly 33,000-acre landscape of woods and prairies with hundreds of waterfalls and talus caves, enjoy the area's lakes, or amble through the city's expansive hiking trails that traverse nature reserves and former remnants of the Ohio and Erie Canal.

Urbanites can enjoy the city's world class cultural institutions including the Akron Art Museum, a modern architectural marvel with a renowned collection of 1950's Pop Art, and Akron University's Cummings Center for the History of Human Psychology, the most extensive museum of its kind.

Last and certainly not least, for the sports enthusiasts, the city offers an abundance of options. While King (Lebron) James' loyal subjects continue to take in basketball games at his alma mater St. Vincent-St. Mary High School, few realize that fellow inevitable Hall of Famer Steph Curry was also born in Akron just three years later, in the same hospital nonetheless. Additionally, the Akron region is the proud home of Firestone Country Club, a regular professional tournament destination and three-time PGA Championship host, NCAA soccer powerhouse Akron University, and most notably, the Pro Football Hall of Fame in nearby Canton. And while Ohio will forever be regarded as a football state, as evidenced by their passionate fanbases at all levels, baseball is not far behind. Even though Akron residents loyally support Cleveland's major franchises, they still love their local clubs including 2021 Double-A Northeast League

Champion and Cleveland Guardians' affiliate the Akron RubberDucks, who draw over 200,000 per season and remain near the top of league attendance rankings.

Proud Baseball Tradition

Founded in 1825 for workers on the nearby Ohio and Erie Canal, the city quickly prospered as a milling and manufacturing hub after the canal segment's completion in 1827. While already a growing community, Benjamin Franklin Goodrich's founding of Goodrich, Tew and Company (later known as B.F. Goodrich) began Akron's journey as the "Rubber Capital of the World".[147] Goodrich's success and the city's robust manufacturing and transportation infrastructure made Akron an ideal hub for the rubber industry, which exploded after the emergence of the automobile in the late 19th century. Shortly thereafter, Goodrich became just one of the major tire producers in town alongside Goodyear and Firestone. By 1950, the city had more than 130 rubber manufacturers employing over 85,000 workers.[148]

As the city's population grew with the manufacturing industry in the late 19th century, so did the sporting scene. While never a hub to major league baseball due to its size and close proximity to Cleveland, Akron has a proud tradition supporting America's Pastime at all levels, especially their minor league teams.

Like most of the country after the Civil War, the newfound game of base ball flourished in Akron as a welcomed distraction from postwar tensions and outlet for returning veterans. As early as 1867, Akron formed an amateur squad known as the Akrons to compete against regional clubs. In fact, a June 1867 article in the local *Sunday Gazette* reported a 41-26 Akrons' victory over the neighboring Middlebury Mechanics, noting that "heavy hitting was the order of the day".[149] The heavy hitting continued into the season with 53 and 52 run outbursts against Cleveland's Western Reserve and in a rematch with Middlebury, respectively. Given the prevalence of Chadwick's *1860 Beadle's Dime Base-Ball Player* rules, which encouraged slow, underhand pitching to contact, the offensive prowess of the era is hardly surprising.

Despite the "Old Akrons'" success as an amateur club, the emergence of professionalism was inevitable after 1869's Cincinnati Red Stockings. In brazen defiance of Chadwick and the National Association of Base Ball Players' longtime stance against player compensation (although legalized by 1869), the Red Stockings, under the ownership of local lawyer Aaron Champion and his roughly $10,000 payroll, formed an all-professional team of hand-picked players from across the country. In their first full professional season, the Red Stockings challenged local clubs from coast-to-coast winning all 57 matches (plus seven exhibition wins to boot) and averaging over 42 runs a game.[150] Given the Red Stockings' success on the field and at the gates, where the price of admission reached as high as $1, several other clubs quickly followed suit, which led to greater competition, occasional defeats and the original club's demise after the 1870 season.

After the founding of the all-professional National Association in 1871 and enduring National League in 1876, which included large market clubs like the Boston Red Stockings, New York Mutuals and Philadelphia Athletics, Akron residents organized an independent club under the legacy Akrons moniker in 1879. To finance the club, a joint-stock company with $5-$10 shares was formed within the local business community. Unlike the National League, the Akrons initially competed solely against nearby clubs like Orrville, Garrettsville, Elyria and Warren. While labeled as amateurs, the Akron club dominated its initial campaign with 17 wins, including a 30-run drubbing of nearby Kent. Of the club's three total losses, two were at the hands of the National League's Cleveland Blues, including a game in Akron that drew over 2,000 or more than 10% of the city's population.[151]

Following a successful maiden campaign, the club resumed in summer of 1880 after relocating to new grounds that featured an 800-seat grandstand. In response to last season's lucrative series against the Cleveland Blues, the Akrons challenged additional National League clubs, including a 4-3 upset of the eventual champion Chicago White Stockings aided by stellar pitching from Tony "the Count" Mullane, who later went on to win 284 games over an exceptional 13-year career in the majors. While losing their other nine matches against professional opponents, including a 14-0 setback against Cleveland, the Akrons dominated their amateur slate in route to a 19-12-1 record. The club's success and passionate fanbase even prompted the local *Summit County Beacon* to report:

"The question has been frequently asked why Akron could not join the (National) *League. According to the rules of the association only cities with a population of 75,000 can belong to it, consequently Akron* (1880 population was less than 20,000) *is barred. But then, Akron will be situated that she will have nearly all the advantages of a league club."*[152]

Despite the on-field success, the club reported a $925 loss, which exceeded 20% of its total revenues, due in part to increasing player salaries, lost receipts from frequent rainouts and capital improvements that included a new grandstand roof.[153]

Financial hardship aside, the club resumed in 1881 thanks to a $2,500 guaranty fund raised by area business leaders and a plan to convert the grounds into a skating rink during the offseason. Not only did the club return, they also upgraded their roster, retaining star pitchers Tony Mullane and John Neagle and acquiring John "Bid" McPhee, who is now enshrined in Cooperstown for his brilliant 18-year professional career that included over 2,200 hits and 1,000 RBI, from the Davenport, Iowa club.

Despite high expectations, the 1881 campaign began with a 25-1 thud against their perpetual nemesis Cleveland Blues. The setback proved ominous as the club mounted losses against professional clubs, including a 17-4 loss to the Buffalo Bisons. While the club remained dominant against amateur opponents and competitive against soon-to-be professional clubs like Louisville's Eclipse and St. Louis' Brown Stockings, attendance dwindled, sometimes falling well below 500 and bringing in less than $100 per game, further intensifying financial pressures on ownership.

If the club's imperiled finances were not enough, the 1882 formation of professional baseball's American Association, which expanded the total professional clubs from 8 to 14 including the addition of the nearby Cincinnati Red Stockings and Louisville Eclipse (with two more American Association clubs added the following season), were the coup de grace for the beleaguered Akrons. With around 100 new professional roster spots (and the higher salaries to boot) suddenly available, the Akrons were gutted seemingly overnight, seeing 10 of their 16 players taken, including Akron native and infielder Sam Wise joining Boston and pitcher John Neagle fleeing for the New York

Metropolitans and their $100/month salary. Adding insult to injury, pitcher Tony Mullane went to Louisville, where he won 31 games as a rookie, and second baseman Bid McPhee began a Hall of Fame career with Cincinnati.

Undeterred by the dissolution of the legendary Akrons, the city has maintained a proud baseball tradition including an early 20th century industrial league with clubs from Firestone and Goodyear, Akron University's sesquicentennial program, and the city's beloved Double-A RubberDucks, whose franchise has accumulated 23 league titles including six while in Akron (through 2022).

The Early Black Stockings

While full season vintage clubs began emerging in the 1980's, including the Ohio Village Muffins in nearby Columbus, the vintage revival was still very much in its infancy by the mid-90's. In fact, only 13 clubs (albeit from five different states) were represented at the inaugural assembly of the Vintage Base Ball Association (VBBA) in Columbus, Ohio in 1996 to commemorate the 150th anniversary of the first recorded base ball match between organized clubs, where the New York Nine thrashed the Knickerbockers 23-1 over four innings at Hoboken, New Jersey's Elysian Fields. One of those 13 founding clubs was Akron's Black Stockings, who had organized the prior year under local museum curator Mark "Capt'n" Heppner.

As the VBBA's initial delegation agreed to use the National Association of Base Ball Players (c. 1858) as their model, the Black Stockings are not an homage to their iconic hometown Akrons, who did not ascend to prominence until their storied run from 1879-1881, but rather the aforementioned Cincinnati Red Stockings and their legendary 57-0 national campaign in 1869. While the club's look and attire, which includes short-brimmed caps, bibs with Old English font, knickers and high socks, are inspired by the 1869 Red Stockings, the Black Stockings moniker and black-and-white color scheme are an homage to Akron's tire industry and their home grounds Stan Hywet Hall, the former home of Goodyear Tire and Rubber Company founder Frank Seiberling.

Since their inception, the Black Stockings have played their home matches at picturesque Stan Hywet Hall and Gardens in Northwest Akron, where club founder Mark Heppner served as curator. Now a museum and conservatory, the site's meticulously preserved, three-story, 64,500 square foot 1915 Tudor revival mansion and surrounding 3,000 acres previously belonged to Frank Seiberling, who wanted the estate for his growing family and as a venue for community events. Seiberling named the estate Stan Hywet, the Old English term for "stone quarry", as the grounds served as one prior to his acquisition. Seiberling, along with his wife and seven children resided at the estate, which boasts 65 rooms, 23 fireplaces, 12 chimneys and an astounding 21,455 panes of glass.[154] The Seiberling's remained there until Frank's passing in 1955. In 1957, as a testament to the family's crest and motto *"Non Nobis Solum"* (Not for Us Alone), Frank's children gifted the estate to the city as a museum, giving Akron its first and largest National Historic Landmark. While the mansion remains fully intact, the facility's grounds now cover approximately 70 acres including the "Great Meadow", which offers a flat, open space for vintage base ball games. And while the Meadow offers plenty of space for a single game, it can present challenges during tournaments like the Akron Cup, where up to three matches can be played simultaneously. Depending on how the fields are configured, outfielders can be forced to navigate trees, drainage basins and other topography. Yet despite the occasional "quirks", Black Stockings' captain Scott "Tiny" Hamblin praises the grounds for their vintage nostalgia:

"I don't think I have had a single bad playing experience at Stan Hywet, other than when mother nature decides differently. Many teams tell us that Stan Hywet is one of their favorite places to come play. We usually do not have too many quirks on our playing fields as the "Great Meadow" is large enough to avoid obstacles like trees most of the time and is relatively flat. The only except to that is when we set up three separate fields in the meadow (yes, it is just large enough to get three fields that just overlap slightly). When the three fields are set up, one field will have trees in right field, while the other two will have a few trees in the left field."[155]

While the club has always prioritized history and camaraderie over wins, the Black Stockings have remained competitive throughout their existence, often enjoying winning seasons, which Hamblin recognizes as a testament to the club's cohesiveness:

"I don't know exact records of the earlier years of the club as stats and records of game play were not kept, that only started about six years ago. At the time, we did not really even have a league but rather just scheduled exhibition games with other clubs. I do know that the club as a whole has been relatively competitive throughout its existence. Club members, while individually may not have been the strongest of athletes or ballists, played well together and displayed a formidable team every outing."[156]

Despite the club's diverse composition, which includes a wide range of professions including accountants, engineers, artists, students, construction and warehouse workers, the members are united by their common goal of historical preservation. They also relish the bonding opportunities afforded by their annual trips, which have included Columbus' Ohio Cup; Waynesville's (OH) Caesar's Creek Festival; Upstate New York's National Silver Ball Tournament; and Frankenmuth's Michigan Vintage Base Ball Festival. Additionally, the club is planning a trip to Dyersville, Iowa's majestic Field of Dreams.

Fearless Leader

Today's Black Stockings are led by the one and only Scott "Tiny" Hamblin, ironically nicknamed for his imposing stature, which measured at 6'2" and 350 pounds during his rookie campaign, and self-proclaimed love of sarcasm. Although Hamblin has slimmed down considerably since then and is no longer the tallest or biggest on the team, he still commands the respect of his teammates and adversaries. Despite his intimidating presence on the bases and in the batter's box, Hamblin is a beloved captain, club manager, innovative marketer and ambassador of the vintage game. In addition to being a family man, successful business professional and amateur furnituremaker, Hamblin has spent over a decade with the Black Stockings, most of which as their captain and general manager. Beyond leading his club on the field and handling the administrative tasks (e.g., scheduling, roster management, travel arrangements, website maintenance) with his co-captains Don

"The Beard" Jarvis and Chase "Freight Train" Zonfa, Hamblin has fostered the Black Stockings brand through club-themed merchandise sales and promotional sponsorships with local businesses:

"Behind the scenes, the club is run like a non-profit business. We sell merchandise at games, participate in fundraisers for other non-profit organizations, and market the team and events to the public to gain more fans and improve our influence on the community."[157]

One way Hamblin and the Black Stockings have been able to promote the game and awareness is through hosting the Akron Cup, a tournament played annually in mid-July. While overshadowed by the state's (and country's) premier vintage base ball showcase the Ohio Cup, the Akron Cup has become an immense source of pride for the host Black Stockings and Hamblin. Attracting clubs from across Ohio, Pennsylvania, Michigan and further destinations like New York, the Akron Cup began in 1998 and has remained at the Black Stockings' home Stan Hywet Hall and Gardens.

While a lifelong baseball fan, whose career extended into college, Hamblin recalls how he incidentally discovered the vintage game in 2009 while noticing a co-worker's desk photo of her husband and former Black Stockings captain Rich "Juggler" Blasick in vintage attire. After mistaking the image for a novelty costume photo, Hamblin was intrigued by Wendy's explanation of vintage base ball and immediately accepted her invitation to come to a Black Stockings practice. As a former corner infielder and catcher, Hamblin quickly adapted to the lack of gloves using his body to block balls and soon became the club's primary third baseman.

Soon thereafter, Hamblin established a reputation as a sure-handed third baseman and left fielder, hard hitter and intelligent player. In an October 2020 edition of his *Roller Out the Barrel Podcast*, Matthew "Barrel Roller" Barnard recalls his introduction to Hamblin and the Black Stockings at the 2019 Ohio Cup. Suffice it to say, they did not make a great first impression. While substituting for a Minnesota club, Barnard recalls hitting a clean single and running through first before leisurely returning to the bag. Adept in the 1860's rules, Hamblin and his teammates rushed the ball back to first before Barnard. Realizing he was out, an agitated Barnard later remarked on his podcast "so these guys were thinking while they're playing base ball. And now I know who the Akron Black Stockings are." Barnard was not alone in his sentiment. On the same podcast, Rudy "Swamp Fox" Frias, captain of the Columbus Capitals, the Black Stockings' main "frenemy", added that he "hated" playing defense against Hamblin because he knew "it was gonna be a line drive, and it was gonna hurt to catch".[158] Despite the rocky first impression, both Barnard and Frias expressed their respect and admiration for Hamblin and his innovative marketing, dedication to the vintage game and willingness to help other clubs.

While a passionate competitor, Hamblin lives by the club's motto "playing the game of base ball as it was meant to be played" and provides the calming influence sometimes needed by his fellow ballists:

"My club, at times, may not have the most gentlemanly play. In terms of when a call doesn't go our way, we do have guys that get a little vocal. And you just have to reel them back in and remind them that this isn't modern baseball. This isn't men's slow pitch softball. That's not the way we go at this. We don't complain that way. If you have an issue, you wait until afterward and discuss it with the other team's captain or with the arbiter quietly and get it sorted out."[159]

Not only does Hamblin promote good sportsmanship, but also camaraderie, which extends beyond his own club:

"With the other clubs, I feel there is a solidarity and common bond that regardless of it being the first meeting or the 101st, teams can look across the field and call the other team their brothers and no one would bat an eye."[160]

Not Your Muffin Nine

While Hamblin acknowledges that the club has not kept robust win and loss records until recently, the Black Stockings have historically been an above .500 club, a trend that has continued in recent years. In fact, the Black Stockings have adorned their trophy case with a pair of tournament titles in recent years, including the 2019 Battle for Ohio, where they swept nearby Alliance's Crossing Rails and Columbus' Capitals. Hamblin fondly recalls that memorable October Sunday at the Norton Cider Festival:

"Between our two matches we tallied somewhere near 60 aces, winning both. The final match against Columbus was won in the bottom of the last inning with us starting out trailing by one ace. It also marked the first time the Capitals had not won the Battle for Ohio since it started, which was several years earlier. Any time we beat Columbus, I am happy to gloat, sorry Rudy (the aforementioned Rudy "Swamp Fox" Frias).*"*[161]

In 2020, the Black Stockings joined the nascent Northern Alliance of Vintage Ballists, a seven-team, two-division "Super League" of storied clubs from across Michigan, Ohio and Pennsylvania. Featuring familiar foes like the Columbus Capitals, Canal Dover Redlegs and Alliance Crossing Rails along with regional powerhouses like the Addison (PA) Mountain Stars, Flat Rock (MI) Bear Clan BBC and reigning Akron Cup champion Cornshuckers BBC of Canton (OH), the league represents one of the nation's most competitive. However, as Hamblin points out, the NAVB is far more than just a competitive alliance:

"The games that were scheduled were always exhibition games. By forming and joining the league, it makes games mean a bit more. The teams that helped form and join the league are all like-minded in that we want to play competitive games but also maintain the gentlemanly spirit of vintage base ball. With each year, the league learns a little more to foster the spirit of the game while making the games competitive and exciting to watch."[162]

In a pandemic-shortened season that saw the cancellation of the NAVB's inaugural league tournament, the Black Stockings nobly fought to a 12-11-1 record. While always competitive in defeats, the Black Stockings managed to score notable wins against storied clubs including Kentucky's Bluegrass Barons, Michigan's Rochester Grangers and even the pioneering Ohio Village Muffins.

Despite 2020's mixed results, the ever-competitive Black Stockings were poised for a breakout 2021 campaign thanks to the return of over 80% of their roster including prior season statistical leaders like captain Scott "Tiny" Hamblin (44 RBI), pitcher Billy "Bulldog" Gay (68 innings pitched), and slugger Keith "Stitch" Patterson (.688 average, 5 home runs and 1.054 slugging percentage). Nonetheless, the Black Stockings' talented hitters needed time to shake off the rust after a long offseason hiatus, as evidenced by the 12-4 season opening setback to conference foe Addison at Stan Hywet. And while the slump lingered into the next match against the Canal Fulton Mules, an offensive outburst in the seventh secured the 12-9 victory.

The Black Stockings took their hot bats with them to the Caesar's Creek Festival in Waynesville, Ohio the following weekend (May 1-2). Perhaps in homage to the 1867 Akrons' debut, where "heavy hitting was the order of the day" in their 41-26 dismantling of Middlebury, the Black Stockings smashed their way to 23-5 and 23-10 victories over the Moscow (OH) Monarchs and Indianapolis Blues. After another strong showing to begin the next day with a 13-6 victory over the Blackbottom 9 (OH), the four-game win streak came to an end with a 16-4 setback to the Columbus Buckeyes.

After another heavy-hitting performance in the following weekend's 27-6 triumph over the Cincinnati Red Stockings, the Black Stockings enjoyed an early bye week before heading to the National Road Festival in Scenery Hill, PA. After a heartbreaking, 0-3 opening day, punctuated by a 7-6 loss to league rival Addison, the resilient Black Stockings reversed their misfortunes and salvaged their trip with a pair of wins over the Eastwood (OH) Iron Horses.

The Black Stockings carried their momentum into the Quail Cup in Wooster, Ohio's idyllic Quailcrest Farm on Sunday, May 30th. After watching the vaunted (and eventual NAVB champion) Alliance Crossing Rails dispatch the Mansfield (OH) Independents BBC 19-4, the Black Stockings seized the opportunity and avenged last season's consecutive extra-inning losses by defeating Alliance 4-2. Needing a win to avoid a dreaded three-way tiebreaker, the Black Stockings did not take well-rested Mansfield lightly, as they cruised to a 19-1 win and their second cup in three years.

After capping a five-game win streak with a 22-7 triumph at their rival Canal Fulton (OH) Mules, the Black Stockings returned to the friendly confines of Stan Hywet for the Akron Cup on July 10-11. Despite playing stout defense, the Black Stockings dropped a pair of tightly-contested 7-5 and 13-9 matches to Canal Dover and eventual champion Canton Cornshuckers, respectively. While out-of-contention for the top prize, the unflappable Black Stockings ended the tournament on a high note with a 10-7 victory over the Oaks of Locust Corner BBC (OH) and a 15-2 statement over their perpetual frenemy Columbus Capitals.

Following another bye week, the Black Stockings headed to Alliance, Ohio for the Carnation Cup held at the beautiful Glamorgan Castle. After dropping the opener 9-2 to host Alliance, the Black Stockings rebounded with comfortable wins over Spiegel Grove (9-2) and Canal Dover (15-4).

After splitting a four-game set the following weekend while representing 29th US President Warren G. Harding at Spiegel Grove's State of Eight Tournament (commemorating Ohio's eight presidents), the Black Stockings headed north two weeks later to Mumford, New York's Silver Ball Tournament played at Silver Park, which Hamblin describes as "just about as perfect of a vintage ballpark that you could imagine." Facing a challenging slate of New York clubs, the Black Stockings fought throughout earning an 8-4 victory, ironically over Phelps' Victory BBC, before falling 22-6 to Flower City BBC. Undeterred by the lopsided defeat, the Black Stockings rallied to preserve a winning weekend with victories over Live Oak (24-13) and Rochester BBC (16-9).

The Black Stockings returned home with their bats fully intact, as evidenced by dominant doubleheader victories over Lexington's (KY) Bluegrass Barons (22-7) and the anything but lucky Whiskey Island (OH) Shamrocks (27-1).

After a competitive 14-11 defeat to Canal Dover at the Green Shake Cup, the Black Stockings headed southwest to Columbus for the grandaddy of them all.

The Ohio Cup is hosted by Columbus' Ohio Village Muffins, one of the first organized vintage revival clubs dating back to 1981, at picturesque Muffin Meadow in the Ohio Village Museum complex, which is modeled after a 19th century village with historical reenactors and craftsmen. From its humble beginnings in 1992, the Ohio Cup has emerged as one of the largest and most celebrated vintage base ball events welcoming over 30 clubs from around the country every Labor Day Weekend. But contrary to its name, no "cup" is awarded or champion named for that matter, as the event is a celebration of the vintage game and the fellowship it brings. As the aforementioned Rudy "Swamp Fox" Frias of the Columbus Capitals describes it:

> *"The game, the score, everything takes a backseat to just connecting with people."*[163]

While the Akron Black Stockings adhere to the same common values and relish each experience at the Ohio Cup regardless of the outcome, they are certainly not precluded from putting forth their best efforts, and 2021 was no exception.

After opening with an impressive 7-3 triumph over the Union BBC of Minnesota, the Black Stockings followed with an emphatic 19-1 statement over Indiana's Deep River Grinders. And while the Black Stockings' 2021 Ohio Cup ended with a 5-1 defeat to Black Flags BBC of Drovertown (IN), the weekend was a resounding success.

With the inaugural league playoffs looming, the Black Stockings headed to nearby Cleveland for a doubleheader against familiar foes in the Whiskey Island Shamrocks. While not as dominant as in their first encounter, a 27-1 victory, the Black Stockings coasted to a doubleheader sweep (15-4 and 11-2).

Having won eight of their last ten, the Black Stockings entered the Northern Alliance of Vintage Ballists league tournament in Dover, Ohio brimming with confidence, which showed in their 13-8 opening win over the host Red Legs, guaranteeing a 2-2 season split with their league rivals. But despite another strong offensive showing, the Black Stockings fell just short in their next match, a 16-12 loss to Alliance Crossing Rails, who proceeded to outlast the Columbus Capitals 18-15 in the championship match.

Despite their 4-8 league record, which included five losses by four runs or less, the Black Stockings proved they belonged in the elite NAVB. League record aside, the Black Stockings dominated their "non-conference" slate resulting in a 26-14 overall record, which included 23 double-digit scoring performances (with nine of them over 20), and one tournament crown.

Despite the club's sustained success, Captain Scott "Tiny" Hamblin keeps a watchful eye towards the future, recognizing the importance of continued recruitment:

"That is the only way these teams stay alive. There will be a point in time that will no longer be able to throw a ball or pick up a bat. It will be on the younger members of the team to step up and continue running and growing the team above and beyond what it is today."

Hamblin's advice to new and interested players, particularly those with a modern baseball background, is this:

"Get out and try it. This game is not for everyone. I have tried to bring in phenomenal baseball players but they could not handle not having a glove."[164]

And while the ever-competitive Black Stockings look towards continuing their momentum in future seasons, they certainly recognize the importance of celebrating success and recognizing greatness. In fact, the club inducted its first Hall of Fame class in 2020 welcoming 15-year veteran and former captain Rich "Juggler" Blasick, longtime arbiter (umpire) Ed "Honest" Searle, and club founder and former VBBA president Mark "Capt'n" Heppner, who graciously admits:

"The success of the Akron Black Stockings has truly surpassed any dream that I had!"[165]

While a club MVP and imminent Black Stockings' Hall of Famer, Hamblin refuses to rest on his laurels, acknowledging there is further work to be done by the club and the vintage game as a whole:

"We do see teams each year cease to exist as players retire or get to busy with life and a team can no longer be sustained. On the flip side, new teams pop up every so often to add new blood to the vintage base ball community. I'd like to see the popularity grow and get at least as many people interested in vintage games as our local minor league team's games. I'd also like to get our club to the point where we are recognized as a pillar in the community,

not only for our base ball but for outreach to other organizations and causes."[166]

Akron Black Stockings' Statistics

While history, sportsmanship and camaraderie come first, the Black Stockings, like their inspiration 1869 Cincinnati Red Stockings, also play to win. And while uncommon amongst today's vintage base ball clubs, the Black Stockings have maintained robust statistics since 2020 which, as noted below, were not all that different from their Red Stockings heroes:

Pitching Stats
Club Totals

Club	Year	W	L	IP	ER	ERA (per 9)
Cincinnati Red Stockings	1869	57	0	470	528	10.11
Akron Black Stockings	2020	12	11	179	207	10.41
Akron Black Stockings	2021	26	14	274	328	10.77

Club Leaders

Club	Year	Player	G	IP	ER	ERA (per 9)
Cincinnati Red Stockings	1869	Asa Brainard	55	338	405	10.78
Akron Black Stockings	2020	Billy Gay	14	68	77	10.19
Akron Black Stockings	2021	Billy Gay	21	135.34	150	9.97

Hitting Stats
Club Totals

Club	Year	G	H	HR	AVG	SLG
Cincinnati Red Stockings	1869	57	2020	169	.504	.830
Akron Black Stockings	2020	24	487	8	.545	.644
Akron Black Stockings	2021	40	903	11	.576	.668

Hitting Stats
Club Leaders

Club	Yr.	Player	G	H	HR	AVG	SLG
Cincinnati	1869	George Wright	57	304	49	.633	1.279
Akron	2020	Keith Patterson	24	64	5	.688	1.054
Akron	2021	Scott Hamblin	38	109	0	.686	.748

Notes:
1. The comparison between today's Akron Black Stockings and the 1869 Cincinnati Red Stockings is for entertainment purposes only and far from "apples to apples" due to:
    a. Rules – While the Black Stockings play by varying eras depending on opponents, they most commonly play by early 1860's rules, which allow for the bound catch in fair territory, a rule abolished after 1864, thus promoting more offense.

b. Statistics – As several key statistical categories were either not invented or consistently tracked in 1869 (e.g., RBI, pitcher wins-losses), applicable categories were either omitted from this analysis or recomputed based on available and verifiable data points.

c. Quality of competition – The 1869 Red Stockings played a national schedule that featured at least 29 professional clubs.

d. Games and innings played – Even in a full season, the Black Stockings rarely exceed 40 matches, with inning totals varying by match based on circumstances.

e. Equipment – While the Black Stockings go to great lengths to preserve historical authenticity. 19th century replica equipment can vary significantly in terms of quality, consistency and authenticity and is inherently difficult to compare to the actual player experience from over 150 years prior.

2. Statistics for the Black Stockings are courtesy of club captain Scott Hamblin.

3. Red Stockings Statistics were obtained from Greg Rhodes, John Erardi and Greg Gajus' 2019 book *Baseball Revolutionaries: How the 1869 Red Stockings Rocked the Country and Made Baseball Famous*. Further note that those totals were compiled based on stats published in the *Cincinnati Commercial* based on Harry Wright's scorebooks. Stats may vary slightly from other sources as they only cover official league contests and not exhibitions or matches against picked nines.

Billy "Bulldog" Gay pitches against the Addison Mountain Stars at the 2020 Akron Cup on their home field at picturesque Stan Hywet Hall and Gardens. Photo courtesy of the Akron Black Stockings.

The Black Stockings outfielders navigating some obstacles in a 2018 contest against the Spiegel Grove Squires in Fremont, OH. Photo courtesy of the Akron Black Stockings.

The proud Black Stockings after their 2019 Battle for Ohio Championship. Photo courtesy of the Akron Black Stockings.

The Black Stockings at the 2021 Silver Ball Tournament at the Genesee Country Village & Museum in Mumford, New York. Photo courtesy of the Akron Black Stockings.

9: Lafayette Square Cyclone (St. Louis, MO)

"The best advice to new players is to relax and focus on the experience; those who come in with a must-win attitude tend to ruin it for everyone. We cheer outstanding plays by opposing players, we congratulate each other, win or lose, and mingle after the games as friends. That's when the game is as its best."[167]

- Cyclone Base Ball Club (BBC) Manager
Chris "Bookworm" Duggan

St. Louis - The Best Baseball Town in America?

While the debate over America's most passionate baseball town will rage on in perpetuity between several cities with legitimate claims (i.e., New York, Boston, Chicago, Los Angeles and Bay Area among others), St. Louis is seemingly always in the conversation. Despite being only the 21st most populous metropolitan area (2.8 million residents as of the 2020 census), St. Louis has comfortably remained atop Major League Baseball's attendance reports, drawing well over three million fans a year (or over 40,000 per night) from 2004-2019, trailing only the Dodgers over the past decade. And not to discredit the Dodgers' feat, but one could argue their attendance advantage is aided by a larger park (with over 10,000 more seats) and a metropolitan area with over ten million more residents.

So why does the relatively small market of St. Louis do so well at the turnstiles? How about winning? The Cardinals' eleven World Series titles, including two since 2006, trail only the New York Yankees' 27. Beyond world championships and National League pennants (19), the club seems to be, much to the chagrin of Cubs fans, always in the hunt, as evidenced by their 32 postseason appearances (through 2022), including 16 since 2000. And because of this phenomenon, the Cardinals have yet to embrace the polarizing rebuild philosophy that pays off for some (e.g., 2016 Cubs and 2017 Astros) and prolongs the misery for others, but always begins with empty seats, rows and (sometimes in Florida) whole sections. In fact, the Cardinals have logged only one losing season this millennium, a gutting 78-84 failed Word Series title defense in 2007.

Apart from the winning product on the field, the Cardinals have continued to dazzle fans with superstar talents, including the 12 enshrined in Cooperstown[168] like Stan "the Man" Musial, Jay "Dizzy" Dean, Bob Gibson, "Sweet" Lou Brock and Ozzie "the Wizard" Smith. And that excludes inevitable Hall of Famers Albert Pujols and Yadier Molina. Even in down years, like 1998's third-place, 83-win campaign, the Cardinals managed to draw 3.2 million thanks to Mark McGwire's 70 home runs, asterisk or not.

Beyond the gaudy records and laundry list of Hall of Famers, Cardinals fans get to experience a relatively light commute to a beautiful, open-air park with views of the iconic St. Louis Arch and adjacent Ballpark Village entertainment district, daily giveaways, diverse concession options, and camaraderie with their fellow self-appointed "best fans in baseball".

As an aside on the whole best fans thing, the moniker, while contrived and unanimously decried by opposing fans, is not entirely baseless. If you've had the pleasure of catching the Cards at Busch Stadium, you'll notice (with exceptions, of course) a relatively cordial and knowledgeable fan base that appreciates the game both locally and around the league. While web gems are applauded regardless of jersey color, Cardinals fans welcome back former players with open arms. Of course, Albert Pujols received an extended ovation after returning as a Dodger in 2021, both before and after hitting a homer in his opening at bat, but moving polarizing second baseman Kolten Wong to tears in his return as a Brewer? Unprecedented.

While St. Louis' disproportionate MLB attendance and diehard fanbase is likely due to a combination of franchise success, star power and ballpark experience, detractors have argued that the city's love for its team is partly out of necessity, either due to the lack of NFL and NBA teams or lesser recreation and entertainment options than other larger and geographically desirable MLB markets. While the NFL's Rams or (prior to 1988) Cardinals, NHL's Blues or NBA's (prior to 1968) Hawks never threatened the Cardinals' reign atop St. Louis' sporting pantheon, the latter point may have merit. After all, St. Louis is devoid of beaches, mountains, Great Lakes, sprawling skyscrapers and Hollywood A-Listers, except for the occasional visit from native son Jon Hamm. But regardless of why St. Louisans love their Cardinals and the game of baseball, the sentiment is nearly unanimous and extends well beyond the major leagues.

To understand this phenomenon, one can simply drive seven miles southeast of Busch Stadium to see the Gateway Grizzlies of the independent Frontier League (and be sure to order Baseball's Best Burger, a bacon cheeseburger wedged between glazed donuts), or to the western suburb of O'Fallon for the Mother's Day Tournament, which can attract over 180 youth teams in a single weekend,[169] or even St. Louis' Forest Park for a full slate of co-ed softball games.

Not only has the city's love for the game transcended all levels, but it's also withstood the test of time, even predating their beloved Cardinals, who were established in 1882 as the Brown Stockings (although the club's origin is also associated with 1892 when they joined the National League). Note that the Browns/Brown Stockings name stuck until 1899 when it was replaced by the Perfectos, which is also the name of a current St. Louis vintage base ball club, for one year before settling permanently on the Cardinals. The Browns nickname returned after the 1901 season when the American League's Milwaukee Brewers relocated. But from the onset, the Browns remained in the shadow of their big brother due largely to their shorter tenure and comparative lack of success, with the exception of the 1944 AL pennant and resulting "Streetcar Series" where the Cardinals prevailed in six. Unfortunately, the town just wasn't big enough for both franchises as the Browns, after a brutal 54-100 campaign, were jettisoned off to Baltimore in 1954.

But St. Louis' love of baseball and its many preceding bat and ball games is nearly as old as the city itself. Founded in 1764 by French merchants Pierre Laclede and Auguste Chouteau, St. Louis inherited many aspects of French culture including its pastimes. While the exact dates, nature and extent of games played remain debated, bat and ball games in the city likely predated the 19th century, as inferred from accounts of childhood ball games from prominent settler Henry Gratiot and the 1809 prohibition of gambling on ball games in the adjacent Illinois territory.[170]

The city's passion for these games intensified after becoming an American territory with Thomas Jefferson's 1803 Louisiana Purchase. In fact, St. Louis became a hotbed for baseball precursor town ball by the mid-19th century. Similar to its modern successor, town ball involved four bases, a pitcher, catcher and hitter. Unlike today's game, the batter started at the mid-point between home and first, fielders were free to station themselves anywhere as there was no foul territory and outs were commonly registered by striking the runner with the ball.

The Original Cyclone Club

Although the city fielded an abundance of town ball clubs, a formal base ball club was not established until Brooklyn native and ballplayer Merritt Griswold moved to St. Louis in 1859. While base ball was well established in Griswold's native New York, dating back to at least the Knickerbocker Club in 1842, St. Louisans were initially reluctant to adopt this newer and more structured game. In fact, Griswold wrote of his initial experiences trying to convince a local town ball club (Morning Star Club) to adopt the new game:

"After considerable urging and coaxing on my part they passed a resolution at one of their meetings that they would try the national rules for one morning if I would...teach them, which I consented to do if they would agree to stick to it for a full hour without 'kicking' (complaining), for as I told them they would not like it until after playing it for a sufficient length of time to be familiar with some of its fine points, all of which they agreed to and kept their words like good fellows as they were, but in ten minutes I could see most of them were disgusted, yet they would not go back on their word and stuck to it for their hour's play. At the breaking up of the game to go home they asked me if I would coach them one morning as they began to 'kindly like it'.[171]

In the Fall of 1859, with the encouragement and financial support of his boss at the Missouri Glass Company Ed Bredell, Griswold formed the city's inaugural base ball team: the Cyclone Club. While finding players was not an issue after the successful experiment with a local town ball club, arranging for suitable grounds proved far more challenging. As the city's (and Western United States') oldest urban park, Lafayette Park, with its over 30 acres, was the logical choice. And with Bredell's father, Edward Bredell, Sr., on the park's board of improvements, the club received permission to use the space...with one big condition. The park was neglected, overgrown with Osage Orange trees and needed significant landscaping to be playable. Luckily, in addition to Bredell, the club included several "high rollers" like

Louis Hutchinson, John Stetinius, Paul Prewett, and John Riggin, who rounded up the $600 (or around $20,000 today) to get the grounds in playable condition.[172]

On July 9, 1860, Griswold's Cyclone Club hosted the very same town ball club he helped convert over to the new game. While equally new to base ball, the Morning Star Club, comprised primarily of associates from national retailer Ubsdell, Pierson & Lake were a seasoned town ball club whose skills transferred over to the new game, as evidenced by the 49-24 drubbing they handed the Cyclones that day, in what marked the first official base ball game west of the Mississippi.[173]

While the game quickly gained traction, with at least ten clubs competing that year, the fledgling game ground to a tragic halt the following spring as the country and city were fiercely divided by Civil War. The Cyclone Club's newly restored home of Lafayette Park was commandeered by the Union Army in July of 1861 and became Camp Jessie, which housed 23 companies or roughly 2,300 soldiers. With no home field and a loss of players to the wartime efforts, the Cyclone Club effectively dissolved. As a microcosm of the national and regional divide, the Cyclone Club saw teammates join both ends of the fighting, including co-founders Merritt Griswold, who enlisted as an officer with the pro-Union local militia, known as the Home Guard, and Bredell, who served as a staff officer and aide for Confederate General John Bowen. In a cruel twist of fate, Bredell and former teammate John Riggin, then serving as an aide to General Ulysses S. Grant, crossed paths in 1863's bloody Siege of Vicksburg. Neither were part of the more than 32,000 Confederate or nearly 5,000 Union casualties.[174] While Riggin went on to a successful military (attaining the rank of Brigadier General) and real estate career, Bredell did not survive the war, perishing in combat on November 16, 1864 in Berry's Ferry, Virginia. His body was returned home to St. Louis and temporarily buried behind the family's home across from Lafayette Park, until it was transferred to the prestigious Bellefontaine Cemetery following his father's settlement of a lengthy burial permit dispute with the pro-Union city administration.

While a few clubs like the Empires managed to survive during the war through scrimmages, the game largely went dormant in St. Louis until after the war when an abundance of clubs formed or reunited. The Cyclone Club unfortunately was not one of them. In addition to the original club's tragic undoing by the Civil War, their beautiful home at Lafayette Park was also inflicted by tragedy. Just after 5 p.m. on Wednesday, May 27, 1896, an unprecedented tornado swept across the Mississippi and laid waste to a ten-mile path through the city, killing 255 and damaging nearly 9,000 buildings in just 20 terrifying minutes.[175] The Lafayette Square neighborhood and park sustained some of the worst damage, including destroyed homes and fallen trees, and took decades to rebuild.

Rebirth

Much like the Greek myth of the phoenix emerging from the ashes, the Lafayette Square neighborhood and its centerpiece park re-emerged after the devasting tornado, and were painstakingly restored to their original grandeur, which endures to this day. And after nearly a 150-year hiatus, the Cyclone Base Ball Club (BBC) reorganized at its original home in Lafayette Park in 2009.

But while the majority of St. Louisans had since embraced the ever-evolving modern game championed by their beloved Cardinals, who play less than two miles from Lafayette Park, the Cyclone BBC intended to pick up exactly where and when their predecessors left off. From the rulebook, based on the "Father of Baseball" Henry Chadwick's publication *1860 Beadle's Dime Base Ball-Player*, to the nicknames, vernacular and uniforms, which are custom-stitched and often cost upwards of $200 each, nearly every known detail from the 1860's game has been adopted by the club to preserve the "living history and vintage aesthetic".[176] Clearly, the Cyclone BBC has accomplished this mission as evidenced by club manager and historian Chris "Bookworm" Duggan's recollection:

"Renowned baseball photographer Jean Fruth visited the GSLBBHS (Greater St. Louis Base Ball Historical Society) annual Sheppard Barclay Vintage Base Ball Festival a couple years ago and said, though she had photographed baseball at all levels all over the world, from the MLB to the sandlots, she had never seen anything like it."[177]

And while efforts to preserve this history are often painstaking, like wearing full-length wool uniforms in sweltering heat, they can at times be pragmatic. For instance, the Lafayette Park field, the same site that the original club spent $600 to landscape in 1860, has proven to be an ideal setting for today's club as Duggan notes:

"The field is commonly regarded as among the best sites for vintage base ball in the region with the classic architecture of the neighborhood and the historical beauty of the park itself, as well as the flat playing surface. Because the field is elevated and falls away toward the street on two sides, it tends to drain very well after rain."[178]

While recreating a team that had not played for a century and a half may seem like a daunting, if not impossible task, the Cyclone BBC had the benefit of their brother club and Lafayette Park co-tenant St. Louis Perfectos, who organized in 2002 as one of the first clubs in the city's vintage revival.

While the Cyclone BBC was founded by longtime Perfecto Rick "Sting" Rea, the club was far from a carbon copy or even rival of the Perfectos. Rather, the Cyclone BBC was established as a complementary club to absorb players from the overcrowded Perfectos roster, thus freeing up playing time all around. Further dispelling the notion of a rivalry, the clubs occasionally join forces in the Ohio Cup, where they have competed as the St. Louis Maroons in homage to baseball's (arguably) most dominant team. In fact, the original Maroons played only a single season in 1884, where they roared to a 20-0 start, a professional sports record that stood for 131 years before Stephen Curry and the Golden State Warriors rattled off 24 straight to begin the 2015-2016 campaign. Unlike those Warriors, who lost an epic seven-game Finals to Lebron James' Cavaliers, the Maroons claimed top honors in their league, the fledgling Union Association, posting a 94-19 record, 21 games clear of the second-place Cincinnati Outlaw Reds. The Maroons' success was hardly surprising when considering their ownership, which included brewing tycoon Adolphus Busch, and loaded roster that featured "Buttercup" Dickerson, "Sleeper" Sullivan, "Orator" Shafer and .412-hitting Fred Dunlap. While the Maroons' record campaign may have been great for their players and fans, the Union Association's competitive disparity and lack of top talent dominated the headlines, leading to its "Onion League" moniker and inevitable dissolution after just one season. And while the club joined the National League the following season, they were never able to rekindle their early success and relocated to Indiana in 1887 (renamed the Hoosiers).[179] And while the 2017 Maroons revival was far less dominant, a 1-4-1 rain-soaked weekend in Columbus, the club honorably represented its namesake with a hard-fought, sportsmanlike performance.

As a welcomed consequence of being originally designated as the less-competitive squad, the Cyclone BBC quickly established a reputation as a relaxed and fun-loving group. For example, prior to his retirement, club manager Rick "Sting" Rea was often seen playing with a lit cigar in his mouth.

And to say that the club is a close-knit group may be an understatement. Whether it's founding member Mark "Wheels" Olmsted playing alongside his sons Tim and Alex; husband and wife Tom "Shakespeare" and Katie "Dubs" Duggan; or the occasional all-Neil infield with brothers Ryan "Big Red", Adam "Little Red" and Alec "Young Red" joining their father Troy "Red Senior"; the club has prided itself on its family atmosphere.

The club in not only close-knit, but also eclectic. A simple inventory of notable members and their nicknames illustrates the well-rounded roster including cartographer Ross "Atlas" Gallentine, liquor distributor Karl "Moonshine" Krekeler, Joe "Tavern Keeper" Pecaut, photographer Dave "Shutterbug" Moore, Indiana-native Wil "Hoosier" Grundon, and (for one glorious guest appearance in September 2017) Justin "the Freshest Man Alive" Rohour.

But the Cyclone BBC is known for much more than their relaxed vibe, close camaraderie and diverse composition, they're also renowned for their vast knowledge of the vintage game and eagerness to teach newcomers and (in my case years ago) random bystanders. In addition to club founder Rick "Sting" Rea, who helped lead the local vintage revival, the Cyclone BBC is endowed with a brain trust that's included two university professors, cartographers, actors and authors. In fact, club manager Chris "Bookworm" Duggan boasts that the club "could credibly claim one of the largest collections of advanced degrees of any vintage club with multiple master's degrees and a couple of doctorates."[180]

One of the aforementioned professors is none other than Dr. Debra "Little Egypt" Reid, whose laundry list of accomplishments includes a professorship at Eastern Illinois University, a curatorship at Michigan's Henry Ford Museum, and several award-winning publications ranging from agriculture to social equality. While not an Egyptologist or native of the African country, Reid's vintage base ball nickname "Little Egypt" is an homage to her roots in Southern Illinois, a region given the nickname by frontier settlers for its abundance of grain and Native American mounds resembling pyramids. Yet despite the rigors of academia, publication and philanthropy, Reid has managed to "squeeze" in a remarkable 30-year vintage base ball career. Playing for a dozen clubs from the Cooperstown Leatherstockings in Upstate New York to the Cyclone BBC and driving upwards of 35,000 miles annually between work, matches and (on at least one occasion) tornadoes, Reid is a national legend in the vintage base ball community and pioneer for women in the sport. Even though vintage clubs like the Cyclone BBC go to great lengths to preserve the rules, traditions and ideals of the 1860's game, they ensure modern virtues of equity and inclusiveness are ingrained in everything they do, welcoming players regardless of gender, race, age or even skill level. Nonetheless, in her 30 years in a predominately male game, Reid has encountered occasional opposition while with other clubs including unequal playing time, inappropriate comments, overprotective teammates and even one opponent's open protest. While such incidents are indicative that the vintage game (and society as a whole) still has significant progress to make, Reid fondly recalls her stint with the Cyclone BBC and other welcoming clubs:

"I have great memories of days spent with friends, with wonderful events like the Barclay Cup (Sheppard Barclay Vintage Base Ball Festival) at Lafayette Square in St. Louis, the Ohio Cup and sharing rides there and back, and sitting with a beer at the end of a long day watching a game on Muffin Meadow (Columbus, Ohio)."[181]

Although best known for her dedication to the vintage game and its equity, Reid's on-field success has garnered the respect and admiration of her fellow ballists, culminating in the prestigious J. "Dinnerplate" Merrick Glory of the Game Award at Decatur, Illinois' Douglas Cup. And while Reid has since retired from the game, her exceptional career remains an inspiration to vintage ballists young and old, female and male.

While the Cyclone BBC's primary values are historical preservation and camaraderie, the club has managed to win some games along the way. As manager Chris Duggan points out:

"The teams of the bygone era were playing to win, and that is part of representing the game, so there is a balance."[182]

But like any expansion team, apart from the Las Vegas Golden Knights, who won the NHL's Western Conference in their maiden 2017-2018 campaign, the Cyclone BBC endured some early growing pains. With an inaugural roster comprised of reserves from the St. Louis Perfectos and newcomers from recreational softball leagues, a daunting schedule against established local and regional clubs, the odds were clearly stacked against the nascent Cyclone BBC.

Similar to their namesake and predecessor, who fell 49-24 in their 1860 debut, the Cyclone BBC struggled out of the gate. In their inaugural matches in 2009, a doubleheader against the formidable St. Louis Unions, the Cyclone BBC were swept, including a whitewash (shutout) where they failed to reach third base.

Not to be discouraged, the Cyclone BBC proved they were no muffins by showing continued improvement. In fact, the club returned the favor from their flat debut with a hard-fought, 6-3 triumph over the Unions in 2011, highlighted by a tiebreaking four-ace sixth inning. True to form, sportsmanship prevailed and the clubs socialized afterwards.

By 2017, the Cyclone BBC had emerged as a contender. In their home opening weekend against the nearby Alton (IL) Giant, named after 8' 11" resident Robert Wadlow, the Cyclone plated 14 runs by the third inning in an eventual rout. The Cyclone continued their winning ways, including a doubleheader sweep of the Belleville (IL) Stags, a 12-5 drubbing of the Indianapolis Hoosiers, a pair of wins against Illinois squads, including a game-ending, double-play to preserve an 8-7 win over the Vermilion Voles at the St. Louis Cup, and a 13-12 walk-off against the St. Louis Brown Stockings.

And while the Brown Stockings and Cyclone have enjoyed several memorable, hard-fought contests since both clubs were founded in 2009, the clubs are far from rivals. In fact, Brown Stockings founder Tony "Lightning" Wicker credits the Greater St. Louis Historical Baseball Society, the parent organization of the Perfectos and Cyclone clubs, for their fundraising assistance that allowed the Brown Stockings to get up and running by the 2010 season. Further underscoring the mutual respect and camaraderie among St. Louis area clubs, Wicker notes:

"I really don't look at any clubs for rivalries because we all love to play this great game and the camaraderie among all the players and their friends.... Our club is designed to treat everyone as part of one big family. I think that is why we have always been able to field a full team wherever we go. We don't strive to win or lose but to re-create how the game was played and to educate the fans who come to watch. We try to interact with the fans to answer questions, go over the rules, and to show them the equipment...As this game is played, most teams in the Midwest will help each other out. If teams are short on players, other teams will help fill in. If a player on a team gets hurts and can't play, then another player from the other team will help fill in when necessary. We all just want to play the game."[183]

Going into the Cyclone's September 2017 stretch-run at a very respectable 11-11, which included six losses by three runs or less, the Cyclone BBC was poised to make a statement. After joining forces with their comrades from the Perfectos to form the St. Louis Maroons at the Ohio Cup, which proved to be a fun yet overmatched 1-4-1 weekend, the Cyclone reconvened in Decatur, Illinois to compete for the prestigious Douglas Cup.

While the Cyclone BBC are lauded for their sportsmanship, they proved to be ungracious guests that warm, mid-September day in Decatur, tallying eight aces in the opening frame against the host Rock Springs Ground Squirrels. The inning saw the entire lineup score runs, including fill-ins from the aforementioned Vermilion Voles, with the exception of Duggan, who uncharacteristically accounted for the first two outs. The club needed every bit of that cushion as the Squirrels roared back with a late seven-run frame, but ultimately fell short 10-7. The Cyclone followed their opening victory with a more tactical, defensive performance against the Voles, highlighted by a three-run fifth that ensured the 5-3 victory.

Despite the championship stakes in the finale against the storied Deep River Grinders (IN), the Cyclone stayed true to form by playing free and easy. The result? A complete team effort that featured a nine-run outburst over the first two innings and stout defense that culminated in an 11-3 clinching victory.

Since 2017's breakthrough, the club has sustained its burgeoning success through continually strong campaigns, highlighted by a "magical" trip to Dyersville Iowa's Field of Dreams. Despite their on-field success, the club has not deviated from its founding ideals as Duggan recalls:

"I did not realize (the winning record) *until I reviewed the score book at the end of the season. This, to me, means we were enjoying the experience, which is what it's all about."*[184]

Despite a 2020 hiatus due to the pandemic, the club triumphantly re-emerged in 2021 as a perennial contender both locally and nationally. In fact, the club took on the nation's best at the Ohio Cup on Labor Day Weekend. And while the club kept with tradition and played under the St. Louis Maroons moniker, they fielded an all-Cyclone lineup. The result? A club-record three wins on the weekend, even after falling just short in three other one-run contests, none of which prevented the great times throughout the weekend.

And while tempting in today's statistically dominated world to measure this team by results, the Cyclone BBC's legacy will continue to be one of living history, sportsmanship and camaraderie, as their universal respect and acclaim from other clubs far outweigh the wins and trophies they've graciously accumulated.

1896 photograph of the post-tornado damage to Lafayette Park's Northwest corner, including the ballfield. Photo credited to the St. Louis City Public Library and obtained from the Lafayette Square Archive. https://www.archives-lafayettesquare.org/archive_files/pdf_files/18A_2021_039_d.pdf

Joe "Tavern Keeper" Pecaut pitching at picturesque Lafayette Park. If not for the photo quality and (city-mandated) light fixtures and lake's water pump in the background, one might struggle to guess the decade or even century for that matter. Photo courtesy of the Cyclone BBC.

Cyclone BBC Founder Rick "Sting" Rea digging in against his former club, the St. Louis Perfectos. While no cigar this time, the merriment is palpable. Photo courtesy of the Cyclone BBC.

10: Ohio Village Diamonds Ladies Vintage Base Ball Club (Columbus, OH)

"It's almost like Muffin Meadow (home grounds of the Ohio Village Diamonds and Muffins) brings a calming sense of peace. It brings out the child in me and lifts the rest of the world away for a couple of hours while playing. It's were I have 25 years of fun, laughter and memory making with my Muffin and Diamond family (and we are a family). It's on the Meadow where many players have earned their nicknames through mishaps that are now unforgettable."[185]
- Former Diamonds' captain Jackie "Thumper" Forquer

Not Just for the Boys

Overshadowed by softball and obscured by a historical dearth of coverage, organized women's baseball has often been relegated to a small niche following. Sadly, many have little knowledge of the sport beyond what they learned from Penny Marshall's 1992 smash hit film *A League of Their Own,* which celebrated the 1943 Rockford Peaches of the All-American Girls Professional Baseball League. And while the film was a critically acclaimed and commercial success that broadened awareness of women's vast contributions to the game, it represents just one impressive chapter in a distinguished history dating back to at least the 1860's.

While women had been playing base ball recreationally for years, the first known organized clubs would not surface until 1866 at Poughkeepsie, New York's nascent and prestigious Vassar Female College. Educating women of high society, founder Matthew Vassar's emphasis on physical conditioning to complement mental discipline defied societal norms, where women were often perceived as fragile and shielded from rigorous activities including most sports. In addition to physical education classes and calisthenics, students participated in various sporting clubs including croquet, boating and the newly popular game of base ball. In fact, student interest in base ball was so high that two clubs (Laurel and Abenakis) were formed to accommodate the 23 interested young women that represented over 5% of the entire student body. And while the clubs were formed primarily as recreational outlets, founding member and class valedictorian Annie Glidden expressed her optimism in a letter that April to her brother John:

"They are getting up various clubs now for out-of-door exercise. They have a floral society, boat clubs, and base-ball clubs. I belong to one of the latter, and enjoy it, hugely, I can assure you. Our ground was measured off this morning. We think, after we have practiced a little, we will let the Atlantic Club (reigning National Association of Base Ball Players' champion Brooklyn Atlantics) play a match with us. Or, it may be, we will consent to play a match with the students from College Hill (nearby boy's preparatory school): but we have not decided yet."[186]

Despite Glidden's excitement, both clubs and their successor (the Precocious Club) would only last a year, likely due to a combination of factors including social and familial pressures, academic priorities (student schedules were fixed from 6 a.m. to 10 p.m. with less than an hour for recreational activities),[187] poor organization and a general lack of amenities including a serviceable field and school-subsidized equipment. Concurrent experiments at California's Mills College and Connecticut's Miss Porter's School were also short-lived for similar reasons. To make matters worse, many of the sport's most outspoken critics were in the media. For example, an 1867 *Utica Morning Herald and Daily Gazette* article decried the women's game:

"Imagine a fair creature arrayed in all the paraphernalia of dress, hoop skirts, and sun bonnet making a home run!... Who would wish to see his sweetheart's eye done in mourning (black eye) for a week or her fair hand battered and bruised and soiled by a 'foul' ball, or her fair hair all pulled out or her ankle swathed in bandages, or her—oh! The subject is too heart rendering for discussion. Don't play base ball girls, that is we would be understood to say, don't do it unless you wish to and then of course "all creation couldn't."[188]

This continued onslaught reached a crescendo in October 1867 when newspapers across the country inaccurately attributed the death of Amaret Howard, a 21-year-old in Allen's Prairie, Michigan, to overexertion from playing ball. While the official cause of death was later determined to be typhoid fever, the catastrophic damage to women's base ball had been done.[189]

But while organized women's base ball initially struggled at schools like Vassar, Miss Porter's and Mills College, the game was enjoying modest success in other parts of the country. By 1869, at least 20 organized women's clubs had emerged, most notably in the Upstate New York town of Peterboro (formerly "Peterborough"). Founded in 1868 as the first non-collegiate organized women's club, the Peterboro club was aided by various factors including a prominent captain, a large and experienced roster, a passionate fanbase and powerful media proponents.

For starters, club captain and founder Miss Nannie Miller was the granddaughter of renowned abolitionist, politician, philanthropist and landowner Gerrit Smith and daughter of women's rights activist Elizabeth "Libby" Smith Miller. Leveraging her high social standing in a community at the forefront of the women's rights movements, Nannie Miller was able to organize around 50 women to play for the town's junior and senior clubs. To ensure the clubs were prepared before playing for spectators, Miller held practices and scrimmages outside of town to avoid the same kind of disparaging media coverage that plagued their predecessors. Even their uniforms were well-planned. Regardless of whether the decision was based on comfort or solidarity with the women's rights movements, the Peterboro club played in "bloomer" dresses, which were puffy, Turkish-style pantaloons covered by knee-length dresses (in lieu of the prevalent yet cumbersome hoop skirts) and were widely viewed as a symbol of liberation.

Leadership, preparation and uniforms aside, the club's prominence is largely attributable to their most renowned fan and media proponent: Elizabeth Cady Stanton. Best known as co-author of the *Declaration of Sentiments*, which endorsed the same freedoms of the Declaration of Independence for women, formed the basis for the 1848 Seneca Falls Convention and inspired various women's rights and suffrage movements, Stanton had become a national celebrity through her activism, speeches and writing, most notably through the National Woman Suffrage Association's journal *The Revolution*. Fortunately for Nannie Miller and her teammates, Stanton happened to be cousins with Miller's grandfather, the aforementioned Gerrit Smith. While visiting her cousin in Peterboro during the Summer of 1868,

Stanton quickly took note of the burgeoning club and lauded their efforts in a letter published in *The Revolution*, which included the following passage on their July 25th match against the junior club, whom they defeated 29-5:

"We were delighted to find here a base ball club of girls. Nannie Miller, a grand-daughter of Gerrit Smith, is the captain, and handles the club with a grace and strength worthy of notice. It was a very pretty sight to see the girls with their white dresses and blue ribbons flying, in full possession of the public square, last Saturday afternoon, while the boys were quiet spectators at the scene."[190]

Further complementing the impressive club, Peterboro's local newspaper added:

"The young women of Peterboro, N.Y., jealous of the popular sports enjoyed by the more muscular portion of mankind, have organized a baseball club, and have already arrived at a creditable degree of proficiency in play. There are about fifty members belonging to it, from which a playing nine has been chosen, headed by Miss Ninnie [sic] Miller as captain. The nine have played several games outside the town and away from the gaze of the curious. Having thus perfected themselves, this nine lately played a public game in the town of Peterboro, as may well be supposed, before a multitude of spectators."[191]

Although little else is known of the Peterboro club beyond Stanton's letters and their re-publication shortly thereafter in various newspapers across the country, the club's legacy remains one of early success and advancement of women's base ball as evidenced by subsequent accounts from various Northeastern and Midwestern newspapers, including the following *Brooklyn Daily Eagle* account from September 10, 1868:

*"Following in the example of the 'Gushing Girls' of Peterboro, a movement is on foot in Brooklyn to organize a Club of female base ball players. They are to discard hoops and skirts utterly, and appear in a genuine Arab rig (*Bloomer dresses*). Most of them*

are undergoing physical discipline, and all of them are making preparations for a match."[192]

Despite the encouraging accounts from Peterboro, the preponderance of women's base ball coverage remained overwhelmingly negative, most notably Harvard Physician Edward H. Clarke's bestselling 1873 book *Sex in Education; or, A Fair Chance for Girls,* which warned of dire consequences for ongoing participation in exerting activities like sports:

"But it is not true that she can do all this, and retain uninjured health and a future secure from neuralgia, uterine disease, hysteria, and other derangements of the nervous system, if she follows the same method that boys are trained in. Boys must study and work in a boy's way, and girls in a girl's way."[193]

And while many heeded Clarke's misinformed warnings, others were emboldened by them like the women of Vassar College, who organized at least seven clubs in 1875, or Springfield, Illinois' Blondes and Brunettes clubs, who were the first to play before a paying crowd and receive compensation on September 11, 1875.

The profitable exhibition in Springfield ushered in an influx of professional "Bloomer Girls" clubs ranging from the theatrical, as was the case in Springfield, to the highly competitive, like New York's oddly named Cincinnati Reds, who barnstormed throughout New York and Pennsylvania in the 1890's. Besides their misleading nickname, the Reds boasted some of the game's greatest talents including pitcher Lizzie Arlington, who went on to pitch a scoreless frame in an 1898 men's minor league game, and Maud Nelson. Born Clementina Brida circa 1881, Nelson left Italy as a child for America, where she quickly embraced the National Pastime and began pitching professionally for Boston's Bloomer Girls around age 16. After successful stints with Boston and Chicago's Bloomer Girls clubs, where local press noted her pitching skills "attracted attention, and some men found to their chagrin that they couldn't get a hit off her."[194] Similar to her Reds' teammate Lizzie Arlington, Nelson thrived against both male and female competition, including stints with the mixed Bloomers Baseball Club of Indianapolis and Cherokee Indian Baseball Club. In addition to being a dominant pitcher, Nelson went on to manage, scout and even own various clubs.

With the newfound celebrity and wealth that professional ball afforded some of the early Bloomer Girls came occasional exploitation. And without question, the biggest villain of early women's professional base ball is none other than Sylvester F. Wilson. In his tenure as an owner and manager of various women's clubs throughout the Northeast, Midwest and South from 1879-1903, Wilson was arrested several times and served approximately 15 years (including his final days) in various prisons for a laundry list of heinous crimes ranging from kidnapping and sexual misconduct with underage players to defrauding business partners. And while Wilson was brought to justice, women's base ball was further suppressed amid fears of similar transgressions. In fact, New York State Representative Edward McCormick proposed a bill "An Act to Prohibit Female Base-Ball Playing" in 1892, which was fortunately and immediately discarded by the state's Committee on General Laws, who proceeded to mock McCormick's bill by proposing outlandish amendments like restricting the hiring of only "red-headed" players, exempting random counties and proposing an enactment date over a century later (2009).[195]

While common sense prevailed in the legislative chambers, women's base ball continued to struggle in the Court of Public Opinion. Making matters worse, another barnstorming club known as the American Female Base Ball Club (formerly the American Stars) embarked on an ambitious international tour in Almendares, Cuba. Unfortunately, the visit ended after a single game as hostile spectators incited a full riot that destroyed the venue and injured one of the players.

Despite the growing list of naysayers which now included politicians, media and physicians, women's base ball persevered in subsequent decades thanks largely to the success of various barnstorming Bloomer Girl clubs like Maud Nelson's Western Bloomer Girls in the 1910's and the All-Star Ranger Girls in the 1920's. But, like many industries, women's base ball was ravaged by the Great Depression in the 1930's. Even Major League Baseball, which was in the midst of a Golden Age thanks to iconic personalities like Babe Ruth, Lou Gehrig and Rogers Hornsby, was not impervious as ticket sales plunged by as much as 40%.[196] To make matters worse, legendary Cardinals and

Dodgers' General Manager Branch Rickey's development of the first modern farm system led to a proliferation of minor league clubs across the country, further displacing market share from the barnstorming female clubs, which largely dissolved by the 1930's. Lastly, while softball had been played recreationally since the 1880's, it had largely eclipsed baseball as the leading women's bat and ball game by the 1930's.

Largely gone but not forgotten, women's baseball would briefly return to the national forefront during World War II, when over 500 major leaguers including Ted Williams, Joe DiMaggio and Stan Musial joined the fight. At the behest of Chicago Cubs' owner and chewing gum magnate Philip K. Wrigley, the All-American Girls Professional Baseball League (AAGPBL) was formed in 1943. Although the league only lasted 12 seasons, it was a resounding success, attracting upwards of 900,000 spectators per season at its peak. During its tenure, the league featured over 500 players across 15 clubs throughout the Midwest, including the famed Rockford (IL) Peaches, the inspiration for the 1992 film *A League of their Own*. And while the end of the war and subsequent ascent of major and minor league men's baseball led to the eventual demise of the All-American Girls Professional Baseball League in 1954, its legacy of hope and inspiration endures, punctuated by a permanent exhibit in Cooperstown that was dedicated in 1988. Moved by the gesture, Dottie (Wiltse) Collins, the former Fort Wayne Daisies' hurler and league alumni committee member that lobbied for and helped design the exhibit, remarked:

"We are thrilled to be accorded a place of honor in the history of our national pastime. At the time we were just kids having fun. Not until it was all over did we realize that we had been pioneers as far as women's sports are concerned. This is the thrill of a lifetime for us."[197]

Diamonds in the Rough

As has been the case with the men's game, historical research and interest around women's baseball has skewed heavily towards the early and mid-20th century, most notably the aforementioned Bloomer Girls barnstorming tours at the onset and the wartime All-American Girls Professional Baseball League. But with the renewed interest in men's 19th century base ball, perpetuated by the emergence and success of vintage clubs in the 1980's and early '90's, also came interest in the women's game of the same era. Even though women had played essential roles since the very beginning of vintage base ball's revival, they were largely limited to supporting roles like recordkeepers and historical interpreters for the spectators. And while not uncommon for individual players to join men's teams, a dedicated women's vintage club would not formally organize until 1993 in Columbus' Ohio Village. This decade-plus gap between the formation of men's and women's vintage clubs may be attributable to a historical dilemma that longtime Ohio Village Muffin "Gentleman" Jim Tootle articulates in his book *Vintage Base Ball: Recapturing the National Pastime:*

"Women were playing base ball in college in the mid-1860's but other examples have been difficult to find. This puts historical societies in a bit of a dilemma. With so little evidence of women playing base ball in its early days, and since vigorous physical activity for women was often discouraged in that era, questions have emerged regarding the historical accuracy of sponsoring a women's team and presenting it to the public as something that would have actually existed in the 1850's or 1860's. On the other hand, the vintage base ball community is very welcoming to anyone who wants to get involved in playing the game. In that spirit of inclusiveness, opportunities have been made available for women to play vintage base ball."[198]

In that spirit, volunteers from Columbus' Ohio Historical Society (now the Ohio History Connection) met on November 23, 1993 to organize the first ladies' vintage base ball club, which would play by 1860's rules and customs (including usage of wooden bats and prohibition of gloves) on the same grounds (Muffin Meadow) as their brother club and aforementioned vintage base ball pioneers the Ohio Village Muffins. Like the Muffins, the ladies' club was founded upon and remains true to their shared mission:

"The Ohio History Connection's (vintage base ball) program is an integral part of the organization's Visitors Experience Department. As museum volunteers, participants in the vintage base ball program extend the Ohio History Connection's mission

to spark discovery of Ohio's stories and embrace the present, share the past, and transform the future. The demonstration and interpretation of nineteenth-century base ball, along with its related social and recreational histories, is a significant contribution to this mission. Historical authenticity is an important objective of the program in order to accurately portray the game as it was played in the 1860s. The competitive nature of the games are of secondary importance."[199]

While the ladies' quickly and unanimously agreed upon their mission, deciding on a name proved far more challenging. Amidst a plethora of clever and authentic suggestions like the College Ladies, Daisies and Lady Birds, the group ultimately decided on the Diamonds, an abbreviation of "Diamonds in the Rough" and homage to the women that attained the moniker in the 19th century for their quality play outside of the public eye. Next, the group appointed two captains (both wives of Muffin ballists) in Pam Koons and Dianna Frias, the mother of the aforementioned Rudy "Swamp Fox" Frias (Chapter 8), who leads the *Vintage Base Ball Podcast* and Columbus Capitals Base Ball Club. Lastly, the group agreed upon uniforms, which were modeled after the dark blue 1860's exercise uniforms synonymous with the early women's collegiate clubs, although they would switch to simple dresses from the same period by the 1996 season to more accurately depict the unsung recreational players that inspired the "Diamonds" nickname.

While historically accurate, the 1860's ankle-length dresses present their share of challenges, particularly while running. As longtime Diamond (and daughter-in-law of the club's first captain) Brandy Frias noted in a 2021 interview on the local *Down Home with Tina Show,* running must be done "very carefully" and that "if you fall and trip over your dress, then you're an official ballplayer." Taking great pride and fun in their steadfast commitment to preserving history, the Diamonds even award the Golden Safety Pin to the player that requires the most safety pins to fix a dress during a game.

As expected of the only organized club of its kind, the Diamonds struggled early on to find opponents and, much like the early women's clubs they sought to re-create, had to resort to creative means to stay sharp. Ranging from co-ed matches with their Muffin brethren to intrasquad scrimmages to simple demonstrations, the Diamonds managed to not only survive their first couple seasons, but also inspire the formation of other women's clubs. Beginning with the Sycamore (OH) Crickets (later the Katydids) in 1996, the Diamonds' influence continually spread with the 1998 formation of Ohio's fourth club the Akron Lady Locks, who were established as the sister club to the aforementioned Black Stockings.

At its peak in the mid-2000's, ladies vintage base ball had expanded well beyond Ohio with clubs in New York, Minnesota and even Colorado, which promoted more competition but also required significant travel. Yet the travel was hardly a deterrent early on for the Ohio clubs, who had grown tired of playing one another. And as one might expect, the far more experienced Ohio clubs dominated their out-of-state competition. Former Diamonds captain Jackie Forquer recalls a 2004 tournament in Rochester, Minnesota where the Diamonds, Lady Locks (Akron) and Clodbusters (Dayton) took on the host and newly formed Hens club in a round-robin tournament. Despite their best efforts, the outmatched Hens were swept by the seasoned Ohio clubs on Saturday. Uninterested in the next day's slate of games against their all too familiar in-state foes, and with the Mall of America just over an hour's drive north, the Ohio clubs were scarcely represented on the grounds that Sunday, causing them to form a makeshift "All-Ohio" club to close the weekend with another impressive performance.[200]

The Ohio ladies' dominance was not limited to the Midwest. In 2005, the Akron Lady Locks traveled to picturesque Genesee Country Village and Museum in Mumford, NY to challenge the two local clubs, the Brooks Grove Belles (Belles) and Priscilla Porter's Astonishing Ladies Base Ball Club (Porters), during the prestigious Silver Ball Tournament. Given the distant locale, the Lady Locks were unable to field a full squad.

Yet in the true spirit of camaraderie, two members of the Diamonds including Forquer came to the aid of their sisters. And much like the prior year trip to Minnesota, the Ohio ladies convincingly defeated the host clubs, with one ballist earning her permanent nickname "New York" for her incredible play over the weekend. Needless to say, the local clubs were not interested in an encore, as the Sunday competitions were restructured into a more equitable "top hat game", where rosters were drawn out of a hat.

While today's Diamonds continue to thrive thanks to the inspiration of the "pioneering spirit and grit of those first Lady Diamonds"[201] and the unwavering support from their brother Muffins and the Ohio History Connection, nearly all other organized vintage ladies base ball clubs have disbanded. Based on her more than 25 years around the game, Jackie Forquer attributes the dwindling numbers to changing priorities and succession planning:

"Ladies Vintage Base Ball is strongly affected by priorities. From the time I started playing in 1997 to 2019, I played every game because I had placed it as a priority. As soon as I felt my priorities changing, I started an exit plan making sure there were players in a position to make the Diamonds more of a priority in their lives."[202]

In addition to proactive succession planning, the Diamonds' sustainability can be attributed to their diverse roster that (as of the 2022 season) ranges in age from 19 to 53. This broad age range is not only the product of the game being passed over generations, like when founder Dianna Frias was succeeded as captain by her daughter-in-law Brandy, but also successful, multi-faceted recruiting practices. In addition to serving as volunteers and historical interpreters at the Ohio Village Museum and during Muffins base ball matches, various Diamonds like Jackie Forquer have given vintage base ball talks and demonstrations at local schools and festivals to raise awareness and interest in the game. Further, to recruit new players and fill their match schedule, the Diamonds frequently compete against makeshift local clubs in various host communities.

Today's Diamonds are not only diverse in age, but also in profession as their roster includes a college student, an elementary school teacher, an accountant, a human resources manager and even a veterinarian. And in true vintage base ball fashion, each ballist takes great pride in her nicknames and the stories behind them including Tumbleweed (trips on her dress frequently), Tipper (good catcher known for snagging foul tips), Momma Bear (played while pregnant three times), Fun Size (a short, fun-loving player), Pole Cat (hit a ball so hard that when it hit a utility pole, it came back and landed about a foot in front of home for a fair ball), New York (played her best games ever in New York).[203] Even Forquer has long embraced her nickname of "Thumper", based on her size 11 shoes and her toe-touching hamstring stretches that teammates associated with the lovable rabbit from Disney's *Bambi*.

Despite their varying ages, backgrounds and nicknames, the Diamonds, Muffins and their alumni are a family. In addition to the literal family members that play together or support their parents or spouses as fans, the Diamonds have forged bonds with their teammates and even competitors as Jackie Forquer notes:

"Vintage Base Ball is a nationwide family. In my 25 years of playing, I have seen a lot of players come and go on both the women's and men's teams, but no matter how long they stayed around, they are still family. Members of the Muffins and Diamonds get together all the time off the field. Whether it's mid-week or mid-winter, there's always an email going out about meeting up somewhere to grab a bite. Anytime I meet a fellow ballist, there is a bond that forms automatically. I am still in regular contact with many of the Lady Clodbusters many years after they folded. Through tournament play, I know players from across the country by name. I may not know them well, but that family bond is there."

But Forquer, and the Diamonds for that matter, are not alone in this familial sentiment, as former Dayton Lady Clodbuster Heather Shively echoes:

"I definitely miss our days of vintage base ball! I agree that family is a great word. One thing I loved about our games and those my husband played too was that each game felt like a family reunion. Everyone played fiercely on the field but would sit in the shade of the trees together to eat a meal after and families would sit and chat and catch up while our kiddos played together. Vintage base ball was a community and not only did we re-create base ball from the early days, I think we re-created the community feel of the early days too. Families would be spread apart but would come together for special occasions to play and reconnect and (enjoy) fellowship. We all seemed to know each other well and watched our families grow and change over the years. I'm so

thankful for the lifelong friendships I gained from my experiences and am so glad my children got to grow up with their base ball friends and family too. I miss it greatly and am thankful for the modern inventions of social media to check in on some of the "family" and I wonder about others often and how they are doing. I'm sure it's how families felt back in earlier times as well; missing their extended families and waiting for opportunities to come back together again someday!"[204]

Despite the overall attrition in women's vintage base ball in recent years, longtime Diamond Jackie Forquer maintains a hopeful outlook on the game's future, offering encouragement to those interested in learning more:

"People especially younger generations should pick up vintage base ball in order to understand how baseball has come to be. To better respect those players that came before us, the rules, and the sacrifices that many gave during war times to get us to where we are today in the sport. This is our history and it's our (Civil War) history that spread the game of base ball leading us to call it America's Pastime...Get a veteran to be your mentor in the finer points of playing the game. Don't just learn the game, but what life in the country was like during the period your team is playing. To get the best first-person impression you can, you need to learn and adopt the mannerisms, dress, look (eye glasses, hair, adornments, etc.), and speak of the time.... The one thing that has never changed is the focus of education. Education in both the history of base ball and the rules, and the ways of the time period we are portraying."[205]

Drawing of woman in the Bloomer dress (c. 1851), named after suffragist and editor Amelia Bloomer. Public domain. Photo from National Park Service and Library of Congress. https://www.nps.gov/wori/learn/historyculture/amelia-bloomer.htm.

The Diamonds posing in front of the 17th Avenue Fields outside the Ohio Historical Center during the 2011 Ohio Cup. Photo courtesy of Jackie Forquer.

The Diamonds and Hens meet with the umpire prior to their 2004 match in Rochester, MN. Photo courtesy of Jackie Forquer.

Jackie Forquer striking while playing with the Akron Lady Locks in the 2005 Silver Ball Tournament in Upstate New York's Genesee Country Village and Museum. Photo courtesy of Jackie Forquer.

11: Westward Expansion: Fort Verde Excelsiors (Camp Verde, AZ) & Whatcom Aces (Bellingham, WA)

"It's a great way to learn something more about base ball than only how they do it today. People tend to be myopic about the world we live in, honestly behaving as if something only started when they discovered it. Baseball existed for more than a century before I got here, and it will go on after I am in the ground. Learning its history, playing its history, helps us understand how really small each of us is in such a big thing."[206]
  - Whatcom Aces Founder and Former Ft. Verde Excelsiors' Captain Bill "Shutterbug" Helm

Baseball in Arizona: More Than Just Spring Training
Since the warmth and intrigue of its seemingly endless deserts lured Horace Stoneham's New York Giants and Bill Veeck's Cleveland Indians into making it their permanent Spring Training homes in 1947,[207] Arizona has, despite the relative lack of rain and arable soil, served as baseball's metaphorical garden, where half of Major League Baseball's clubs sow and cultivate talent every spring and thereafter in various prospect leagues. And regardless of whether the clubs are bracing for a title defense or plotting an exodus from perpetual futility, hope springs eternal for every club, player and fan in these rejuvenating deserts. Even after the big clubs break camp in late-March and (with the exception of the resident Diamondbacks) flee for literally greener pastures, the state remains a baseball incubator through its Arizona Complex League, a short-season rookie league of around 20 affiliated clubs often played at Cactus League venues, and its prestigious Arizona Fall League, where elite prospects showcase their talents and make compelling arguments for promotions to their top clubs.

Yet Arizona and baseball have been intertwined far longer than the Cactus League. Furthermore, baseball has played a prominent role in the region since at least the 1870's, over four decades before attaining statehood in 1912. In fact, the earliest recorded game in Arizona dates back to 1872 at the notorious Camp Grant, where just a year earlier, a vigilante group of approximately six American and 48 Mexican settlers and 92

Tohono O'odham ambushed an encampment of Apache refugees killing over 100[208] in what became known as the "Camp Grant Massacre" and exacerbated the ongoing war between the US Army and Apache.

Just as base ball had provided Civil War soldiers relief from the horrors of war and monotony of camp, the soldiers at Camp Grant quickly took to America's Pastime. On Christmas Day 1872, troops from the 23rd Infantry and 5th Cavalry organized a friendly game. Perhaps tired of intramural competition or military campgrounds, the troops quickly spread the game to civilians in surrounding towns like the territorial capital Prescott, where a club known as the Champions formed and has since been revived as a vintage club. By 1876, the civilian-led Prescott Champions became a regional powerhouse, as evidenced by their 49-22 triumph over the soldiers of the Fort Whipple Base Ball Club for the inaugural Championship of the Arizona Territory on May 21st, 1876. The *Weekly Arizona Miner* recounted the game and noted that the Champions received additional players from Boston's major league club (then the Red Caps), a rumor that has been widely debunked and has provoked much speculation on its potential root causes, which range from confusion over the similar uniforms to a mere publicity stunt.

Regardless of whether it was the fellowship, recreation, entertainment or pervasive gambling that marked these early games, base ball quickly ascended as the leading pastime in the booming mining territory of Arizona, where the population grew from less than 10,000 in 1870 to roughly 40,000 by 1880 and over 120,000 by 1900. To keep up with growing demand and provide a recreational outlet for its employees, the Calumet and Arizona Mining Company built Warren Ballpark in 1909 in the territory's then-largest town of Bisbee, roughly ten miles north of the Mexican Border. In addition to countless recreational matches, Warren Ballpark hosted major league exhibitions including the New York Giants' 9-1 victory of the Chicago White Sox on November 7, 1913 during both clubs' international tour that reached as far as Hong Kong and Australia. Despite being over 110 years old, Warren Park remains in use primarily for high school sports (and occasionally vintage base ball games), making it perhaps the oldest continuously used ballpark in the country, eclipsing Fenway (1912) and Wrigley (1914).

And like the rest of the country, Arizona baseball rapidly evolved in the early 20th century. With large scale ballparks sprouting up and periodic visits from major league clubs, homegrown professional baseball soon arose in Arizona beginning with the short-lived Rio Grande Association. In the newly formed state's first official professional baseball game on April 27, 1915, the Old Pueblos of Tucson routed the visiting Phoenix Senators 10-2 at Elysian Grove in a wild contest that the *El Paso Herald* characterized as:

"A slugfest throughout, and the reason Tucson made such a strong showing was due to excellent team work, while the Phoenix players seemed to be unacquainted with each other and at critical moments went to sleep."

And while the article complemented the crowd, including their collection of $5 to reimburse Tucson's catcher after being fined for arguing the strike zone, it lamented the sparse attendance and effectively foreshadowed the league's inevitable demise three months later:

"The attendance was small compared with what it should have been. After this big crowds will be on hand, as there is plenty of enthusiasm but not much cash around."[209]

After nearly a decade hiatus, a semi-professional league resurfaced in 1925 in Douglas, Arizona, where the local Blues joined the Frontier League (also known as the Copper League) with clubs from El Paso (TX), Fort Bayard (NM) and Juarez, Mexico. The Blues were led by 15-year major league first baseman, longtime Highlander/Yankee and 1916 National League Batting Champion (with Cincinnati) Hal Chase. And despite amassing over 2,100 hits and 900 RBI, Chase's legacy remains clouded by scandal. Dubbed by critics as the "Black Prince of Baseball",[210] Chase was often accused of throwing games including in 1910 with the Highlanders and 1918 with the Reds. While Chase was able to narrowly skate most of these charges throughout his career, often by switching clubs, his association with the 1919 Black Sox Scandal, for which he was indicted (but never stood trial) for allegedly serving as an intermediary between White Sox first baseman Charles Arnold

"Chick" Gandil and gamblers. And while Chase was not among the eight White Sox players assessed lifetime bans, his major league career was behind him. Seeking new beginnings in Arizona, Chase welcomed his alleged accomplices including Gandil, infielder Buck Weaver and pitcher Lefty Williams onto the Blues' roster in what quickly became known as an outlaw league. And despite nearly winning the second half league championship in 1925, the foursome split up during a disappointing 1926 campaign.

While semi-professional leagues like the Arizona State and Arizona-Mexico followed, Arizona's baseball legacy was irreversibly shaped in 1947 with the advent of Major League Baseball's Cactus League. Like the rest of the country, most baseball fans wholeheartedly flocked towards the modern professional game, embracing its continued adaptation and, in a sense, forgetting its past. But thanks to the tireless, continued efforts of a small yet influential community, local residents can reconnect with the region's early base ball roots via the Arizona Territories Vintage Base Ball League.

Arizona Territories Vintage Base Ball League
While clubs had been playing for decades throughout the Northeast and Midwest, and isolated exhibitions had been played in the state since at least the 90's, the vintage revival did not fully make its way into Arizona until local baseball historian and author John Tenney formed the Bisbee Bees in 2007. Tenney is not only known for his renowned books *Baseball in Territorial Arizona: A History, 1863-1912* and *Death by Baseball*, but also as a distant relative of baseball legend Fred Tenney, who played and managed for the National League's Boston Beaneaters/Doves/Rustlers and New York's Giants from 1894-1911 and accumulated over 2,200 hits.

Despite Fred Tenney's amazing accomplishments on the field, he is often associated with one particularly infamous moment while away from it. By 1908, Tenney is in twilight of his career with the New York Giants and the perpetual wear and tear of nearly 15 major league seasons had taken its toll on the 36-year-old first baseman. Even though the Giants (87-50) were in a dogfight for the NL Pennant with the Pittsburgh Pirates (88-54) and their current, visiting opponent Chicago Cubs (90-53) heading into the season's final stretch, the ailing Tenney was given a rest day in favor of 19-year-old rookie Fred Merkle. In a 1-1 stalemate in the bottom of the ninth at Upper Manhattan's Polo Grounds, the unproven rookie delivered a clutch, two-out single that brought the winning runner Moose McCormick to third. After shortstop Al Bridwell followed with another single, Merkle is widely believed to have abandoned the basepaths to join the team's celebration. While debated, popular accounts maintain that amidst the rush of thousands of fans on the field, Cubs' second baseman and 1946 Cooperstown inductee Johnny Evers noted Merkle's oversight and rushed to recover the ball. After literally wrestling the ball away from Giants' pitcher Joe McGinnity and a couple of fans after it was tossed into the stands, the Cubs' proceeded to tag second base before the celebrating Merkle could correct his mistake. However, some conflicting accounts (including Merkle's) maintain that Merkle eventually arrived at second during the commotion, only to depart after receiving assurances the match was over. Regardless, umpire Hank O'Day ruled that Merkle was out and the Cubs and officials fled from the angry mob. With the game ruled a 1-1 tie, the Giants and Cubs would finish the regular season gridlocked at 98-55 (one loss clear of Pittsburgh). In a one-game playoff at the now hostile Polo Grounds, the unflappable Cubs methodically dispatched the Giants 4-2 on the way to a five-game World Series victory over Detroit. And despite a stellar 16-year major league career that included over 1,500 hits and 700 RBI, fans and historians have never let Merkle off the hook, garnering the unshakeable nickname "Bonehead" for that fateful 1908 incident widely regarded as the "Merkle Boner".[211]

While John Tenney's Bees are inspired by Bisbee's minor league club from 1928-1941, the club plays by the 1860's rules both as an homage to Arizona's baseball origins and to ensure a broader pool of competitors including clubs from Colorado and California.

The vintage game was immediately well-received not only in Bisbee, which formed a second club in 2009 known as the Black Sox (an homage to aforementioned White Sox castoffs that played in nearby Douglas), but also across the state, where clubs also formed in Phoenix (Senators) and Tucson (Saguaros) in 2008 and 2010, respectively.

The clubs began competing as members of the Arizona Territories Vintage Base Ball League and introduced their premier event in 2010: the Copper City Classic at storied Warren Ballpark. Attracting clubs from across Arizona, Colorado and California, the event remains a premier showcase for the Southwestern vintage base ball community featuring 1860's rules, brass bands and historical presentations. Not only has the event been a player and fan-favorite, but its proceeds continue to support the upkeep of the century-old ballpark.

With the exception of Phoenix, all of the league's original clubs played in Southern Arizona until an influx of four clubs from Central Arizona joined including Tempe's Tip-Tops (2013), Prescott's Champions (2016), Camp (Fort) Verde's Excelsiors (2016) and Mesa's Miners (2017). True to their early roots, the clubs generally play by the rules of 1860, including underhand pitching, bound catches (fair or foul territory) and prohibition of gloves. Furthermore, the clubs often adhere to the unofficial rules of gentlemanly play including prohibition of stealing and assessment of fines (typically capped at 25 cents) for misconduct like profanity and arguing with the umpire. In fact, the league's home page even includes a Code of Conduct, which emphasizes sportsmanship, historical preservation and respect for others including umpires, opponents and volunteers.

But, like many other vintage leagues, adherence to the authentic 1860's rules and customs has its limits and occasional exceptions are warranted as noted on the league's site:

"We strive to stick as closely to the 1860 rules as we possibly can. At times, the playing field or other conditions may force us to bend the rules just a bit."[212]

Some of these notable departures include the field configuration, where bases are recommended to be 80 feet apart (versus the authentic 90) and pitcher/striker lines or circular iron home plates are infrequently used as games are often played on smaller fields primarily intended for youth or softball leagues. Other departures are out of safety and necessity due to the region's intense sunlight (sunglasses are permitted) and heat (substitutions are allowed even though prohibited in 1860 unless due to injury/illness).

Fort Verde Excelsiors

While Fort Verde had occasionally hosted historical base ball exhibitions since 1996, the Fort Verde Excelsiors did not formally join the Arizona Territories Vintage Base Ball League until 2016. And while they may be one of the newer additions to the league, the Excelsiors' historical roots arguably run the deepest. Located in Camp Verde, roughly 90 miles north of Phoenix, the Excelsiors' home grounds are part of Fort Verde State Historical Park, a former Army outpost from 1871-1891 and now living history museum. The Excelsiors' founder and longtime Fort Verde State Historic Park Manager Sheila Stubler describes the park experience:

"Through the preservation of Fort Verde, we're able to tell the story of the early pioneers, the military, miners and the Indian Scouts. Once you dive into history, there's no turning back, as everything seems to connect one way or another and link together."[213]

And as the story of the 19th century Arizona territorial solider is not complete without base ball, Stubler organized the Excelsiors (named after the 1860's Brooklyn powerhouse club) to "carry on the traditional baseball game played by soldiers stationed at Fort Verde back in the 1880's", and organized a roster of "energetic, caring people who share the same mission"[214] beginning with former club captain Bill "Shutterbug" Helm, a longtime vintage base ball veteran, historian and, as indicated by his nickname and the photographs included in this chapter, photographer.

As a master recruiter and ambassador of vintage base ball, Helm immediately went to work building the Excelsiors' roster. Unbeknownst to him, he would face stiff competition at the onset:

"For me the most comedic story for the Excelsiors was the day we met Mike Adrian. In 2016, Mike and his wife Susan moved to Arizona from the Chicago area where he had formed, captained and played for the Somonauk Blue Stockings. Mike came out to Fort Verde for an Excelsiors recruiting event. Living in Prescott, a town nearby, Mike decided to form his own team, the Prescott Champions. What made this funny is that Mike managed to recruit several very good players for his own team, and he recruited them at the home of the Fort Verde team. Mike was such a nice man; all you could do was appreciate his passion for the

game and be happy that his team would provide healthy competition."[215]

As an aside, Mike "Ace" Adrian passed away in December 2021 after a courageous battle with cancer. The vintage base ball community is forever grateful for his immeasurable contributions and this book is dedicated to his memory. As Bill Helm so eloquently wrote in his tribute to his lost friend in the VBBA's *Base Ball Players Chronicle:*

"(Mike) was so excited to live life to the fullest. As I and so many people miss our dear friend Mike, we can be happy that he is playing ball right now with Buck O'Neil, Ernie Banks, Minnie Minoso, Doc Adams and so many other ball players from the past. Sure would love to play ball with that group. Sure would love to play ball again with Mike. Man, I miss my friend."[216]

With challenges maintaining a highly competitive roster in a geographically isolated town of roughly 12,000, stiff competition from clubs around the densely populated and talent-laden Phoenix area, and an unwavering prioritization of authenticity over accolades, Helm acknowledges the club's inevitable growing pains on the field:

"The Fort Verde Excelsiors have not been one of the ATVBBL's better teams (in terms of win-loss record). Primarily a function of Fort Verde, and in a community of mostly older people, the team I left behind (in 2021) had an 81-year-old catcher and an 85-year-old second baseman. Historically, the team had about 5-7 players who would consistently show up for games, the others were people who would play from time to time. Those extra players were rarely people who had much baseball experience."[217]

While the Excelsiors' have had minimal luck finding experienced substitute players, they were awestruck by one on the opposing side. After father-son Prescott Champions teammates Travis and Zach Storey invited their friend and retired Dodger legend Maury Wills, who accumulated 2,134 hits and 586 stolen bases in his 14-year major league career primarily at shortstop, to attend their January 6, 2018 doubleheader against the Excelsiors at Fort Verde, the 85-year-old proved he still had it by taking a guest at-bat that resulted in a single. Even though the Excelsiors ended up on the losing end of both matches, the priceless memories from that experience far outweigh the day's results, as Excelsior Brian Lane noted:

"It was really an honor to meet Mr. Wills and actually play a little ball with him. Mr. Wills was kind enough to sign autographed photos for all our vintage base ball players."[218]

Despite these challenges and mixed results on the field, the club's success is best measured by their continued accomplishment of their primary mission as noted on their website:

"Though we finished with a handful of wins, the whole reason we play is to emphasize the sport's great history."[219]

Reinforcing that point, club founder Sheila Stubler notes that the club is "really just about having a good time",[220] which is clearly evident in the photographs at the end of the chapter.

Bringing the Game Back to the Northwest

In May 2021, former Excelsior captain Bill "Shutterbug" Helm left the warmth of the Arizona deserts for the majestic beauty of the Pacific Northwest Coast in Bellingham, Washington. While this flourishing city of nearly 100,000 is an adventurer's dream with access to ocean waterways, dense forests, national parks and breathtaking mountain ranges, vintage base ball is not (yet) high on the community's list of pastimes. In fact, Helm noted of his initial experiences:

"My wife and I have been up here less than a year and, as far as I know, I am the only person in my area who is even trying to do vintage base ball. Should you find anyone who is also doing it, please send them my way."[221]

While Helm's initial observations are not without merit, the Pacific Northwest can at least boast a proud baseball history dating back to the 19th century. Like most of the West, the game was largely introduced and popularized in the Washington territory by soldiers following the Civil War. In fact, the first organized base ball clubs in the Pacific Northwest formed in Oregon in 1866, including Portland's Pioneer Base Ball Club, founded by Midwest transplant Joseph Buchtel, and Oregon City's Clackamas Base Ball Club. The clubs played the region's first official game to much fanfare on October 13, 1866, which resulted in a 77-45 Pioneers' triumph (despite a late Clackamas rally that included 21 runs scored in the final two frames) that the *Morning Oregonian* declared as "the first match game ever played in the state" and "a splendid beginning."[222] This newfound pastime quickly made its way north into Vancouver, Washington Territory (would not become a state until 1889) with the 1867 formation of two clubs: the Occidental and Sherman (also known as the Garrison) Base Ball Clubs. The latter, as presumed by their name, consisted of cavalry and artillery soldiers stationed at the city's barracks. The two clubs faced off in one of the territory's first official games on May 11, 1867, a lopsided affair that saw the more-conditioned soldiers humble the Occidental side 45-5 in what the local *Enterprise* declared as a "pretty bad flaxing."[223] Despite the anticlimactic debut, base ball quickly became the territory's favorite pastime as more clubs emerged and competitive matches extended all the way until mid-November's cold and wet season when the *Vancouver Register* declared:

"We have an idea from what we heard on the ground that the season is becoming unpropitious for a further continuation of this favorite sport. Since we are to be driven indoors for our winter's amusements, let's try and select some recreation as developing to the mind as base ball has been to the muscle of our citizens."[224]

The Register proved especially prescient when the Oregon, Washington and Idaho Territories Association of Base Ball Players formed in 1868. Although the inaugural edition only featured five clubs, including the aforementioned Pioneers, Clackamas and Occidentals, it was abundantly clear that the National Pastime had taken hold in the Pacific Northwest. And with the nationwide proliferation of clubs and budding fan interest, aided by widespread press coverage of the NABBP, National Association of Professional Base Ball Players and subsequent National League, came the inevitable advent of professionalism in the region. By 1884, the aforementioned

Portland Pioneer Club founder Joe Buchtel established the first professional club in East Portland's Willamettes. The club's success and popularity soon led to 1890's formation of the Pacific Northwest League, the region's first all-professional league. In addition to Portland's club, which later became known as the Webfeet in homage to the area's duck population, various clubs joined from across Washington including Tacoma's Daisies, Spokane's Bunchgrassers and Seattle's Blues (also known as the Hustlers). Despite a brief hiatus during the economic depression or "Panic of 1893", the league remained a successful independent professional league, attracting talent nationwide until merging with the broader Pacific Coast League in 1903, which has remained a primary pipeline to the big leagues for over a century. And after a cameo with the oft forgotten Seattle Pilots of 1969, Major League Baseball found a permanent home in the Pacific Northwest with the Seattle Mariners in 1977.

Like the rest of the country, baseball in the Pacific Northwest continuously adapted in unison with Major League Baseball and, as a result, deviated from its 19th century roots, which motivated some to rekindle the vintage game including Alexander Joy Cartwright IV, the great-great-grandson of the original Knickerbocker, author of their 1845 rules, Hall of Fame inductee and one of the "Fathers of Baseball". And while the vintage base ball revival was in full swing in the Northeast and Midwest, the Pacific Northwest followed in 2006 with Cartwright's formation of the now-defunct Pacific Northwest Vintage Base Ball League. An advertisement for the prospective league's initial meeting in Milton, Washington stated:

"Vintage Baseball is strong everywhere in the country except the Pacific Northwest. The time for Vintage Baseball has arrived in the Northwest with such a rich history of baseball here. Alexander Cartwright will promote the new league to townships, city councils, homeowner associations, and other organizations. The region for the new vintage league will extend from Seattle, Washington to Eugene, Oregon. Cartwright expects to start four teams in 2006 and include teams from Portland, Oregon and Fort Vancouver, Washington in the league."[225]

Despite Cartwright's pedigree and relentless marketing, vintage base ball has only gained traction in parts of the Pacific

Northwest, particularly in Portland, where the Pioneer Base Ball Club (inspired by the region's first organized club in 1866) continues to thrive. In a 2008 *Seattle Met* piece on Cartwright's quest to bring the vintage game back to the region, author Sarah Anderson notes:

"When the Washingtonian from Lake Tapps made a pilgrimage to his ancestor's home field in Hoboken, New Jersey, for baseball's 150th-anniversary celebration in the '90s, he was amazed to see the variety of reenactors who came together to play by the outdated rules...Cartwright came home and did what any self-respecting Washington State obsessive does: He created a web site. On the Pacific Northwest Vintage Base Ball League site (pnwvbl.mrbaseball.com) Cartwright earnestly chirps: "The time for Vintage Base Ball has arrived in the Northwest." It most certainly has not. Teams had already formed in Portland and Vancouver, Washington, but around Puget Sound, no dice—the Mariners, Rainiers, and various city councils have rejected Cartwright's pleas for sponsorship."[226]

Although far more prevalent in Oregon, vintage base ball has made cameos into Southern Washington, most notably through intermittent exhibitions in the 2010's at Fort Vancouver National Historic site, where volunteers competed under the monikers of the region's first clubs from the 1860's including the aforementioned Sherman and Occidental clubs. And while these exhibitions were well-received, they have not led to the formation of organized vintage clubs and leagues in Washington, that is until Bill "Shutterbug" Helm's arrival in 2021.

With a proven track record of growing the vintage game in Arizona, and a firm belief that the game can thrive anywhere with the right exposure, Helm left no time to waste:

"I learned before our big move that there were no vintage base ball teams north of Portland. Something had to be done about that. So, I have placed classified ads in my local paper (Lynden Tribune), a paper I fortunately work for – as editor. I have also written a few columns and have dutifully mentioned my quest to bring vintage base ball to the area. At our second practice and recruiting event, held in early September (2021), 10 people showed up. For vintage base ball to flourish in the PNW, it won't

be enough to put together a team, or even two teams. We must cultivate some sort of fanbase. Or else, we'll be in danger of entertaining only ourselves."[227]

Using print, social media and various grassroots marketing tactics, including a speaking engagement at the local Lions' Club, to broaden awareness and recruit new talent, Helm's message to prospective ballists is simple:

"I like that the vintage base ball movement prioritizes sportsmanship, camaraderie, friendship, authenticity and good competition. We all want to win of course, however nobody is a jerk about it. As for the rules, there was a whole lot of "what if" that got us to the modern game. The 1860 game is before much of the game's evolution. It's a lot of fun to play the way they did before the Civil War."[228]

Having seen its rise in Arizona over the past decade, Helm is confident his new community will embrace the vintage game. To begin this journey, Helm founded the Whatcom Bay Stars as a charter member (along with the aforementioned and established Pioneer Club of Portland) of the newly formed Pacific Northwest Vintage Base Ball Association. While the Bay Stars moniker is not attributable to an actual 19th century club, Helm chose the name for a couple of reasons. For starters, by choosing the name of the county (Whatcom) instead of the host city (Bellingham), Helm is able to access more talent from the broader region. And as the club recruits players from throughout the county, the club is an all-star team in a way. Yet despite the appealing new moniker, Helm renamed the club the Aces in June 2022 to honor the memory of his longtime friend, the aforementioned Mike "Ace" Adrian of Arizona's Prescott Champions.

Within a year of his arrival, Helm has managed to hold a couple of open practices for prospective ballists with hopes of scrimmages and even organized matches in the near term. He also remains proactive in his marketing and recruiting offering the following open invitation on social media to attend an upcoming practice:

"Play base ball the way they did before the Civil War: No gloves, no showboating... Base ball in 1860 was a gentleman's game. It was civilized, leisurely, fun. Although competitive, base ball was a game of sportsmanship. Base ball was a game of fielding. The batter was out when a ball was caught on the fly or on one bounce, or when the batter swung and missed three times. The pitcher delivered the ball underhand. Balls and strikes were not called. Foul balls were not considered strikes. Also, base ball in 1860 was two words."

But with encouragement, Helm also cautions those who may think playing the 1860's vintage game appears easy or that their slow pitch softball skills are seamlessly transferrable:

"It may look easy, but it isn't, especially catching the ball with your bare hands. If you are a young person who wants to play the modern game, try vintage base ball. Once you learn how to catch a ball barehanded, you'll be even better catching a ball with your glove."[229]

While the Whatcom Aces, and the vintage base ball revival in the Pacific Northwest as a whole, are slowly beginning to take shape, a phenomenon Helm attributes to a combination of the area's perpetually damp conditions and softball-centric culture, he remains bullish on the game's growth in his new community:

"If you build it, they will come. That's my attitude about vintage base ball up here. We have a way to go before we have something significant, but we will get there."[230]

Mike "Ace" Adrian and his Prescott Champions prepare to bat in a 2017 game at Warren Ballpark in Bisbee, Arizona. Photo by Bill Helm.

Mike "Ace" Adrian of the Prescott Champions demonstrates his pitching motion before a game against the Fort Verde Excelsiors. The game was played at Fort Verde State Historic Park in Camp Verde, Arizona. Photo by Bill Helm.

Bill "Shutterbug" Helm of the Fort Verde Excelsiors takes a swing in a 2013 game against the Glendale Gophers. The game was held at Fort Verde State Historic Park in Camp Verde, Arizona. Photo by Teresa Helm.

Laz Apostolis of the Fort Verde Excelsiors bats in an exhibition against the Phoenix Senators. The game was held at Fort Verde State Historic Park in Camp Verde, Arizona. Photo Bill Helm.

Josh "The Voice" Freeman of the Fort Verde Excelsiors at Fort Verde State Historic Park in Camp Verde, Arizona. Photo by Bill Helm.

Joe 'Twinkle Toes' Weber pitches to a member of the Bisbee Black Sox in a game at Fort Verde State Historic Park in Camp Verde, Arizona. Photo Bill Helm.

Epilogue – Those Were and These Are the Days

While writing this book in early 2022, Major League Baseball was in the midst of yet another crisis, this time in the form of an owners' lockout prompted by a collective bargaining stalemate with the players' union. Key points of contention included service time requirements before arbitration and free agency, minimum salaries, competitive balance and payroll taxes. While I have not been privy to these secretive negotiations (nor would I care to be), the common denominator for each of these wedge issues is and will undoubtedly continue to be money.

While this lockout was the first in nearly 30 years, the concept of baseball labor stoppages is hardly novel. In fact, the league has now seen nine, with the first in 1972, the same year as the landmark Supreme Court Case Flood v. Kuhn. And while most stoppages were resolved within a few days or weeks, others have left lasting scars like that infamous 232-day stoppage that abruptly ended the 1994 season and broke the hearts of the league-leading Montreal Expos and their long-suffering fans. Yet labor disputes are just one of many factors that have fragmented baseball's fanbase over the years and provoked some to resurrect the vintage game and rekindle baseball in its purest form.

Chapter 3 explored the advent of professionalism through one of the first clubs of its kind: 1869's Cincinnati Red Stockings. And while those Red Stockings are widely remembered for their 57-0 record, electric offense and national celebrity, their insolvency and inevitable dissolution after the following season are merely a historical footnote. Further, Chapter 4 followed the game's meteoric rise at the dawn of the 20th century as the product on the field elevated commensurately with salaries, but also opened the floodgates to gambling and corruption that reached a crescendo at the 1919 "Black Sox" World Series. Even though the game's reputation was largely restored during the oft romanticized Golden Era (c. 1920-1960), thanks in part to the game's wartime connotation with national pride and the era's many heroes like Babe Ruth, Ted Williams, Jackie Robinson and Willie Mays, the seemingly unanimous sentiment would shift dramatically in subsequent decades.

Chapter 5 expounded upon some of those watershed

moments since the 1960's that irreversibly shaped the modern game's identity including 1972's Flood v. Kuhn Supreme Court decision and advent of free agency, which has remained a lightning rod for controversy and perpetual catalyst of work stoppages even half a century later. While most of these formative shifts like free agency, collective bargaining agreements and competitive balancing rules are inextricably tied to economic factors, others are fueled by hyper-competitiveness and the relentless pursuit of another "edge" over one's opponent. Chapter 5's discussion of the notorious "Hackgate" and sign-stealing scandals underscores the dangers of the "win at all cost" mentality and the heavy toll it has taken on individual clubs and the game's overall integrity. On the other hand, the recent and growing list of rebuilds to World Series champions and abundance of competitive balancing incentives like higher draft picks and larger prospect signing bonus pools have ushered in a "lose at all cost" mentality that has further alienated the fanbase. And lastly, with the rapid and universal adoption of advanced analytics and recent experimentation with computer-assisted umpiring, data and science now prevail over hunches and emotions, and as a result, diminish the unpredictable human element that characterized the earlier game.

Yet the game's economic and scientific progress has been a boon for many stakeholder groups like owners, whose individual club assets are now valued in the billions; managers, who can use computers both to assist in decision-making and to provide justification when wrong; and players, including middle relievers with desirable situational stats that ink eight-figure deals, with around 5% going to their agents. Fans, on the other hand, are far more divided. While some embrace the game's rapid evolution and abundance of data, using it to fortify their fantasy rosters or attempt to tilt the gambling odds in their favor, others long for far simpler times. The latter are highly unlikely to get their wish, at least at the major league level, as evidenced by the game's accelerating rate of change and accompanying, sustained revenue growth, including 2019's leaguewide gross revenues of $10.7 billion that marked the 17th consecutive year of record growth.[231]

Instead of stoically accepting the modern game or abandoning baseball altogether, the growing community of vintage ballists continue to revive the game in its most elemental form. And while today's roughly 400 vintage clubs may seem like a small niche following, the vintage revival's burgeoning success, including doubling the number of clubs over the past decade, provides hope for those longing for the earlier game.

Beyond the encouraging growth trajectory, the vintage game's bright future is most evident in the stories of the individual clubs, ballists and their communities. For instance, Chapter 7's account of Fleischmanns, New York's Mountain Athletic Club shows how a club can help a community not only rekindle its rich history but also heal in the wake of tragedy, as was the case after 2011's Hurricane Irene. Chapter 8 discusses the Akron Black Stockings' Scott "Tiny" Hamblin, whose innovative marketing and outreach have made the Black Stockings' a pillar of the local community. Chapter 9's overview of St. Louis' Lafayette Square Cyclone Base Ball Club, where the three Neil brothers have played alongside their father, provides even more cause for optimism on the vintage game's future. Additionally, Chapter 10's account of the Ohio Village Diamonds Ladies Vintage Base Ball Club offers yet another reminder that baseball has never been just for the boys. And finally, Chapter 11's accounts of Arizona's Fort Verde Excelsiors and Washington's Whatcom Aces underscore how the vintage game can thrive in the most unlikely places with the right exposure.

While the clubs profiled herein are but a small subset, their dedication to historical preservation, sportsmanship and camaraderie as well as their optimistic outlook on the vintage game's future are shared throughout the entire vintage base ball community, as evident at national gatherings like the Ohio Cup and the Vintage Base Ball Association's annual conference. So, what I mean by the epilogue's byline "Those Were and These Are the Days" is this: Thanks to the dedicated women and men behind the ongoing vintage base ball revival and their over 40 years of tireless efforts to grow the game across the country and beyond, vintage base ball is no longer just a means to revisit the game's past, but also carry it forward, providing a refreshingly pure alternative to the modern game's often overwhelming complexities. And while these poetic words from Official MLB Historian John Thorn in his renowned essay *Mangled Forms* were specific to the Upstate New York village of Fleischmanns, they too are analogous of the greater vintage base ball community:

"In this somewhat remote place, determined individuals and families who love the old ways are working to be sure of the past; the extent of their success will indeed predict the future of Fleischmanns and so many other communities whose histories, if properly understood and conveyed, are their principal assets."

Appendix –
Vintage Base Ball Terminology

The following section has been reprinted with permission from the website of the Vintage Base Ball Association (https://www.vbba.org/dictionary-terms-1850-1860).

The mission and purpose of the Vintage Base Ball Association shall be to preserve, perpetuate, and promote the game of base ball as it was played during its formative years in the nineteenth century and other historic eras.

A Dictionary of Documented Base Ball Terms Late 1850s – 1860s
The use of many terms in base ball has not changed since the 1860s. A few examples: pitcher, catcher, shortstop, first/second/third baseman, base players, infielders, right/center/left fielder, outfielders, umpire, runs, outs, assist, put out, double/triple play, fair ball, foul ball, foul tip, over/wild throws, bases on hits, bases on errors, safe hit, strike out, base on balls (1864 on), pop up, home run, left on base.

The terms provided here are all documented as being in common use in base ball in the era we portray – the late 1850s through the 1860s.

Ace: See Run.

Amateur Players: Chadwick describes two classes of amateurs; the first class are highly skilled *(a club's first, and maybe second, nine)*, and second class are unskilled but are better than muffins.

Appeal: In the modern game an appeal is a claim of violation of the rules made by the defense. In the vintage period, virtually all calls made by the umpire, including calls on the bases, were by appeal, the players typically calling for *"judgment"*. The exceptions were balks, fouls ball, and the calling of balls (1864) and strikes (1858), which the rules specify the umpire should make *"unasked."* However, it's important to remember that most decisions about outs were not made by the umpire, but were made by the players recognizing the correct outcome of a play.

Artists: The most experienced players of a nine, not only physically active and expert, but mentally quick, and shrewd in judgment of the *"points"* in the game.

Ash, Hickory, Timber: Slang terms for bat. The most common 19th century term was the bat. The term willow is an anachronism for our era, as it emerged as a term for bat only in the 1870s.

Balk: A balk or baulk is committed when the pitcher fails to deliver a ball after making any of the preliminary movements to deliver it; if he steps outside the lines of his position, before the ball leaves his hand, when in the act of pitching; or, if he jerks or throws the ball to the batsman. *(By 1864, it was also a balk if the pitcher had either foot off the ground at the time of delivering the pitch. This was removed from the rules in 1868.)* Balk rules were instilled in the original Knickerbocker rules to allow runners a fair opportunity to steal bases.

Ball *(the object):* The period term is the ball. The terms Apple, Pill, Onion, and Horsehide are all 20th century slang.

Ball *(called):* The period term is ball. Only in use after 1864, when called balls were introduced to the rules.

Ballist, Base-ballist: Slang term for a base ball player.

Base: The period term is also the base. Although the rules specify the field bases be *"canvas bags,"* the slang terms of sacks or bags are from later.

Base ball: It is common for vintage ballists to point out that *"base ball was two words back then."* John Thorn, Historian of Major League Baseball has pointed out that on occasion, the word would be printed as base-ball or even baseball, but that the one-word version was quite uncommon. It didn't become the most common form of the game's name until 1897.

Base on Balls: Is the period term. The term *"walk"* arrives several years after the 1864 rule providing for a base on balls.

Bat *(noun)*: The bat was most commonly called the bat. Ash, Hickory, Timber and Club were seen used as slang terms. The term w*illow* is an anachronism referring to a bat. This slang term emerged after 1870.

Bat *(verb)*: The period term is bat. Also: go in, strike Batsman: The striker at the bat.

Batter: The term arrives at the very end of the 1860s. The more common terms are ***striker*** or ***batsman***.

Battery: In the mid-19th century, this term referred to the arsenal of the pitcher's pitches (e.g., "Smith has quite a battery on display today."). Substantially later it came to refer to the pitcher and catcher together.

Bias or Twist: Rotation put on the ball by the pitcher with his wrist, not with the intent for the ball to curve in flight, but for the ball to be misdirected off the bat. The term ***curving*** is seen used to describe pitches that are tossed with the curve referring to the arc.

Blank, Blank Score: When no runs are scored during a club's inning. Also, a batsman makes a blank score when he fails to score a run in a game. In New York a blank score is also called a ***"Skunk"***, in the West it is also called a ***"Whitewashing"***, and in the East a ***"Blinder"***.

Bounder, Grounder, Ground Ball: Technical terms for a bounding ball from the bat which strikes the ground within the lines of the in-field, vs. a ***daisy cutter*** which does not bound at all.

Clean Home Runs: A home run can include errors and overthrows. A clean home run does not. Chadwick encourages that only clean home runs are recorded as home runs in the box score.

Captain: The player that directed the club. In the professional era he became a Manager.

Catch: Is also a period term. The ball needed be held (i.e., taken from the air and kept still, without touching the ground) for a catch to be considered completed. If it were trapped under an arm, etc., it was considered held.

Catcher: The period term is Catcher. *(See also* **Behind** *on the* Misused Terms page*)*

Caught Napping, Run Out: Picked off base, or out being caught between bases *(as in a run down or a pickle, both of which are 20th century terms)*, or outwitted on a point of play.

Chances: Opportunities for a fielder to make an out, such as a pop up, fly ball, or to put a player out at first base. A *"chance"* is *"accepted"* (caught, the out made) or *"not accepted"* (dropped, made an error).

Club: Is a period term. In the modern day the terms of club and team are almost synonymous, but in the period; team was a term infrequently used to describe the men chosen to be on the field on the day of the game. A period term would be a nine or side. A club was the entire group or association from which the team or nine were chosen.

Country Club: A somewhat derisive term for a rural, less skilled club
First Nine: Refers to the best nine players in a particular club. *Second Nine* would be the next best, etc. depending on the number of men on the club. The *Muffin Nine* would be the least skilled.
A *Picked Nine* would be a team assembled from various clubs for a particular game. A nine that purported to be a pre-existing club for a tournament, but which was alleged to have been pulled from multiple clubs, was sometimes referred to derisively as a scraped nine.
A *Non-Playing Member* was a member of a club who does not play in matches. Usually, such members are not talented enough, do not have time to devote to the sport, or merely want to be associated with the club for its social aspects (maybe umpires, scorers, or simply friends and colleagues).

Corker: A hard hit ball.

Country Club: A rural, less skilled club.

Daisy Cutter, Skimmer: A low pitched ball, hit sharply along the surface of the ground, through the grass, without rebounding to any extent. A grounder that does not bounce.

Dead Ball: A dead ball in the modern sense is a ball out of play due to a suspension of play. In the period, a ball could become dead with play continuing. A ball is said to be *"dead"* when no player can be legally put out by a fielder, such as when a ball is hit foul or stopped by outsiders.

Double Play: Has the same meaning in the period.

Drawn Game, Tie Game: When the score is equal in a game, and at least five even innings have been played, and there is no opportunity to play the game to a close *(generally because of rain or darkness)*, it becomes a drawn game.

Facing For a Hit: Batsman facing the position in the field he desires to send the ball.

Fair Ball: Has the same meaning in the period, and could also be referred to as fairly struck. Also used to refer to a ball pitched within the batsman's reach, in which case it could also be referred to as *fairly pitched*.

Field: Is a period term. *Ground* or *Grounds* are also period terms for the playing field. Garden is an anachronism, referring to the outfield. This slang term emerged after 1870.

Fielder: Has the same meaning in the period. The commonly used terms were **fielder** *(left, center, right)*, **shortstop** *(occasionally referred to as the short fielder)*, and **baseman** *(first, second, third)*. *Ballist* and *Base-ballist* are period slang term for a base ball player.

First Nine: Refers to the best nine players in a particular club.

Fly Ball: Has the same meaning in the period. Slang period terms for a fly ball are ***High Ball, Air Ball, Riser, got up a fly, raised a flyer.*** For a high fly ball, period terms are ***Sky ball, Skyer.***

Fly Game: Up until the NABBP Convention of (December) 1864, the rules stated that fair and foul balls which were caught on one bounce were considered outs. Any games prior to this that were played by agreement with an out on fair balls only counting on the fly were called *"fly games"*. Such games do not count as NABBP games as they were not played by official NABBP rules.

Forced: When referring to a runner required to advance, the term means the same today as in the era we portray. The use of forced to mean that a runner was out when the ball was held at a base before the runner got to the base (e.g., *"the runner was forced at second"*) is an anachronism that emerges in the 1870s.

Foul Ball: Same meaning as today. Infrequently seen referred to as a ***foul strike*** *(which is a term that in the 1870s came to have a very different meaning)*. It is a myth that all or any foul ball was called a foul tick and not a foul ball. A ball straight back from the bat was called a ***foul tip***.

Foul Tip: also ***fly tip.*** Has the similar meaning in the period. In the modern day a foul tip is a ball that is caught and ruled a strike. In the period, a foul tip that was caught was an out, but you could also hit a foul tip that was not caught for an out. To hit a foul tip which is caught by the catcher was often referred to as having ***tipped out.***

Fungoes: Then as today, this term refers to a batsman tossing up balls to hit to the fielders on the fly, as a form of practice.

Friendly Match: Refers to a match between two clubs which is not of consequence for any championship or as part of a series. An informal or practice game.

Game: Is a period term. A ***match*** is period term for a game, or series of games, played between two organized clubs that resulted from a formal challenge and was played for a specific stake *(the game ball, or to claim a championship)*. Although similar to the modern term series, Match is sometimes also used as a synonym for game.

Prior to 1860 a match was the best 2 of 3 games.

After 1860 a match was decided by a single game, unless mutually agreed upon by the contesting clubs.

In 1867, matches reverted to the best 2 of 3 games, unless a single game was mutually agreed on by the contesting clubs.

A Friendly Match refers to a match between two clubs which is not of consequence for any championship or as part of a series. An informal or practice game.

A Scrub Game was an informal game between members of the same club, or multiple clubs *(in which players choose sides and no records are kept)*.

The Fly Game referred to games in which a fair ball had to be caught without it having struck the ground to count as an out. Up until the NABBP Convention of *(December)* 1864, the rules stated that all balls which were caught on one bounce were considered outs. Any games prior to this that were played by agreement with an out on fair balls only counting on the fly were called *"fly games"*. Such games do not count as NABBP games as they were not played by official NABBP rules.

Get His First/Second/Third: To get his base or make his base. To advance a base by any means. Single/double/triple, or steal second/third base.

Ground, Grounds: Slang term for the playing field.

Grounder: Has the same meaning in the period. Also, a ground ball. A grounder from a low-pitched ball, hit sharply along the surface of the ground, through the grass, without rebounding to any extent was often referred to as a daisy cutter or skimmer. The term *bug bruiser* is an anachronism referring to a sharply hit grounder. This slang term emerged after 1870.

Head-Work: Pitcher utilizing his knowledge of a batsman's weak points to bother them in batting.

Hands down, Hands out, Hands lost: The old way of saying outs in an inning. Like ace, this was already an archaic term in 1860 but had not yet disappeared from use. ***H.L.*** *(for Hands Lost)* or ***H.O.*** *(for Hands Out)* continued to appear in some box scores as late as 1869, but ***Outs*** had become much more common in both newspaper box scores and game accounts.

High Ball, Air Ball: Ball hit high into the air.

Home base: Is a period term. Home plate was used by the 1870's with *"plate"* referring to the gauge of the iron, not its shape. More often ***Home Base*** was used. Dish is not a period term. Home Point is a myth of unknown origin referring to the home base.

Home Run: Is a period term. A period distinction was a ***Clean Home Run***. A home run can include errors and overthrows. A clean home run does not. Chadwick encourages that only clean home runs are recorded as home runs in the box score. Four Baser is an anachronism referring to a home run. This slang term emerged after 1870.

Hot Ball: A very swiftly thrown or batted ball.

Hurrah: A well-documented American cheer of the 19th century was three *"Hip, Hip, Hurrahs"*. This cheer, for emphasis, was sometimes followed by a *"tiger"*. This was an *'additional cheer with greater emphasis'*; or *"one more"* (often the word *"tiger"*) or a *"growl, screech or howl"* (1842). *(For more detail, see the entry "A note on Cheering" in Misused Terms.)*

Innings, Rounds: Not frequently seen in the singular (i.e., inning). An innings, in 1860s base ball, is played when three men on the batting side have been put out. The moment the third hand is out, that club's innings terminates. Each club has 9 innings in a game. Thus, you might say *"In the Eckfords' third innings..."* rather than *"In the Eckfords' third inning..." **Rounds*** was a less used slang term for innings.

Judgment: In the period, virtually every call was what would be referred to in the modern day as an *"appeal play"*, in which the umpire only made a decision when an appeal was made. By the 1860s, there were calls added that were to be automatically made by the umpire *"unasked"*, but the umpire would still not typically make a call on a close play unless asked for *"Judgment"* by the defensive player *(since the assumption is always that the player is not out unless declared out, the offensive team would not request judgment on a close play)*. Players might also call ***"How's that?"*** when requesting judgment. This is possibly the most underused term in modern vintage base ball.

Kicking, Chafing: Slang terms for complaining.

Knee High, Waist High, and Shoulder High: These are the three points generally requested by the batsman to show the pitcher where he wants the ball delivered.

Left hander: Is a period term. Wrong Hander is a myth of unknown origin. Hook is a 20th century term for a left hander as well as a curve ball. The common period term is left-hander.

Line Ball: A ball sent swiftly from the bat to the field almost on a horizontal line. Other period terms are ***stinger, whizzer, corker, hot shot, shooter,*** or ***straight-outer.*** *A **hot ball** meant a very swiftly thrown or batted ball.

Long Balls: This is a common name for balls hit to the outer field.

Match: A game, or series of games, played between two organized clubs that resulted from a formal challenge and was played for a specific stake *(the game ball, or to claim a championship)*. Prior to 1860 a match was the best 2 of 3 games. After 1860 a match was decided by a single game, unless mutually agreed upon by the contesting clubs. In 1867, matches reverted to the best 2 of 3 games, unless a single game was mutually agreed on by the contesting clubs. Although similar to the modern term series, Match is sometimes also used as a synonym for game.

Muffed Balls, Muff: Muffed balls are treated as errors of fielding. *(Interestingly, Muff is still in the scoring section of MLB's official rules)*. Also: ***miss, failed to take***.

Muffins: Least skilled players.

Non-Playing Member: A member of a club who does not play in matches. Usually, such members are not talented enough, do not have time to devote to the sport, or merely want to be associated with the club for its social aspects *(maybe umpires, scorers)*.

Not Out, In: Safe on the bases. The term safe was not used as the opposite of out until later, although you would occasionally read that a base runner *"achieved his base safely"*.

Obstruction: In the period, a runner, even having been touched with the ball while off the base, cannot be put out if the fielder in any manner hindered him. Even if waiting for the ball or possessing the ball, the fielder must allow full access to the base.

Out: Is a period term. Also, Hands down, Hands out and Hands lost were in use in the 1860s, and were already considered *"The old way of saying outs in an inning."* H.L. *(for Hands Lost)* or H.O. *(for Hands Out)* continued to appear in some box scores as late as 1869, but **Outs** had become much more common in both newspaper box scores and game accounts. **Hands** was an archaic term yet had not yet disappeared from use. Vintage base ball players also frequently use the term **dead** instead of out. **Dead** was apparently used in early forms of the game where a runner would be put out by being plugged or soaked with the thrown ball. Death and dying on the bases still found infrequent use for color in sportswriter's accounts in early base ball throughout the 19th century. Knowledgeable umpires would have been very unlikely to have used those terms after the first convention in 1857. ***The common term was out.***

Outfielder: Is a period term.

Over-Pitch: Wild pitch over the heads of the batsman and catcher. A mark of too great an effort to pitch swiftly.

Pace: As early as the mid-1850s, pitchers were known to deliver the ball with *"exceeding velocity"* *(Stevens of the Knickerbockers, 1856)*; the most common term for the speed applied to the ball was *pace*. Also: ***swift pitching***.

Passed Ball, Ball Past Catcher: A ball muffed by the catcher on which a base is run. Through most of the 1860s, ball past catcher would have been the more common of these terms.

Picked Nine: A team assembled for a particular game, somewhat akin to a modern all-star game *(for example, the 1858 Fashion Course games, which featured picked nines from Brooklyn and New York).*

Pitcher: The period term is *Pitcher*. Term originally meant to convey that the ball could not be thrown *(i.e., delivered with a bent elbow, either overhand or underhand). (See also the entries for **Hurler, Bowler, and Feeder** in the **Misused Terms** document.)*

Play: As the umpire calling for the game to begin; is a period term.

Points: *Playing points* is having a thorough understanding of the rules and applying that knowledge *(strategy)* in playing the game. Having a thorough knowledge of the rules, and making use of that knowledge to your club's advantage, was something that was generally admired, and not seen as inappropriate.

Professionals: was a period term. The first professional association formed in 1869. Among professionals; *revolvers* were players who play for the highest bidder and who change teams frequently. Prior to the late 1860s, professionalism was generally banned by the rules, and payment was often in the form of jobs for which no work was required, or other disguisable means of payment.

Punishing The Pitcher: When the pitcher is giving up lots of hits, the offense is *punishing the pitcher*.

Put Some Steam On: Encouragement to run faster. The terms leg it and stir your stumps are myths of unknown origin, possibly created in recent years by vintage base ball players.

Revolvers: As early as 1856, *"the movement of the ablest players from weaker clubs to stronger ones"* was referred to as revolving, and was seen as a problem in the New York game. In later years, revolvers were understood to be players who played for the highest bidder and who changed teams frequently. The use of revolver to refer to a substitute player is not consistent with the usage of the term in the era we portray.

Run: It is a myth that ace was used exclusively and run was not. ***Run*** was in common use from the 1850s. *Ace* was used in the Knickerbocker rules of 1845, and was being weeded out as archaic by the early 1860s. Like many archaic base ball terms, it can still be found being used for color in later years. ***Tally*** was used in the 1860s as slang for run, most commonly for the cumulative run total of an inning or a game *(as in "the tally stood at 5 to 4")*. ***Run*** was the common term used in the rules. The phrase *"Tally your ace"* has not been documented as having been used in the 1860s, nor has any requirement to *"check in with the scorer"* in order to *"tally your ace."* ***Blank*** and ***Blank Score*** were when no runs are scored during a club's inning. Also, a batsman makes a blank score when he fails to score a run in a game. In New York a blank score is also called a ***Skunk***, in the West it is also called a ***Whitewashing***, and in the East a ***Blinder***.

Runner: Is a period term. A period call for a runner to run faster may be ***Put Some Steam On***. The terms leg it and stir your stumps are myths of unknown origin. Period terms for a runner advancing to a base would be ***to get (or make or achieve) his base*** or ***to get (or make or achieve) his first (second, third, run)*** whether he did it by a batted ball, stolen base, or by any means.

Safe hit: A batted ball that gives the batsman his base.

Scorer: Is a period term. The term Tallykeeper is an anachronism from some archaic forms of base ball. The commonly used term is ***scorer***.

Scrub Game: An informal game between members of the same club, or multiple clubs *(in which players choose sides and no records are kept)*.

Second Nine: Gentlemen's Clubs of the middle 19th century sometimes had hundreds of members. The first nine were presumably the best players and represented the club in important games. The second nine were presumably of lesser skills and played against less important clubs or against their own first nine.

There may have been third nines, or beyond as well, in larger clubs.

Side, Nine, Club Nine: Team.

Side Out: End of a club's innings, three outs.

Sky ball, Skyer: High fly ball. *Also: **riser, flyer, skyscraper***

Spectators, Audience: When referring to those people witnessing a game of base ball, the most common terms used in the period were spectators or audience, and occasionally you might read about followers. If there were a large group, it might be referred to as a Throng. Fans is an anachronism from much later in baseball's history. Crank is an anachronism for our era of base ball, as it emerged only in the 1880s professional era, and even then, it didn't refer to attendees at a game, but rather to the rabid follower of the game *(see the Misused Terms document, under Cranks)*.

Steal: A common term, then as now, meaning to take a base with neither a hit, nor a muff, nor a passed ball. Stolen bases were recorded differently than bases taken on passed balls.

Stinger, Whizzer: Hard hit ball. Also: ***corker, shooter, hot shot***

Strike: Per the rules as of 1858; On balls delivered by the pitcher within fair reach of the bat, the umpire is required, after a warning, to call a strike, when he deems that the striker was allowing such a pitch to pass to delay the game or give advantage to a player – typically one in position to steal a base. Chadwick says this rule *"should be strictly enforced" (1860 Beadles)*

Striker, Batsman: Batter.

Stump Match: A game that is a challenge match with another club. Suspended Game: Suspended play due to rain etc. was understood.

Tally: See *Run*.

Team: See *Club*.

Tip Out: When a foul ball is caught by the catcher, the batsman is said to *tip out*.

To Bat: The batsmen did not need to be told when they were to bat as there were no infield balls or practice pitches between innings. They were expected to take their position and indicate where they would like their pitch without prompting. We can document a call of *"to bat"* or *"[striker's name], to bat!"* when needed. The call of striker to the line is a myth that was created in the modern day.

Triple Play: Is a period term. Also *treble play*.

Umpire: Is a period term. Arbiter and Arbitrator were not in use to refer to umpires.

Language Used for Color and Interest

None of this is to say that those talking and writing about base ball were not creative and clever in their language. One game account notes that *"Cornell sent his compliments to third base" (meaning he hit the ball towards third)* and that *"Witherspoon, by a low ball to first, was put out by the worthy keeper of that hotel."* The language was interesting – often more so than today. But in no case would we think that the first baseman was commonly called a hotel keeper, or that a hit was called a compliment. Following are some such phrases found in period base ball writing. What constitutes a colorful phrase *vs.* a period term can be a grey area. Some of the very frequently used language is included as a term above.

In the list below, we provide a topic that one might want to talk about, followed by several terms that are documented as having been in use in the era we portray.

Catching: *"took handsomely"* (caught), *"nicely caught out"*, *"promptly secured"*, *"shut upon"*, *"grabbed the leather in style"*, *"fielded prettily to the first baseman's trap", "held the swiftest balls like a vise", "stopped in his hands as if it belonged there", "bottled it in style", "thankfully accepted"*

Excellent Play: crack (as in crack player or crack club (team)), *"took handsomely" (caught), "handsome fielding and throwing" "well guided there" (throw), "caught the ball tip top", "passed it sharply" (throw), "caught on the fly in style" "in the highest style of the art"*

Muffs: *"Fielded the ball poorly to..." (bad throw), "beautifully missed", "failed to take", "another chance to miss an easy bound"*

A Ball Well Struck: Cannon Ball, *"sent a strong ball", "raised a strong one", "knocked a splendid ball", "Howitzer shot", "hit a corker"*

Playing with spirit: Showing sand, Pluck and perseverance, vim For going in to Bat: go in, strike, *'take a turn at the ball", "use the hickory", "throw the club at"* Coming in to strike after giving up runs: *"do justice to their reputation", "get square with their opponents", "hard piece of work cut out for them"*

Strong hitter: "heavy hitter"

Rallying: "presented a bold front"

Close Play: 'close shave', 'tight squeak'.

Reacting to an umpire's judgment against you: *"accepted with quiet acquiescence" (properly), "roused his dander" or "kicked" (angered, improperly)*

Picked off base: *"his sharp dodge caught him napping"* Looking a runner back: *"showed the whites of his eyes"* Pitching with spin: *"peculiar twist put on to the ball"*

Good Game: *"Lively match", "sharp contest", "good display", "well-contested display" "strongly contested"*

Winning the Game: *"Resulted in favor of...", "Victory perched on the bat-sticks of...", "Victory perched on the new banner of the Eckford club", "retrieved their laurels"*

Complaining: chaffing, kicking

Ruffians: short hair class, blackguards

Put Out: *"sent to the grass", "took a back seat", "tame hit, as means of his retirement".*

Bibliography

"1869 Cincinnati Red Stockings". *Baseball Reference.* https://www.baseball-reference.com/bullpen/1869_Cincinnati_Red_Stockings

"1908: The Merkle Boner." *This Great Game.* https://thisgreatgame.com/1908-baseball-history

Akron Black Stockings. https://www.facebook.com/AkronBlackStockingsBBC

Al Reach Historical Marker." *ExplorePAHistory.com*, 2019. https://explorepahistory.com/hmarker.php?markerId=1-A-3

Allardice, Bruce. "Baseball 1858-1865: By the Numbers." *SABR Baseball Research Journal, Spring 2020.* https://sabr.org/journal/article/baseball-1858-1865-by-the-numbers

Allardice, Bruce. "Sport Sullivan." *SABR*, June 2014. https://sabr.org/bioproj/person/sport-sullivan

American Battlefield Trust. "Vicksburg." https://www.battlefields.org/learn/civil-war/battles/vicksburg Accessed September 2021

Andersen, Don. E-mail interview. Conducted by Jack Pelikan, 24 March 2022

Anderson, Sarah. "Play (Really Old) Ball! One man's quest to set the national pastime back 150 years." *Seattle Met.* 27 Dec 2008. https://www.seattlemet.com/arts-and-culture/2008/12/0708-mud-baseball

Andre, Rebecca. "Irene Five Years Later: Eight Untold Stories from the Catskills Flood." *Watershed Post*, 3 September 2016. http://www.watershedpost.com/2016/irene-five-years-later-eight-untold-stories-catskills-flood

Andrews, Evan. "What Was the 1919 Black Sox Baseball Scandal?" *History*. https://www.history.com/news/black-sox-baseball-scandal-1919-world-series-chicago

Annie Glidden Houts to John Glidden, April 20, 1866. http://digitallibrary.vassar.edu/fedora/repository/vassar:24406

Arango, Tim. "Myth of Baseball's Creation Endures, With a Prominent Fan." *New York Times*, 12 November 2010. https://www.nytimes.com/2010/11/13/sports/baseball/13doubleday.html

Arizona Territories Vintage Base Ball League: Fort Verde Excelsiors Page. https://arizonavintagebaseball.org/leaguehome#/fort-verde-excelsiors

Arizona Territories Vintage Base Ball League: Rules Page. http://arizonavintagebaseball.org/links-information

Associated Press. "Christopher Correa, Former Cardinals Executive, Sentenced to Four Years for Hacking Astros' Database." *New York Times*, 18 July 2016

Associated Press. "Hurricane Irene One Year Later: Storm Cost $15.8 in damage from Florida to New York to the Caribbean." *New York Daily News*, 27 August 2012. https://www.nydailynews.com/new-york/hurricane-irene-year-storm-cost-15-8-damage-florida-new-york-caribbean-article-1.1145302

Associated Press. "Robot Umpires at Home Plate Moving Up to Triple-A for 2022." *ABC News*, 20 January 2022. https://abcnews.go.com/Sports/wireStory/robot-umpires-home-plate-moving-triple-2022-82381464

Aubrecht, Michael. "Baseball and the Blue and the Gray." *Baseball Almanac*, August 2016. https://www.baseball-almanac.com/articles/aubrecht2004b.shtml

Barnard, Matthew and Rudy Frias, hosts. "02-11 ROTB-Scott "Tiny" Hamblin – Akron, OH Black Stockings". *The Roller Out the Barrel Podcast.* From Listen Notes, 18 Oct 2020, https://www.listennotes.com/podcasts/the-roller-out-the/02-11-rotb-scott-tiny-xJmvb0ECkMW

Baseball Rule Changes: A Timeline of Major League Baseball Rule Changes." *Baseball Almanac.* https://www.baseball-almanac.com/rulechng.shtml

Belson, Ken. "Apples for a Nickel, and Plenty of Empty Seats." *New York Times*, 7 Jan 2009

Berlage, Gai Ingham. *Women in Baseball: The Forgotten History.* Greenwood Publishing Group, Inc., 1994

Bernstein, Dan. "Astros Cheating Scandal Timeline, From the First Sign-Stealing Allegations to a Controversial Punishment." *The Sporting News*, 24 July 2020

Biography.com Editors. "Shoeless Joe Jackson Biography." *Biography,* 2 Apr 2014. https://www.biography.com/athlete/shoeless-joe-jackson

Birnbaum, Phil. "A Guide to Sabermetric Research." *SABR.* https://sabr.org/sabermetrics

Blum, Ronald. "The Red Sox Are Over the 2022 Luxury Tax, but All Pale to the Big-Spending Dodgers." *Boston Globe,* 3 June 2022. https://www.bostonglobe.com/2022/06/03/sports/red-sox-are-over-2022-luxury-tax-all-pale-big-spending-dodgers

Boardman, Mark. "The Camp Grant Massacre." *True West*, 4 March 2016

Bogovich, Rich and Mark Pestana. "July 23, 2870: The First "Chicago" Game." *SABR,* https://sabr.org/gamesproj/game/july-23-1870-the-first-chicago-game

Bowers, Jennifer. "Ohio Cup Brings Vintage Base Ball to Ohio Village". *NBC4i.com*. 4 September 2021. https://www.nbc4i.com/news/local-news/columbus/ohio-cup-brings-vintage-base-ball-to-ohio-village.

Branson, Vicki. "Vicki Branson on the Founding of the Ohio Village Muffins". *YouTube,* 22 February 2014. https://www.youtube.com/watch?v=QSrmTDQjKWQ

Brown, Maury. "MLB Sees Record 10.7 Billion in Revenues for 2019." *Forbes,* 21 December 2019. https://www.forbes.com/sites/maurybrown/2019/12/21/mlb-sees-record-107-billion-in-revenues-for-2019/?sh=553834825d78

Carola, Chris. "Suspenders, Yes. Gloves, No. Vintage Baseball Makes a Comeback in the Catskills." *Times Union,* 25 May 2021. https://www.timesunion.com/hudsonvalley/outdoors/article/Vintage-baseball-makes-comeback-in-Catskills-16197922.php

Cartwright, Alexander. "Alexander Joy Cartwright IV Forms Pacific Northwest Vintage Baseball League." *PRWeb*, 20 February 2006. https://www.prweb.com/releases/2006/02/prweb347849.htm

Chadwick, Henry. *1860 Beadle's Dime Base-Ball Player*. New York, Irwin R. Beadle, 1860

Chadwick, Henry. *1870 Beadle's Dime Base-Ball Player*. New York, Irwin R. Beadle, 1870

Chicago White Sox vs Cincinnati Reds October 1, 1919 Box Score." *Baseball Almanac*. https://www.baseball-almanac.com/box-scores/boxscore.php?boxid=191910010CIN

Chicago White Sox vs Cincinnati Reds October 6, 1919 Box Score." *Baseball Almanac*. https://www.baseball-almanac.com/box-scores/boxscore.php?boxid=191910060CHA

Clarke, Edward H. *Sex in Education; or, A Fair Chance for the Girls*. Boston, James R. Osgood and Company, 1873

Dickson, Marcus W. "1867 Winter Meetings: National Association of Base Ball Players Annual Convention." *SABR*, 2018. https://sabr.org/journal/article/1867-winter-meetings-national-association-of-base-ball-players-annual-convention

Dickson, Paul. *New Dickson Baseball Dictionary*. New York, Houghton Mifflin Harcourt, 1999

Duggan, Chris. E-mail interview. Conducted by Jack Pelikan, 22 August 2021

Editors. "Abner Doubleday." *History,* 21 October 2018. https://www.history.com/topics/american-civil-war/abner-doubleday

Elmore, Ed. E-mail interview. Conducted by Jack Pelikan, 11 May 2022

"Female Club in Brooklyn." *Brooklyn Daily Eagle*, 10 September 1868

Fitzgerald, F. Scott (Francis Scott), 1896-1940. *The Great Gatsby*. New York: C. Scribner's Sons, 1925

"Flood v. Kuhn." *Baseball Almanac.* https://www.baseball-almanac.com/law/Flood_v._Kuhn.shtml

Forquer, Jackie. E-mail interview. Conducted by Jack Pelikan, 6 April 2022

Francis, Bill. "Doc Adams Helped Shape Baseball's Earliest Days." *National Baseball Hall of Fame.* https://baseballhall.org/discover-more/stories/pre-integration/adams-doc

Frandsen, Nicholas. "Bovina Offense Rolls Through DelCo Historical Association Hay Fields; Improves to 10-1." Bovina Dairymen, 26 July 2021. https://www.bovinadairymen.org/post/bovina-offense-rolls-through-delco-historical-association-hay-fields-improves-to-10-1

Frommer, Harvey. *Old Time Baseball: America's Pastime in the Gilded Age*. Guilford, Lyons Press, 2016

Ginsburg, Daniel. "The 1877 Louisville Grays Scandal." *SABR.* https://sabr.org/journal/article/the-1877-louisville-grays-scandal

"Girls Base Ball Clubs." *Utica Morning Herald*, 17 Oct 1867

Goold. Derek. "On December 24, 1969, Curt Flood Mailed a Letter that Changed Baseball History." *STLToday*, 24 December 2021. https://www.stltoday.com/sports/baseball/professional/on-dec-24-1969-curt-flood-mailed-a-letter-that-changed-baseball-history/article_fe33784a-553c-52ba-87bb-ac981b077b37.html

Haber, Joel. "How Fleischmann's Yeast built the Jewish Catskills." *Jewish Community Voice*. 14 July 2021. https://www.jewishvoicesnj.org/articles/how-fleischmanns-yeast-built-the-jewish-catskills

Hajducky, Dan. "T206 Honus Wagner baseball card sells or $6.606 million, shattering previous record.". *ESPN*. 16 August 2021. https://www.espn.com/mlb/story/_/id/32031670/t206-honus-wagner-baseball-card-sells-6606-million-shattering-previous-record

Hamblin, Scott. E-mail interview. Conducted by Jack Pelikan, 2 September 2021

Helm, Bill. "Arizona Vintage Baseballer Meets His Idol." *The Base Ball Players Chronicle.* Winter 2022. https://www.vbba.org/wp-content/uploads/2022/01/VBBA-2022-WINTER-Newsletter-.pdf

Helm, Bill. "Getting the Word Out: Drumming up Fan Interest in Vintage Base Ball." *The Base Ball Players Chronicle.* Fall 2021. https://www.vbba.org/wp-content/uploads/2021/11/VBBA-2021-FALL-Newsletter-v3.pdf

Helm, Bill. "Mike Adrian: A Real Ace." *The Base Ball Players Chronicle*. Winter 2022. https://www.vbba.org/wp-content/uploads/2022/01/VBBA-2022-WINTER-Newsletter-.pdf

Helm, Bill. E-mail interviews. Conducted by Jack Pelikan, 5 February and 1 May 2022

Henderson, Robert W. *Ball, Bat and Bishop: The Origins of Ball Games*. New York. Rockport Press, 1947

Hodges, Julia. "1866 Winter Meetings: National Association of Base Ball Players Convention." *SABR,* https://sabr.org/journal/article/1866-winter-meetings-national-association-of-base-ball-players-annual-convention

Holleman, Joe. "St. Louis Maroons Erased from Record Books." *St. Louis Post-Dispatch*, 7 December 2021

Honus Wagner Stats." *Baseball Almanac.* https://www.baseball-almanac.com/players/player.php?p=wagneho01

Honus Wagner." *Baseball Reference.* https://www.baseball-reference.com/players/w/wagneho01.shtml

Honus Wagner". *National Baseball Hall of Fame.* https://baseballhall.org/hall-of-famers/wagner-honus

Jable, J. Thomas. "Aspects of Moral Reform in Early Nineteenth-Century Pennsylvania." *Pennsylvania Magazine of History and Biography,* 102.3 (1978): 344-363

"Jay Kirk." *Baseball Reference.* https://www.baseball-reference.com/register/player.fcgi?id=kirke-002jud

Jernigan, Zachary. "Stubler Keeps History Alive." *JournalAZ.com*, 22 January 2016. http://www.journalaz.com/news/camp-verde/3532-stubler-keeps-history-alive.html

Kaneko, Gemma. "Three Fascinating Stories About Women Who Played Baseball in the 19th Century." *Cut4 by MLB.com*, 17 Jan 2017. https://www.mlb.com/cut4/3-fascinating-stories-from-debra-shattuck-s-book-bloomer-girls-women-baseball-pi

Kelly, Matt. "Every No. 1 Overall Draft Pick in MLB History." *MLB.com*, 11 July 2021. https://www.mlb.com/news/every-no-1-overall-mlb-draft-pick

Keri, Jonah. "Nine Managerial Decisions that Helped Decide Game 2 of the NLCS." *FiveThirtyEight*, 13, October 2014. https://fivethirtyeight.com/features/nine-managerial-decisions-that-helped-decide-game-2-of-the-nlcs

Kittel, Jeffrey. "19th Century St. Louis Baseball Grounds." *This Game of Games*, http://www.thisgameofgames.com/19th-century-st-louis-baseball-grounds.html Accessed September 2021

Kittle, Jeffrey. "Henry Gratiot and Early St. Louis Ball Playing." *This Game of Games*, http://thisgameofgames.com/henry-gratiot-and-early-st-louis-ball-playing.html Accessed September 2021

Koslowski, Jeffrey. "1868 Winter Meetings: 'The Most Brilliant Season' or A Lamentable Failure;" *SABR*, 2018.

https://sabr.org/journal/article/1868-winter-meetings-the-most-brilliant-season-or-a-lamentable-failure

Lineberger, Mark. "Sluggers Send Fans Back in Time." *JournalAZ.com*. 13 July 2011. http://www.journalaz.com/news/camp-verde/918-sluggers-send-fans-back-in-time.html

Locke, Irwin J. S. "Tucson Defeats Phoenix, 10-2; Old Pueblos Are Heavy Hitters." *El Paso Herald*, 28 April 1915

Lynch, Mike. "Pioneer Club Celebrates Origins of Baseball in Pacific Northwest." *Seamheads*, 20 July 2009. https://seamheads.com/2009/07/20/pioneer-club-celebrates-origins-of-baseball-in-pacific-northwest

Martin, Brian. *Baseball's Creation Myth: Adam Ford, Abner Graves and the Cooperstown Story*. Jefferson, MacFarland, 2013

McBane, Richard. *A Fine-Looking Lot of Ball-Tossers: The Remarkable Akrons of 1881*. Jefferson, McFarland, 2005

McGinty, Jo Craven. "Behind Broken Bats, Broken Records." *WSJ*, 26 June 2015

McLennan, Jim. "Baseball's Greatest Scandals, #7: The Louisville Grays." *SB Nation: AZ Snake Pit*. 24 May 2011. https://www.azsnakepit.com/2011/5/24/2131205/baseballs-greatest-scandals-9-the-louisville-greys

Miklich, Eric. "1862 Winter Meetings: Static Rules and Great Conflict." *SABR*. https://sabr.org/journal/article/1862-winter-meetings-static-rules-and-the-great-conflict

Miller, Collin. "2021 Season in Review Part 1: Living History." Mountain Athletic Club, 27 November 2021. https://www.macvintagebaseball.org/post/2021-season-in-review-part-1

Miller, Collin. "2021 Season in Review Part 2: M.A.C. Returns to Queen City 121 Years Later." Mountain Athletic Club, 9 January 2022. https://www.macvintagebaseball.org/post/season-in-review-part-2-121-years-later-m-a-c-returns-to-the-queen-city

Miller, Collin. "Founders' Day & the Hon. Julius Fleischmann – Yeast Magnate, Mayor, Baseball Executive & Ballist." Mountain Athletic Club. 10 June 2020. https://www.macvintagebaseball.org/post/founder-s-day-the-hon-julius-fleischmann-yeast-magnate-mayor-of-cincy-baseball-exec-ballist

Miller, Collin. Phone interview. Conducted by Jack Pelikan, 1 March 2022

MLB.com Baseball Memory Lab. "Earliest Baseball Clubs". http://mlb.mlb.com/memorylab/spread_of_baseball/earliest_clubs.jsp

Monti, Gary. Phone interview. Conducted by Jack Pelikan, 15 April 2022

Morris, Peter. *A Game of Inches: The Stories Behind the Innovations That Shaped Baseball: The Game on the Field.* Chicago, Ivan R. Dee, 2006

Morris, Peter. *But Didn't We Have Fun? An Informal History of Baseball's Pioneer Era, 1843-1870.* Chicago, Ivan. R. Dee, 2008

Mountain Athletic Club Vintage Base Ball. Facebook, 10 Oct. 2021. https://www.facebook.com/page/341511739594891/search/?q=yearning

Mountain Athletic Club Vintage Base Ball. Facebook, 24 Sep. 2019. https://www.facebook.com/page/341511739594891/search/?q=Keator%20Cup

National Baseball Hall of Fame. "Henry Chadwick." https://baseballhall.org/hall-of-famers/chadwick-henry

Newbery, John. *A Little Pretty Pocket Book. First American Edition.* Worcester, Massachusetts: Isaiah Thomas, 1787. Rare Book and Special Collections Division, Library of Congress (005.00.00)

Nucciarone, Monica. *Alexander Cartwright: The Life Behind the Baseball Legend.* University of Nebraska Press, 2014

O'Dea, Janelle. "Youth Baseball Tournament in Cottleville a Sign of Strange New Normal." *St. Louis Post-Dispatch*, 11 May 2020

Ohio History Connection. "Handbook of the Ohio Village Muffins & Lady Diamonds Vintage Base Ball Program."

Passan, Jeff. "Ex-Astros Pitcher Mike Fiers: Team Stole Signs with Camera." *ESPN.* 12 November 2019. https://www.espn.com/mlb/story/_/id/28066522/ex-astros-pitcher-mike-fiers-team-stole-signs-camera

Perry, Dayn. "MLB Lockout: A Brief History of Strikes and Lockouts as Baseball Comes to a Halt for First Time in 26 Year." *CBS Sports*, 5 December 2021.
https://www.cbssports.com/mlb/news/mlb-lockout-a-brief-history-of-strikes-and-lockouts-as-baseball-comes-to-a-halt-for-first-time-in-26-years

Pestana, Mark. "1869 Winter Meetings: Pivot to Professionalism." *SABR*, 2018.
https://sabr.org/journal/article/1869-winter-meetings-pivot-to-professionalism.

Peterjohn, Alvin K. "Baseball in Akron, 1879-81". *1973 Baseball Research Journal*.
https://sabr.org/journal/article/baseball-in-akron-1879-81

Piccione, Peter A. "Pharaoh at the Bat." *College of Charleston Magazine*, 1 July 2003.
https://piccionep.people.cofc.edu/pharaoh_at_bat.pdf

Porter, William. "Out-Door Sports: Base Ball: Base Ball at St. Louis, Mo." *Porter's Spirit of the Times*, vol. 8, no. 21. 17 July 1860

Pruitt, Sarah. "Why the Civil War Actually Ended 16 Months After Lee Surrendered." *History*, 1 September, 2018.
https://www.history.com/news/why-the-civil-war-actually-ended-16-months-after-lee-surrendered

Randhawa, Manny. "Honus Wagner T206 Card Sells for Record $7.25 Million." *ESPN*. 4 August 2022.
https://www.mlb.com/news/rare-t206-honus-wagner-baseball-card-sold-for-7-25-million

Reischel, Julia. "In Fleischmanns recount, Morrell still wins, but only by 2 votes." *Watershed Post*. 17 March 2011. http://www.watershedpost.com/2011/fleischmanns-recount-morrell-still-wins-only-2-votes

Remington, Alex. "The Civil War Christmas Game, Hilton Head, 1862." *FanGraphs*, December 22, 2011. https://blogs.fangraphs.com/the-civil-warchristmas-day-game-hilton-head-1862

Rhodes, Greg, John Erardi and Greg Gajus. *Baseball Revolutionaries: How the 1869 Cincinnati Red Stockings Rocked the Country and Made Baseball Famous.* Printed by authors, 2019

Rhodes, Greg. "June 14, 1870: The Atlantic Storm: Red Stockings suffer first defeat." *SABR*, 2013. https://sabr.org/gamesproj/game/june-14-1870-the-atlantic-storm-red-stockings-suffer-first-defeat

Robert Edward Auctions. "Extraordinary Correspondence Archive Relating to Alexander Cartwright's Induction to the Hall of Fame." 2007. https://robertedwardauctions.com/auction/2007/spring/977/extraordinary-correspondence-archive-relating-alexander-cartwrights-induction-hall-fame

Robert Edward Auctions. "The 1838 Olympic Constitution." 2007. https://robertedwardauctions.com/auction/2007/spring/1/1838-olympic-constitution

Rosenstein, Mike. "Yankees, Mets Each Have 1 Player Making More than Entire A's Roster After Sean Manaea-Padres Trade." *NJ.com*, 4 April 2022. https://www.nj.com/yankees/2022/04/yankees-mets-each-have-1-player-making-more-than-entire-as-roster-after-sean-manaea-padres-trade.html

Rothenberg, Matt. "30 Years Ago, The AAGPBL Came to Cooperstown." *National Baseball Hall of Fame.* 2018. https://baseballhall.org/discover/women-in-baseball-exhibit-made-history-in-cooperstown

"Rubber Industry". *Ohio History Connection.* https://ohiohistorycentral.org/w/Rubber_Industry

Salvatore, Victor. "The Man Who Didn't Invent Baseball." *American Heritage*, Volume 34, Issue 4 1983. https://www.americanheritage.com/man-who-didnt-invent-baseball

Sampson, Bob. "Pioneers of Vintage Base Ball, No. VI: Debra Reid, many teams from Cooperstown, N.Y. to St. Louis Missouri and points between." 6 September 2020. https://www.facebook.com/groups/459820377408533/ 6 September 2020

Schmidt, Michael S. "Cardinals Investigated for Hacking Into Astros' Database." *New York Times*, 16 June 2015

Schwartz, Joel. "Playing Baseball the Old-Fashioned Way." *Sports Illustrated*, 27 April 1987

Severo, Richard. "Rash of Fires in Catskills Points Up Growing Decline." *New York Times.* 27 July 1976. https://www.nytimes.com/1976/07/27/archives/rash-of-fires-in-catskills-points-up-growing-decline-rash-of-fires.html

Sharpe, Abby. "It's Just Something Magical: Bisbee's Historic Warren Ballpark Facilitates Sports in a Small Town." KOLD News 13, 26 August 2021.

https://www.kold.com/2021/08/26/its-just-something-magical-bisbees-historic-warren-ballpark-facilitates-sports-small-town

Shattuck, Debra. "Women's Baseball in Nineteenth-Century New York and the Man Who Set Back Women's Professional Baseball for Decades." *SABR*. 2017. https://sabr.org/journal/article/womens-baseball-in-nineteenth-century-new-york-and-the-man-who-set-back-womens-professional-baseball-for-decades

Sheinin, Dave. "No Longer Sports' Dirty Little Secret, Tanking is on Full Display and Impossible to Contain." *Washington Post*, 2 March 2018

Shine, Gregory P. "The National Game is Decidedly 'on the Fly.'" The Rise of Organized Base Ball in the Portland and Vancouver Area in 1867. Vancouver WA, *National Park Service*, 2006

Short, William R. "Knattleikr, the Viking Ball Game." *Hurstwic*, 2004. http://www.hurstwic.org/history/articles/daily_living/text/knattleikr.htm

Smith, Randy. "The Romance of Baseball." *The Chattanoogan.com*, 26 March 2021. https://www.chattanoogan.com/2021/3/26/425601/Randy-Smith-The-Romance-Of-B aseball.aspx

Spalding, Albert G. *America's National Game*. New York, American Sports Publishing Company, 1911

Sparks, Glen. "Should Doc Adams Be in the Hall of Fame? Of course." *Dazzy Vance Chronicles*, 4, December 2015. https://dazzyvancechronicles.wordpress.com/2015/12/04/should-doc-adams-be-in-the-hall-of-fame-of-course

Spink, Alfred. *The National Game*. Carbondale, SIU Press, 1911

St. Louis Public Library. "The Great Cyclone of 1896". http://tornados.slpl.org

Staff. "Why Cricket Is Getting More and More Popular in the United States." *San Francisco News*, 21 December 2021. https://www.thesfnews.com/why-cricket-is-getting-more-and-more-popular-in-the-united-states/80486

"Stan Hywet Fact Sheet". *Stan Hywet Hall & Gardens*. https://www.stanhywet.org/sites/default/files/assets/docs/Stan%20Hywet_Fact%20Sheet.pdf

"Statistics From the Civil War." *Facing History and Ourselves*. https://www.facinghistory.org/resource-library/statistics-civil-war

Stewart, Doug. "The Old Ball Game." *Smithsonian*, October 1998

The Revolution, August 6, 1868

Thorn, John. "Doc Adams." *SABR*. https://sabr.org/bioproj/person/doc-adams

Thorn, John. "Honus Wagner's Rookie Year, 1895." *Our Game: The MLB.com/Blog of Official MLB Historian John Thorn*. 5 September 2017. https://ourgame.mlblogs.com/honus-wagners-rookie-year-1895-558e7a006f43

Thorn, John. "Mangled Forms." *Our Game: The MLB.com/Blog of Official MLB Historian John Thorn*, 11 October 2016. https://ourgame.mlblogs.com/mangled-forms-b7f73a2e40d9

Thorn, John. "The Making of Baseball's Magna Carta." *Our Game*, 28 February 2016. https://ourgame.mlblogs.com/the-making-of-baseballs-magna-carta-93aac0a08f01

Tiemann, Bob. "November 1, 1870: The Birth of the National Association." *SABR*, https://sabr.org/gamesproj/game/november-1-1870-the-birth-of-the-national-association

"Times and Spirits Change." *Sporting News*, Jan 1918. https://behindthebag.net/2019/02/17/pastime-press-shoeless-joe-jackson-and-the-wwi-draft-chicago-tribune-sporting-news-1918-1919

Tootle, James R. *Vintage Base Ball: Recapturing the National Pastime*. Jefferson, McFarland, 2011

Tygiel, Jules. *Past Time: Baseball as History*. Oxford University Press, 2001

Vintage Base Ball Association. "Code of Regulations (i.e., Bylaws)." https://www.vbba.org/bylaws Accessed 24 May 2022

Vintage Base Ball Association. "Knickerbocker Rules (New York): 1845." https://www.vbba.org/1845-knickerbocker-rules

Waff, Craig B. "September 18, 1862: The 'Silver Ball' Game." *SABR*, 2013.

https://sabr.org/gamesproj/game/september-18-1862-the-silver-ball-game

Weintraub, Robert. "Two Who Did Not Return." *New York Times*, 26 May, 2013. https://www.nytimes.com/2013/05/26/sports/baseball/remembering-the-major-leaguers-who-died-in-world-war-ii.html

Westcott, Rich. "The Early Years of Philadelphia Baseball." *SABR*, 2013. https://sabr.org/journal/article/the-early-years-of-philadelphia-baseball

Whatcom Aces Vintage Base Ball Team. Facebook. https://www.facebook.com/WhatcomBayStars/?ref=page_internal

Wicker, Tony. E-mail interview. Conducted by Jack Pelikan. 17 January 2022

Wilborn, Nubyjas. "Sources: Felipe Vazquez's Fight with Kyle Crick Began Over Locker Room Music." *Pittsburgh Post-Gazette*, 11 Sep 2019

Wilkinson, Howard. "The 1869 Red Stockings: The Team That 'Made Baseball Famous'." *91.7 WVXU,* 22 February, 2019. https://www.wvxu.org/sports/2019-02-22/the-1869-red-stockings-the-team-that-made-baseball-famous

Will, George. "Dred Scott in Spikes," Syndicated newspaper article from November 21, 1993; reprinted in *Bunts: Curt Flood, Camden Yards, Pete Rose and Other Reflections on Baseball* (New York: Scribner, 1998)

Wilson, Douglas L. and Rodney O. Davis. *Herndon's Informants: Letters, Interviews, and Statements About Abraham Lincoln.* Champaign, U Illinois Press, 1998

Wood, Francis. *Earliest Years at Vassar*. Poughkeepsie, Vassar College Press, 1909

Wyss, Robert. "1869 Cincinnati Red Stockings Turned Baseball Into a National Sensation". *The Conversation*. 27 Mar 2019. https://theconversation.com/how-the-1869-cincinnati-red- stockings-turned-baseball-into-a-national-sensation-113299

Index
(bold indicates illustrated pages, Teams notated by sections)

17th Avenue Fields, **186**
1994 MLB Strike, 102-103, 209
2020 Tokyo Olympics, 125
3Com / Candlestick Park, **111**
A League of their Own (film), 172, 178
A Pretty Little Pocket Book (Newbery), 9, **23**
Adams, Daniel "Doc", 15, 16, 18, 20-22, 196
Adams, Marjorie, 21
Adams, Matt, 87
Adrian, Mike "Ace", 195, 196, 201, **203-204**
Aiken, Brady, 90, 94
Akron / Summit County Beacon Journal, 13, 138
Akron Cup, 141, 143, 145, 146, **153**
Akron, Ohio, 13, 136-41
Albany Times Union, 123
All-American Girls Professional Baseball League (AAGPBL), 172, 178
Allegheny League, 115
Allen, Dick, 85
Allison, Doug, 58
All-Star Game (MLB), 38
Alomar, Roberto, 2
Altrock, Nick, 118
American Association, 64, 76-78, 139
American Female Base Ball Club, 177
American League, 77-79, 159
American Way, 103
America's National Game, 51
Amherst, MA, 98
An Act to Prohibit Female Base-Ball Playing (1892), 177

analytics, 3, 5, 32, 83, 86-89, 94, 210
Andersen, Don "Big Bat", **43**, **45**, **46**, 100, 106, **110**, **111**
Anderson, Sarah, 201
Apostolis, Laz, **206**
Appel, Mark, 90, 94
Appomattox Courthouse, VA, 51
arbitration, 209
Arizona (Territories) Vintage Base Ball League, 189-195
Arizona Complex League, 189
Arizona Fall League, 189
Arlington, Lizzie, 176
Army of Northern Virginia, 51
Army of the Potomac, 50-51
Ashes Cup (cricket), 25
Association of Living History, Farm and Agricultural Museums (ALHFAM), 99
Atlantic League (independent), 88
Atlantic League (historic), 116
Attell, Abe, 81
Australia, 25, 190
Balcom, Ken, 98, 102
balls, 6, 7, 10, 15, 16, 28, 31, 33, 35, 40-42, **46**, 100, 107, 108, 143, 200
bankruptcy / insolvency, 76-77, 128, 209
Barnard, Matthew "Barrel Roller", 143-44
Barnes, Ross, 33
Base Ball Players Chronicle (VBBA), 196
Baseball Almanac, 39, 40
Baseball America, 89
Baseball Hall of Fame, 12, 13, 116, 124, 127
Baseball Reference, 38, 62
baserunning, 8, 34, 35

bats, 6, 10, 28, 29, 31, 42, **45**, 100, 128, 146, 147, 179, **206**
Battle for Ohio (tournament), 144, 145, **155**
Battle of Pea Ridge Civil War Reenactment, **109**
Beadle's Dime Base-Ball Player, 9, 12, 25, 26, 31, 32, 36, 39, 62, 137, 162
Bechtel, George, 73
Beer and Whiskey League, 64, 76
Bellingham, Washington, 189, 197, 201
Bernadina, Roger, 125
Best of the West (vintage base ball showcase), 106
Bidgood, J.V., 52
Bisbee, Arizona, 190, 192, 193, **203**
Black Sox Scandal (1919), 36, 78, 82, 89, 92, 191
Blasick, Rich "Juggler", 143, 149
Block, David, 14
bloomer dresses, 174-175, **185**
Bloomer Girls, 176-78
Bloomer, Amelia, **185**
Boetticher, Act. Major Otto, **66**
Boras, Scott, 95
Boston Globe, 103
Brainard, Asa, 57, 58, 63, 150
Branson, Vicky, 99
Bredell, Ed, 160, 161
Bredell, Sr., Ed, 160
Bridwell, Al, 193
Bristol, Connecticut, 10
Brock, Lou, 158
Brooklyn Capitoline Grounds, 63
Brooklyn Daily Eagle, 175
Brooklyn Union Skating and Base Ball Grounds, 48
Brooklyn, New York, 22, 26, 48, 54, 63, 74 100, 102, 122, 160, 175

Brown, Mordecai, 55
Browne, Byron, 84
Buchtel, Joseph, 198, 199
Bulkeley, Morgan, 12, 72
Bullington, Bryan, 94
Burns, Ken, 101
Burr, Bo, 107
Busch Stadium, 158, 159
Busch, Adolphus, 163
Bush, Matt, 94
Cactus League, 189, 192
Caesar's Creek Festival (OH), 142, 146
Camden, New Jersey, 11
Camp Grant Massacre, 190
Camp Verde, Arizona, 189, 195, **204-08**
Canada, 104, 106, 121
Carnation Cup (Alliance, OH), 147
Carnegie, Andrew, 113
Carnegie, PA, 115
Cartwright Day, 19
Cartwright, Alexander (IV), 199, 200
Cartwright, Alexander (Jr.), 15, 18-19
Cartwright, Bruce, 19, 20
Catskill Mountain News, **131**
Catskill Mountains, 112, 114, 118-19, 122
Caylor, O.P., 76
Chadwick, Henry, 9, 12, 14, 17, 22, 25-37, 39, 47, 48, 53, 55, 56, 62, 71, 86, 120, 137, 162, 213, 215, 220, 225
Champion, Aaron, 56-58, 63, 138
Chance, Frank, 55
Chase, Charles E., 74, 75
Chase, Hal, 81, 89, 191, 192
Chicagoed (phrase), 70
China, 108

Chouteau, Auguste, 159
Christmas Day Game (Hilton Head, SC), 49, 190
Cicotte, Eddie, 80, 81
Cincinnati Commercial, 57
Cincinnati Enquirer, 50, 76
Cincinnati, OH, 11, 56, 58, 63, 75-77, 80, 101, 112, 114, 117, 118, 124, 127
Civil War, 1, 7, 12, 14, 47, 51, 57, 98, 101, 106, **109**, 137, 161, 162, 184, 190, 198, 201, 202
Clark, Stephen C., 13
Clarke, Edward H., 176
Cleland, Alexander, 19
Clinton, Bill, 86
Cobb, Ty, 37, 120
Codebreaker (sign-stealing scheme), 90
Cokley, Andy, **131**
Colcolough, Tom, 118
Cole, Gerrit, 94
Collier's, 13
Collins (Wiltse), Dottie, 178
Collins, Eddie, 79
Columbus, Ohio, **43**, 98-100, 140, 142, 147, 164, 165, 172, 179
Comerica Park, 38
Comiskey, Charles, 78
competitive balancing, 3, 5, 83, 92, 975, 210
Confederate Army, 49, 50, 161
Cooperstown, New York 12-14, 18, 19, 21, 64, 97, 99, 106, 121, 126, 139, 165, 178, 193
Coors Field, 28
Copper (Frontier) League, 191
Copper City Classic (AZ), 194
Cora, Alex, 91
Correa, Carlos, 89, 94

Correa, Christopher, 37, 90, 92
Cragin, Peter, **131**
Craver, Bill, 69, 73-75
Cregan, Pete, 117
Crick, Kyle, 39
cricket, 5-10, 16, 26, 33, 56
Crowe, Robert E., 81
Cure, Grant "The Pounder", 120
Currier & Ives, 67
Curry, Duncan, 16
Curry, Steph, 136, 163
Curt Flood Act (1998), 86
Cuthbert, Ned, 70
Cy Young Award, 87
data analytics, 3, 32, 87
Davenport, Iowa, 11
Davis, Henry, 95
Dean, Jay "Dizzy", 158
Declaration of Sentiments, 174
Devine, Bing, 84
Devlin, Jim, 73-75
Dickerson, "Buttercup", 163
Dieckmann, Al "Old Dutch", 103
Dinneen, Bill, 78
Dooin, Charlie "Red", 118, 124
Doon, Bill, **131**
Double-A, 136, 140
Doubleday Field, 12, 106, 121
Doubleday, Abner, 12-14, 18-19, 47, 106, 121
Douglas Cup (IL), 165, 167
Duggan, Chris "Bookworm", 157, 162-64, 166-67
Duggan, Katie "Dubs", 164
Duggan, Tom "Shakespeare", 164
Dunlap, Fred, 163

Duryea's Zouaves, 50
Duryee, Abram (Duryea), 50
Easton IncrediBall, 100, 107
Ebony, 86
Eckersley, Dennis, 87
Egypt, 6
Eight Men Out (film), 101
El Paso Herald, 191
Elmira, NY, 97
Elmore, Ed "Pigtail", 103, 106, 108
Elysian Fields, 6, 16, 17, **67**, 106, 140
England / Great Britain, 5, 7, 8, 12, 25, 26
Evers, Johnny, 55, 193
Farquhar, Danny, 91
Father of Baseball, *see* Chadwick, Henry
Father of Professional Baseball, 64
FBI / DOJ, 89-90
Federal Baseball Club of Baltimore v. National League (1922), 83, 85
Felsch, Oscar "Happy", 79
Fenway Park, 190
Ferguson, Bob, 63
Field of Dreams (film), 5, 101
Field of Dreams (venue), 106, 142, 168
fielding, 7, 32, 70, 80, 105, 202, 221, 227
Fiers, Mike, 91
fines / disciplinary measures, 2, 3, 36-38, 194
First base ball game (official),12, 16, 18-19, 106, 140
Fish, Nate, 124, 125, 127
Fleischmann, Charles, 112, 114, 118
Fleischmann, Julius, 114, 118, 123, 124, 126, **131**, **132**
Fleischmann, Max, 112, 114, 117, 118, 124, **131**

Fleischmanns, New York, 112, 116, 118-20 122-24, 127, 211
Flood v. Kuhn (1972), 84, 209-210
Flood, Curt, 84-86
Foley, Tom, 70
Forquer, Jackie "Thumper", 172, 181-84, **186**, **187**, **188**
Fort Sumter, 14
Fort Vancouver National Historic Site (WA), 199-200
Fort Verde State Historical Park, 195, **204-06**
Founder's Day, 124, **134**
Frandsen, Nicholas "Roughcut", 129
Fraud Triangle, 91-92
free agency, 3, 5, 83-84, 86, 210
Freeman, Josh "The Voice", **207**
Fremont, Ohio, **154**
Frias, Brandy, 180
Frias, Dianna, 180, 182
Frias, Rudy "Swamp Fox", 144-45, 148
Fruth, Jean, 162
Galarraga, Armando, 38
Gallentine, Ross "Atlas", 164
Galloway, Bill "Hipple/Hippo", 117, 118
gambling, 18, 36, 72, 73, 79, 89, 92, 159, 190, 209, 210
Gandil, C. Arnold ("Chick"), 79-81, 192
Garcia, Rene, 122, 123
Gashouse Gang (St. Louis Cardinals), 82
Gay, Billy "Bulldog", 146, 150, **153**
Gedeon, Elmer, 82
Gehrig, Lou, 82, 177
Genesee Country Village and Museum, **44**, 107, **156**, 181, **188**

Gerhardt, Joseph, 73
Gettysburg National 19th Century Base Ball Festival, 107
Gibson, Bob, 158
Gibson, Kirk, 87
Gleason, Kid, 80
Glidden, Annie, 173
gloves, 2, 28, 29, 31, 32, 35, 42, 92, 98, 120, 179, 194, 202
Gold Gloves, 84
Gold Rush, 18
Goldburg, Abe, 117
Golden Era/Age, 3, 82, 209
Golden State Warriors, 163
Gonzales, Marco, 88
Gonzalez, Adrian, 94
Gorman, Arthur, 12, 53
Gould, Charlie, 57, 58, 63, 64
Grant, Ulysses S., 51, 161
Gratiot, Henry, 159
Graves, Abner, 13
Great Awakening, 72
Great Depression, 82, 177
Greater St. Louis Base Ball Historical Society (GSLBBHS), 162, 167
Green Shake Cup (OH), 147
Greenfield Village (MI), 107
Grenelle, William, 20, 21
Grichuk, Randal, 88
Griffin Corners, NY, 112, 113, 118
Griswold, Merritt, 22, 160, 161
Grundon, Wil "Hoosier", 164
Hackgate, 89, 92, 210
Hague, Bill, 74
Haldeman, John, 74

Haldeman, Walter, 73
Hall, George, 63, 73-75
Hamblin, Scott "Tiny", 141-47, 149, 152, 211
Harding, Warren G., 147
Harper, Bryce, 93, 94
Harry M. Keator Cup, 121
Hatfield, John, 57, 58
Helm, Bill "Shutterbug", 189, 195-97, 200. 201, 202, **204-08**
Helm, Teresa, **205**
Heppner, Mark "Capt'n", 135, 140, 149
Hirschbeck, John, 2
Hitt, Orson, **131**
hitting, 6, 10, 25, 31, 32, 80, 87, 91, 137. 143, 146, 151, 158
Hoboken, New Jersey, 6, 8, 16, **67**, 106, 140, 200
Hoerner, Joe, 84
Holliday, James Wear "Bug", 118
Honolulu, HI, 19
Howard, Amarett, 173
Hubbell, Jerrod "J-Rod", 120, **134**
Huggins, Miller James, 117, 118, 124, 127
Hulbert, William, 72, 75
Hunt, Terry, 98
Hunter, Jim "Catfish", 86
Hurley, Dick, 58
Hurricane Irene, 122, 1254, **133**, 211
Inter-State League, 115
Irwin, Will, 13
Israel National Team (Baseball), 125, 127
Jackson, "Shoeless" Joe, 78-81, 932
Jacobs Field, 107, **110**
James, Bill, 87

James, Lebron, 136, 163
Jarvis, Don "The Beard", 143
Johnson, Andrew, 51
Johnson, Ban, 77
Johnson, Jerry, 85
Junior Circuit, *see* American League
Kasten, Stan, 93, 94
Keenan, "Black Jack", 117
Kelly, Bob, 116
Kelly, John, **131**
Kennett, W.H., 64, 76
Keokuk, Iowa, **109**
Kerr, Dickie, 80, 81
Kershaw, Clayton, 87
Kirke, Jay, 124
knattleikr (viking game), 6
Knickerbocker Rules (1845 & 1854), 5, 6, 11, 15-18, 20, 40-42, 47, 199, 224
Koons, Pam, 180
Krekeler, Karl "Moonshine", 164
Krutz, Andrew "Crutches", 128
Kuhn, Bowie, 84-86
labor stoppages / lockouts, 86, 209
Laclede, Pierre, 159
Lafayette Park, 1, 160-163, **169, 170**
Lafayette Square (St. Louis), 1, 162, 165, **169,** 211
Landis, Kenesaw Mountain, 81
Lane, Brian, 197
Larsen, Erik, 93
Las Vegas Golden Knights, 166
Lasorda, Tommy 87-88
Laws of Baseball (1857), 20, 22
Lee, Robert E., 48, 51

lemon peel baseball, 29, **46**, 100, 108
Leonard, Andy, 58, 63
Lewis, Michael, 86
Library of Congress, 20, **23**, **66**, **67**, **68**, **185**
lifetime bans, 36, 75, 92, 192
Lincoln, Abraham, 11, 50
Long Island Star, 26
Long Island, 3, 98, 101
Louisville Courier-Journal, 73, 74
Louisville Grays Scandal (1877), 72
Louisville, KY, 72
Loveday, Amos, 99
Lunhow, Jeff, 89-90, 92
luxury tax, 94
Lynden Tribune (WA), 200
MacClintock, Dave "Shoeless", 126
Maness, Seth, 88
Mangled Forms (John Thorn), 120, 211
Manhattan, New York, 15, 16, 98, 193
Mann, Terence (*Field of Dreams*), 5
Marinak, Chris, 88
Marquez, Winston, 124, 129
Martin, Corbin, 90
Mason-Dixon Line, 47, 53
Massachusetts Game (town ball variant), 5, 10, 11, 15, 17, 20, 22, 97, 98, 106, 159, 160, 161
Matheny, Mike, 87, 88
Matijevic, J.J., 90
Mauer, Joe, 94
Mays, Willie, 82, 209
McCarver, Tim, 84
McCormick, Edward, 177
McCormick, Moose, 193

McFadden, Barney, 117
McGinnity, Joe, 193
McGraw, John, 115
McMullin, Fred, 79
McNally, Dave, 86
McPhee, John "Bid", 139, 140
McVey, Cal, 59, 63, 64
Mendoza line, 88
Merkle Boner, 193
Merkle, Fred, 193
Messersmith, Andy, 86
Miami Dolphins, 55
Miller, Collin "Stumpy", 116, 120, 121, 123-27, 129
Miller, Nannie, 174-75
Mills College, 173
Mills Commission, 13
Mills, Abraham G. (A.G.), 12, 13
Mills, Charles, 70
Miss Porter's School, 173-74
MLB Player Draft, 89, 92, 93-95, 210
Molina, Yadier, 88, 158
Moneyball, 86
Monti, Gary "Reverend", 101, 102, 105, 107, 108
Moore, Dave "Shutterbug", 164
Morning Oregonian, 198
Morell, Dave, 119
Morris, Peter, 33
Moskowitz, Dan "the Man", 97
Muffin Meadow, **43**, 147, 165, 172, 179
Mullane, Tony "Count", 138-40
Murderers' Row (1927 Yankees), 82
Musial, Stan, 158, 178
MVP Award, 87, 149

National Agreement, 77
National Association of Base Ball Players (NABBP), 22, 48, 52-57, 62, 64, 69, 71, 198, 218, 219
National Association of Professional Base Ball Players ("National Association"), 21, 22, 25, 26, 40, 47, 48, 49, 51, 54, 55, 64, 69, 71, 72, 105, 138, 140, 173, 198
National League, 12, 22, 64, 71, 72, 75, 76-79, 84, 85, 115-17, 138, 157, 164, 191-92, 198
National Park Service, **185**
National Register of Historic Places, 119, 124
National Road Festival (Scenery Hill, PA), 146
National Vintage Base Ball Showcase, 143
Neagle, John, 139
Negro League, 117
Neil, Adam "Little Red", 164, 211
Neil, Alec "Young Red", 164, 211
Neil, Ryan "Big Red", 164, 211
Neil, Troy "Red Senior", 164, 211
Nelson, Maud, 176-77
Netherlands National Team (Baseball), 125
New York Clipper, 26, 70, 86
New York Game, 15-17, 21-22, 47, 52, 223
New York Herald, 70
New York Mercury, 17, 21, 26, 52, 86
New York Public Library, **24**
New York Sun, 114
New York Times, 26
New York World, **130**
Nichols, Al, 74-75
Northern Alliance of Vintage Ballists, 145, 148

Nucciarone, Monica, 219
O'Brien, Conan, 105
O'Day, Hank, 193
Ohio Cup, **43**, 101, 107, 142-43, 147-48, 163, 165, 167-68, **186**, 211
Ohio Historical Center, **186**
Ohio History Connection (formerly Ohio Historical Society), 104, 179, 181-82
Ohio Village, 98-100, 104, 106-07, 147, 179, 182, 211
Old Bethpage Village Restoration (OBVR), 98, 102
Old-Timer Exhibition (SABR), **111**
Olmsted, Mark "Wheels", 164
Ommegang Historic Base Ball Festival, 126
O'Neill, Harry, 82
Oregon, Washington and Idaho Territories Association of Base Ball Players, 198
Orta, Jorge, 1
Parker, Alpheris, 49
Pascarella, Todd "Moonshine", 119, 120
Patterson, Keith "Stitch", 146, 151
payroll, 58, 64, 69, 94, 138, 209
Pecaut, Joe "Tavern Keeper", 164, **170**
Pestana, Mark, 56
Peterboro, NY (Peterborough), 174-76
Petersburg, Virginia, 50
Philadelphia, PA, 11, 17, 22, 113
Piccione, Peter, 6
Pioneer Era (Baseball), 3, 65
Players' League, 77
Polo Grounds (Manhattan), 193
Porter's Spirit of the Times, 17, 21
Poughkeepsie Evening Enterprise, 126
Poughkeepsie, NY, 172
Pujols, Albert, 158

Putnam, George H., 50
Quail Cup (Wooster, OH), 146
Railride into Yesteryear (Roxbury, NY), 119
Rea, Rick "Sting", 163-64, **171**
Reach, Al, 12, 54-55
Reid, Debra "Little Egypt", 164-65
Rendon, Anthony, 95
Reserve Clause, 41, 76, 85
Reuther, Dutch, 79
Reynolds, Arthur S., **131**
Richmond, Virginia, 51-52
Rickey, Branch, 87, 178
Riley, Frank, **131**
Rio Grande Association, 191
Risberg, Charles "Swede", 79
Robinson, Jackie 53, 82, 117, 209
Rochester, MN, 181, **187**
Rohe, George "Whitey", 117-18, 124
Rohour, Justin "Freshest Man Alive", 164
Rojas, Cookie, 85
Roller Out the Barrel Podcast, 143
Rose, Pete, 36, 89, 92
Rothstein, Arnold "The Brain", 79
rounders (ball game), 5-6, 8-10, 12, 15, 26
Roush, Edd, 79
Rules, 39-42, 95
Rush, Benjamin, 72
Rush, Jacob, 72
Ruth, Babe, 78, 82, 177, 209
Sabermetrics, 87
Saik, Dr. Brent, 121
Salisbury, NC (Civil War POW Camp), 49, **66**, 106
Sandoval, Pablo, 88

Sands, George, 56
Sandusky, Ohio (Civil War POW Camp), 49, 106
Sarony, Major & Knapp, **66**
Scherzer, Max, 94
Seager, Corey, 95
Seattle Met, 200
Seiberling, Frank (Goodyear Tires), 140-141
Seitz, Peter, 85-86
seker-hemat (Ancient Egypt), 6
Seneca Falls Convention (1848), 174
Sex in Education; or, A Fair Chance for Girls, 176
Shafer, "Orator", 163
Sheppard Barclay Vintage Base Ball Festival, 162, 165
Sherman (Garrison) Base Ball Club (WA), 198
Shively, Heather, 183
Shuefelt, William, **131**
Sidrane, Michelle, **134**
signing bonus pool, 95, 210
sign-stealing, 37, 90-942, 210
Silver Ball Match, 48-49
Silver Ball Tournament (Upstate NY), 107, 142, 147, **156**, 181
Silver Park (Mumford, NY), **44**, 147
Skene, Alexander, 113
Skubish, Chrissy "Showtime", 123
Smith Miller, Elizabeth "Libby", 174
Smith, Doug, 104
Smith, Gerrit, 174-75
Smith, Ozzie, 158
Smithsonian (museum/magazine), 103
Society for American Baseball Research (SABR), **111**

softball, 29, 98, 100, 121, 144, 159, 166, 172, 178, 194, 202
Spalding, Albert Goodwill (A.G., 12-14. 47, 51, 63-64
Spalding's Official Base Ball Guide, 12
Spirit Magazine (Southwest Airlines), 101
Spirit of the Times, 17, 21
Sporting News, 20
Sports Illustrated, 100-01
Sprague, Joe, 49
Spring Training, 88, 189
St. Louis Cup, 166
St. Louis, MO, 1, 11, 22, 113, 157-62, 165, 167
Stan Hywet Hall and Gardens, 140-41, 143, 146, **153**
Stanton, Elizabeth Cady, 174-75
Stargell, Willie, 83
State of Eight Tournament (OH), 147
Stephens, Alexander, 50
Stern-Gluck, Rozalia (Leah), 122
Steubenville Club (OH), 115
Stevens, Harry, **131**, 222
Stewart, Doug, 103
Stoneham, Horace, 189
stoolball, 5-7
Storey, Travis, 196
Storey, Zach, 196
Strasburg, Stephen, 93-94
Streetcar Series (1944), 159
Stubler, Sheila, 195, 197
Sullivan, "Sleeper", 163
Sullivan, James, 12
Sullivan, Joseph "Sport", 79, 81
Supreme Court, 84, 86, 209-10
Sweasy, Charlie, 58, 63

Syracuse Standard, 17

tanking, 3, 83, 92-95

Teams (Historic Clubs)

Akron Base Ball Club (Akrons), 137-140, 146

Blondes and Brunettes Clubs (Springfield, IL), 176

Boston Americans, 78

Boston Braves, 79

Boston Red Caps, 190

Boston Red Stockings, 33, 64, 138

Brooklyn Atlantics, 22, 48, 53, 58, 62, 69, 76, 105-06, 108, 119, 126, 129, 173

Brooklyn Dodgers, 87, 93-95, 125, 157, 178

Brooklyn Eckfords, 49, 53, 55, 71, 220

Brooklyn Excelsiors, **24**, 57

Buffalo Bisons, 139

Carnegie Athletic Club, 115

Cherokee Indian Baseball Club, 176

Chicago White Stockings (Cubs), 54, 70, 72-76, 138

Cincinnati Buckeyes, 56-58

Cincinnati Outlaw Reds, 163

Cincinnati Red Stockings, 36, 55-56, 60, 62, **68**, 69-71, 73, 137, 139-40, 146, 150-51, 209

Cincinnati Reds (NY women's club), 176

Clackamas Base Ball Club (OR), 198

Cleveland Blues, 138-39

Cleveland Forest Citys, 71, 107, **110**

Cleveland Indians, 107, 189

Cleveland Spiders, 77

Cuban Giants / X-Giants, 117-18

Detroit Wolverines, 75

Douglas Blues, 191-92

Fort Wayne Daisies, 178

Fort Wayne Kekiongas, 71
Fort Whipple Base Ball Club (AZ), 190
Hartford Dark Blues, 71
Knickerbocker Base Ball Club, 5-6, 11, 14-22, **24**, 25, 29, 40, 42, 47, 56, 65, 105, 140, 160, 199, 214, 222, 224
Laurel and Abenakis (early women's base ball clubs), 172
Louisville Colonels, 77, 116
Louisville Eclipse, 64, 76, 139-40
Louisville Grays, 36, 72-73, 75, 82, 89
Louisville Olympic Club, 57
Mansfield Indians (PA), 115
Middlebury Mechanics (OH), 137, 146
Montreal Expos, 102, 209
Morning Star Club (St. Louis), 160-61
Mountain Athletic Club / Mountain Tourists (NY), 113-14, 116, 118-19 **130-32**, **135**
New York Eagles, 17
New York Empires, 17, 161
New York Giants, 77-78, 80, 115-, 16, 189-90, 192-93
New York Gothams, 75
New York Highlanders, 78, 191
New York Mutuals, 57-59, 62, 70-71, 73-74, 105, 119, 138
New York Nine, 6, 16, 18, 140
Occidental Base Ball Club (WA), 198, 200
Olympic Club (Philadelphia), 10-11, 22, 60
Paterson (NJ) Silk Weavers, 116
Philadelphia Athletics, 55, 57, 69, 73, 76, 78-79, 138
Philadelphia Pythians, 53
Philadelphia White Stockings (Whites), 73

Phoenix Senators, 191, **206**

Pioneer Base Ball Club (Portland), 52, 198, 200

Pittsburgh Alleghenys, 76

Portland Willamettes / Webfeet (OR), 199

Prescott Champions (AZ), 190, 195-96, 201, **203-04**

Providence Grays, 126

Richmond Base Ball Club (VA), 52

Rockford Forest Citys, 61-62, 71

Rockford Peaches, 172, 178

Seattle Blues (Hustlers), 199

Seattle Pilots, 199

Sherman (Garrison) Base Ball Club (WA), 198, 200

Spokane Bunchgrassers, 199

St. Louis Brown Stockings, 64, 70-71, 76, 139, 159, 166-67

St. Louis Browns, 76-77

St. Louis Cyclone Base Ball Club (1860), 47-48, 160-61

St. Louis Empires, 161

St. Louis Maroons, 76, 163-64, 167-68

St. Louis Perfectos, 159, 163, 166-67, **171**

Steubenville Club (OH), 115

Tacoma Daisies, 199

Troy Haymakers (Union of Lansingburgh), 69, 73

Tucson Old Pueblos, 191

Union Club (Morrisania), 53

Union Club (Richmond), 52

Union Cricket Club (Cincinnati), 56

Washington Olympic Club, 63, 71

Washington Senators, 77, 85
Washington Nationals (19th century), 57-58

Teams (Modern Professional)
Akron RubberDucks, 137, 140
Arizona Diamondbacks, 94, 189
Atlanta Braves, 3, 93
Baltimore Orioles, 64, 76-77, 87
Boston Red Sox, 78, 91-92, 124
Chicago Cubs, 55, 178, 192
Chicago White Sox, 38, 55, 77-81, 91, 117-18, 190-93
Cincinnati Reds, 36, 64, 80-81, 92, 114, 117-118, 126-27, 176, 191
Cleveland Guardians, 137
Detroit Tigers, 38, 77
Houston Astros, 37, 89
Kansas City Royals, 1, 90
Los Angeles Dodgers, 86-87, 93-95, 125, 157, 178
Milwaukee Brewers, 77, 159
Minnesota Twins, 124, 129
New York Mets, 85, 94
New York Yankees, 82, 84, 117, 157
Oakland Athletics, 86, 94
Philadelphia Phillies, 54, 84
Pittsburgh Pirates, 39, 77-78, 95, 101, 106, 126, 192
San Francisco Giants, 79, 88
Seattle Mariners, 55, 199
St. Louis Cardinals, 1, 37-38, 77, 83, 89-90, 92, 117, 157-59, 162
Washington Nationals, 77, 85

Teams (Vintage Clubs)

Addison Mountain Stars (PA), 145-46, **153**
Akron Black Stockings (OH), **44**, 136, 140-152, **153-156**, 181, 211
Akron Lady Locks (OH), 181, **188**
Alliance Crossing Rails Vintage Base Ball Club (OH), 145-48
Alton Giant (IL), 166
Belleville Stags (IL), 166
Bisbee Bees (AZ), 192-93
Bisbee Black Sox (AZ), 193, **208**
Black Flags BBC of Drovertown (IN), 148
Blackbottom 9 (OH), 146
Bluegrass Barons (KY), 145, 147
Boston Union Base Ball Club, 126
Bovina Dairymen (NY), 121, 124-25, 127-129, **134**
Brooklyn Atlantics (NY), 22, 48, 53, 58, 62, 69, 76, 105-06, 108, 119, 126
Brooks Grove Belles (NY), 181
Canal Dover Redlegs (OH), 145, 147
Canal Fulton Mules (OH), 146
Canton Cornshuckers (OH), 145, 147
Columbus Buckeyes (OH), 146
Columbus Capitals (OH), 144-147, 180
Connecticut Bulldogs, 123
Cooperstown Leatherstockings (NY), 106, 165
Dayton Clodbusters (OH), 127
Dayton Lady Clodbusters (OH), 183
Deep River Grinders (IN), 148, 168
Delhi Polecats (NY), 121, 127
Eastwood Iron Horses (OH), 146
Flat Rock Bear Clan (MI), 145

Flower City BBC (NY), 147
Fort Verde Excelsiors (AZ), 189, 194, 196, **204-207**, 211
Freeport Athletics (NY), 102
Glendale Gophers (AZ), **205**
Glen Head Zig Zags (NY), 97
Hempstead Eurekas (NY), 98, 101
Indianapolis Blues (IN), 146
Indianapolis Hoosiers (IN), 166
Lafayette Square Cyclone Base Ball Club (MO), 48, 157, 162-68, **170-71**, 211
Liberty Base Ball Club (CT), 126
Little Falls Alerts (NY), 128
Live Oak BBC (NY), 147
Mansfield Independents (OH), 146
Mesa Miners (AZ), 194
Mineola Washingtons (NY), 98, 101
Moscow Monarchs (OH), 146
Mountain Athletic Club (NY), 112-113, 116, 119-29, **134-35**, 211
Mudville Base Ball Club (MA), 128
New York Mutuals, 105, 119
Oaks of Locust Corner BBC (OH), 147
Ohio Village Diamonds, **43**, 107, 172, 211
Ohio Village Muffins, **43**, 99-100, 104, 106-08, **109-10**, 140, 147, 172, 179, 182
Olneyville Cadets (RI), 126
Phoenix Senators (AZ), 193-94, **206**
Pioneer Base Ball Club (OR), 200-01
Prescott Champions (AZ), 194-97, 201, **203-04**
Priscilla Porter's Astonishing Ladies Base Ball Club (NY), 181
Providence Grays (RI), 126
Rochester BBC (NY), 147

Rochester Grangers (MI), 145
Rochester Hens (MN), 181, **187**
Rock Springs Ground Squirrels (IL), 167
Roxbury Nine (NY), 119-21
Spiegel Grove Squires (OH), 147, **154**
St. Louis Brown Stockings (MO), 166-67
St. Louis Maroons (MO), 163-64, 167-68
St. Louis Perfectos (MO), 159, 163, 166-67, **171**, 198-200
St. Louis Unions (MO), 166
Sycamore Crickets/Katydids (OH), 181
Tempe Tip-Tops (AZ), 194
Tucson Saguaros (AZ), 193
Union BBC (MN), 148
Vermilion Voles (IL), 166-68
Victory BBC (NY), 147
Westburys (NY), 102
Westfield Wheelmen (MA), 125
Whatcom Aces (Bay Stars) (WA), 189, 201-02, 211
Whiskey Island Shamrocks (OH), 147-48

Tenney, Fred, 192
Tenney, John, 192-93
The Athletic, 91
The Great Gatsby, 69
The Lefty Catcher, 93
The Revolution (National Woman Suffrage Association), 174-75
Thomas, Isaiah, **23**
Thorn, John, 18, 20, 21, 112, 120, 124, 211, 214
Thorner, Justus, 76
Three Rivers Stadium, 106

Thutmose III, 6

ticket prices, 58. 63, 75-76, 83, 94-95, 177

Tinker, Joe, 55

Toolson v. New York Yankees (1953), 84

Tootle, James "Gentleman", 179

TrackMan (auto-umpire), 88

Triple-A, 88

Tuchfarber, Walkley & Moellman, **68**

Tucker, Troy "Teabag", 129

umpires, 1, 2, 28, 31-34, 36-41, 70-71, 88, 99, 101, 149, **187**, 193-194, 213, 216, 220, 222-23, 225, 226-27

uniforms, 1, 17, 28, 50, 57, **68**, 96, 98, 104-05, 120, 126-27, 162, 174, 180, 190

Union Army, 12, 48-50, **66**, 161

Union Association, 76-77, 163

Upton, Justin, 94

Utica Morning Herald and Daily Gazette, 173

Vancouver Register, 198

Vancouver, WA, 198-200

Vassar College, 172, 174, 176

Vazquez, Felipe, 39

Veeck, Bill, 189

Vintage Base Ball Association (VBBA), 21, 25, 97, 104, 127, 140, 211

Wagner, Albert "Butts", 115-16

Wagner, Honus, 78, 114-16, 118, 120, 126, **131**

Wall Street Journal, 101

Warren Ballpark (Bisbee, AZ), 190, 194, **203**

Waterman, Fred, 57, 58

Weaver, Earl, 87

Weaver, George "Buck", 79, 192

Weber, Joe "Twinkle Toes", **208**

Weekly Arizona Miner, 190

Wellman, Phil, 3
Western League, 77
Whitaker, Grandal, **131**
Whitaker, Granville, 126
White, Guy Harris "Doc", 118
Wicker, Tony "Lightning", 167
wicket (ball game), 5, 10, 20
Will, George, 86
Williams, Claude "Lefty", 79-80, 192
Williams, P.A., 74
Williams, Ted, 82, 178, 209
Wills, Maury, 196, 197
Wilson, Sylvester F., 177
Wins Above Replacement (WAR), 94, 115
Winters, Ed, **131**
Wise, Sam, 139
Wolters, Rynie, 70
Wong, Kolten, 158
Work or Fight Rule, 78
World Baseball Classic, 125
World Series, 1, 32, 55, 69, 76, 78, 79, 81, 82, 87, 90, 93, 103, 118, 124, 157 193, 209, 210
World Tournament of Historic Base Ball, 107
World War I, 118
World War II, 178
World's Fair, 113
Worrell, Todd, 2
Wright, George, 12, 58, 63-64, 71, 151
Wright, Harry, 56-58, 63-64, 71, 152
Wrigley Field, 190
Wrigley, Philip K., 178
Youkilis, Kevin, 124
Young, Cy, 78, 79, 87

Young, Delmon, 94
Young, Nicholas E., 12
Zonfa, Chase "Freight Train", 143

Endnotes

Cover Photo

Billy "Bulldog" Gay pitches against the Addison Mountain Stars at the 2020 Akron Cup on their home field at picturesque Stan Hywet Hall and Gardens. Photo courtesy of the Akron Black Stockings.

Prologue

[1] "Charlie Brown" was the vintage base ball nickname of former Lafayette Square (St. Louis) Cyclone great Jonathan Farris, whose tragic passing in 2021 is mourned by the St. Louis and national vintage base ball community. This book is dedicated to his memory.

[2] Note the term "Huzzah", although a common cheer amongst today's vintage clubs, is used inaccurately as it pertains to an archaic English cheer. According to the Vintage Base Ball Association, the mid-19th century term used by American clubs was "hurrah", and often used in cheers like "Hip, Hip, Hurrahs". https://www.vbba.org/terms-to-avoid.

Chapter 1: Humble Origins

[3] Piccione, Peter A. "Pharaoh at the Bat." *College of Charleston Magazine,* 1 July 2003.
https://piccionep.people.cofc.edu/pharaoh_at_bat.pdf

[4] Short, William R. "Knattleikr, the Viking Ball Game." *Hurstwic,* 2004.
http://www.hurstwic.org/history/articles/daily_living/text/knattleikr.htm

[5] Henderson, Robert W. *Ball, Bat and Bishop: The Origins of Ball Games.* New York. Rockport Press, 1947.

[6] Staff. "Why Cricket Is Getting More and More Popular in the United States." *San Francisco News,* 21 December 2021. https://www.thesfnews.com/why-cricket-is-getting-more-and-more-popular-in-the-united-states/80486

[7] Morris, Peter. *But Didn't We Have Fun? An Informal History of Baseball's Pioneer Era, 1843-1870.* Chicago, Ivan. R. Dee, 2008.

[8] Chadwick, Henry. *1860 Beadle's Dime Base-Ball Player.* New York, Irwin R. Beadle, 1860.

[9] Newbery, John. *A Little Pretty Pocket Book.* First American edition. Worcester, Massachusetts: Isaiah Thomas, 1787. Rare Book and Special Collections Division, Library of Congress (005.00.00).

[10] Chadwick.

[11] Morris.

[12] Robert Edward Auctions. "The 1838 Olympic Constitution." 2007. https://robertedwardauctions.com/auction/2007/spring/1/1838-olympic-constitution

[13] Westcott, Rich. "The Early Years of Philadelphia Baseball." *SABR,* 2013. https://sabr.org/journal/article/the-early-years-of-philadelphia-baseball

[14] Wilson, Douglas L. and Rodney O. Davis. *Herndon's Informants: Letters, Interviews, and Statements About Abraham Lincoln.* Champaign, U Illinois Press, 1998.

[15] Salvatore, Victor. "The Man Who Didn't Invent Baseball." *American Heritage*, Volume 34, Issue 4 1983.

https://www.americanheritage.com/man-who-didnt-invent-baseball

[16] Arango, Tim. "Myth of Baseball's Creation Endures, With a Prominent Fan." *New York Times,* 12 November 2010. https://www.nytimes.com/2010/11/13/sports/baseball/13doubleday.html

[17] Martin, Brian. *Baseball's Creation Myth: Adam Ford, Abner Graves and the Cooperstown Story.* Jefferson, MacFarland, 2013.

[18] Vintage Base Ball Association. "Knickerbocker Rules (New York): 1845." https://www.vbba.org/1845-knickerbocker-rules

[19] Thorn, John. "Doc Adams." *SABR.* https://sabr.org/bioproj/person/doc-adams

[20] Spink, Alfred. *The National Game.* Carbondale, SIU Press, 1911.

[21] Morris.

[22] Tygiel, Jules. *Past Time: Baseball as History.* Oxford University Press, 2001.

[23] Thorn. "Doc Adams."

[24] Robert Edward Auctions. "Extraordinary Correspondence Archive Relating to Alexander Cartwright's Induction to the Hall of Fame." 2007. https://robertedwardauctions.com/auction/2007/spring/977/extraordinary-correspondence-archive-relating-alexander-cartwrights-induction-hall-fame

[25] Thorn, John. "The Making of Baseball's Magna Carta." *Our Game,* 28 February 2016. https://ourgame.mlblogs.com/the-making-of-baseballs-magna-carta-93aac0a08f01

[26] Sparks, Glen. "Should Doc Adams Be in the Hall of Fame? Of course." *Dazzy Vance Chronicles,* 4, December 2015.

https://dazzyvancechronicles.wordpress.com/2015/12/04/should-doc-adams-be-in-the-hall-of-fame-of-course

[27] Francis, Bill. "Doc Adams Helped Shape Baseball's Earliest Days." *National Baseball Hall of Fame.* https://baseballhall.org/discover-more/stories/pre-integration/adams-doc

Chapter 2: Early Rules

[28] Chadwick, Henry. *1860 Beadle's Dime Base-Ball Player.* New York, Irwin R. Beadle, 1860

[29] National Baseball Hall of Fame. "Henry Chadwick." https://baseballhall.org/hall-of-famers/chadwick-henry.

[30] Chadwick.

[31] Tootle, James R. *Vintage Base Ball: Recapturing the National Pastime.* Jefferson, McFarland, 2011.

[32] McGinty, Jo Craven. "Behind Broken Bats, Broken Records." *WSJ,* 26 June 2015.

[33] Tootle.

[34] Dickson, Paul. *New Dickson Baseball Dictionary.* New York, Houghton Mifflin Harcourt, 1999.

[35] Morris, Peter. *A Game of Inches: The Stories Behind the Innovations That Shaped Baseball: The Game on the Field.* Chicago, Ivan R. Dee, 2006.

[36] Chadwick.

[37] Wilborn, Nubyjas. "Sources: Felipe Vazquez's Fight with Kyle Crick Began Over Locker Room Music." *Pittsburgh Post-Gazette,* 11 Sep 2019.

[38] "Baseball Rule Changes: A Timeline of Major League Baseball Rule Changes." *Baseball Almanac*. https://www.baseball-almanac.com/rulechng.shtml

Chapter 3: Gaining Momentum

[39] Spalding, Albert G. *America's National Game.* New York, American Sports Publishing Company, 1911.

[40] "Statistics From the Civil War." *Facing History and Ourselves.* https://www.facinghistory.org/resource-library/statistics-civil-war

[41] Miklich, Eric. "1862 Winter Meetings: Static Rules and Great Conflict." *SABR.* https://sabr.org/journal/article/1862-winter-meetings-static-rules-and-the-great-conflict

[42] Allardice, Bruce. "Baseball 1858-1865: By the Numbers." *SABR Baseball Research Journal*, Spring 2020. https://sabr.org/journal/article/baseball-1858-1865-by-the-numbers

[43] Waff, Craig B. "September 18, 1862: The 'Silver Ball' Game." *SABR*, 2013. https://sabr.org/gamesproj/game/september-18-1862-the-silver-ball-game

[44] Aubrecht, Michael. "Baseball and the Blue and the Gray." Baseball Almanac, August 2016. https://www.baseball-almanac.com/articles/aubrecht2004b.shtml

[45] Remington, Alex. "The Civil War Christmas Game, Hilton Head, 1862." *FanGraphs,* December 22, 2011. https://blogs.fangraphs.com/the-civil-warchristmas-day-game-hilton-head-1862

[46] Frommer, Harvey. *Old Time Baseball: America's Pastime in the Gilded Age.* Guilford, Lyons Press, 2016.

[47] Frommer.

48 Pruitt, Sarah. "Why the Civil War Actually Ended 16 Months After Lee Surrendered." *History*, 1 September, 2018. https://www.history.com/news/why-the-civil-war-actually-ended-16-months-after-lee-surrendered

49 Dickson, Marcus W. "1867 Winter Meetings: National Association of Base Ball Players Annual Convention." *SABR*, 2018. https://sabr.org/journal/article/1867-winter-meetings-national-association-of-base-ball-players-annual-convention.

50 Dickson.

51 MLB.com Baseball Memory Lab. "Earliest Baseball Clubs". http://mlb.mlb.com/memorylab/spread_of_baseball/earliest_clubs.jsp

52 Koslowski, Jeffrey. "1868 Winter Meetings: 'The Most Brilliant Season' or A Lamentable Failure;" *SABR*, 2018. https://sabr.org/journal/article/1868-winter-meetings-the-most-brilliant-season-or-a-lamentable-failure

53 "Al Reach Historical Marker." *ExplorePAHistory.com,* 2019. https://explorepahistory.com/hmarker.php?markerId=1-A-3

54 Pestana, Mark. "1869 Winter Meetings: Pivot to Professionalism." *SABR, 2018.* https://sabr.org/journal/article/1869-winter-meetings-pivot-to-professionalism

55 Pestana.

56 Morris, Peter. *But Didn't We Have Fun? An Informal History of Baseball's Pioneer Era, 1843-1870.* Chicago, Ivan. R. Dee, 2008.

57 Morris.

⁵⁸ Rhodes, Greg, John Erardi and Greg Gajus. *Baseball Revolutionaries: How the 1869 Cincinnati Red Stockings Rocked the Country and Made Baseball Famous*. Printed by authors, 2019.

⁵⁹ Baseball Reference. https://www.baseball-reference.com/bullpen/1869_Cincinnati_Red_Stockings

Note that the Red Stockings' 1869 schedule/results were also printed in *Chadwick's 1870 Beadle's Dime Base-Ball Player*. While the BR and Beadle's win totals (57) match and results are nearly identical, minor variations exist including:
- 6/24 – Reported as a 47-7 win over Baltimore (vs. 30-8 over Pastime BBC of Baltimore)
- 6/25 – Reported as a 24-8 victory over the Washington Nationals in Beadle's (vs. 30-13 over Baltimore)
- 8/6 vs. Forest City – Reported as 43-27 in Beadles' (vs. 43-20).

⁶⁰ Wyss, Robert. "How the 1869 Cincinnati Red Stockings Turned Baseball into a National Sensation." *UConn Today,* 28 March 2019. https://today.uconn.edu/2019/03/1869-cincinnati-red-stockings-turned-baseball-national-sensation-2

⁶¹ Rhodes, Greg. "June 14, 1870: The Atlantic Storm: Red Stockings suffer first defeat." *SABR,* 2013. https://sabr.org/gamesproj/game/june-14-1870-the-atlantic-storm-red-stockings-suffer-first-defeat

Chapter 4: Meteoric Rise, Commercialization and Scandal

⁶² Fitzgerald, F. Scott (Francis Scott), 1896-1940. The Great Gatsby. New York: C. Scribner's Sons, 1925

⁶³ Tiemann, Bob. "November 1, 1870: The Birth of the National Association." *SABR,* https://sabr.org/gamesproj/game/november-1-1870-the-birth-of-the-national-association

[64] Bogovich, Rich and Mark Pestana. "July 23, 2870: The First "Chicago" Game." *SABR*, https://sabr.org/gamesproj/game/july-23-1870-the-first-chicago-game

[65] Tiemann.

[66] Jable, J. Thomas. "Aspects of Moral Reform in Early Nineteenth-Century Pennsylvania." *Pennsylvania Magazine of History and Biography* 102.3 (1978): 344-363. pp 346-47.

[67] McLennan, Jim. "Baseball's Greatest Scandals, #7: The Louisville Grays." *SB Nation: AZ Snake Pit.* 24 May 2011. https://www.azsnakepit.com/2011/5/24/2131205/baseballs-greatest-scandals-9-the-louisville-greys

[68] Ginsburg, Daniel. "The 1877 Louisville Grays Scandal." *SABR*. https://sabr.org/journal/article/the-1877-louisville-grays-scandal

[69] McLennan.

[70] Ginsburg.

[71] Attendance figures obtained from *Baseball Almanac's* Year in Review pages. https://www.baseball-almanac.com/yearly

[72] "Times and Spirits Change." *Sporting News*, Jan 1918. https://behindthebag.net/2019/02/17/pastime-press-shoeless-joe-jackson-and-the-wwi-draft-chicago-tribune-sporting-news-1918-1919

[73] Allardice, Bruce. "Sport Sullivan." *SABR*, June 2014. https://sabr.org/bioproj/person/sport-sullivan

[74] Andrews, Evan. "What Was the 1919 Black Sox Baseball Scandal?" *History*. https://www.history.com/news/black-sox-baseball-scandal-1919-world-series-chicago

[75] "Chicago White Sox vs Cincinnati Reds October 1, 1919 Box Score." *Baseball Almanac.* https://www.baseball-almanac.com/box-scores/boxscore.php?boxid=191910010CIN

[76] "Chicago White Sox vs Cincinnati Reds October 6, 1919 Box Score." *Baseball Almanac.* https://www.baseball-almanac.com/box-scores/boxscore.php?boxid=191910060CHA.

[77] Andrews.

[78] Biography.com Editors. "Shoeless Joe Jackson Biography." *Biography*, 2 Apr 2014. https://www.biography.com/athlete/shoeless-joe-jackson

[79] Belson, Ken. "Apples for a Nickel, and Plenty of Empty Seats." *New York Times,* 7 Jan 2009.

[80] While not emphasized due to their brief professional careers, outfielder Elmer Gedeon (17 appearances with the Washington Senators in 1939) and catcher Harry O'Neill (one game with Philadelphia in 1939) perished in combat in the European and Pacific theaters, respectively, making them the only two major leaguers lost in the war. https://www.nytimes.com/2013/05/26/sports/baseball/remembering-the-major-leaguers-who-died-in-world-war-ii.html

Chapter 5: Free Agency, Tanking and Analytics, Oh My!

[81] Smith, Randy. "The Romance of Baseball." *The Chattanoogan.com,* 26 March 2021. https://www.chattanoogan.com/2021/3/26/425601/Randy-Smith-The-Romance-Of-B aseball.aspx

[82] "Flood v. Kuhn." *Baseball Almanac.* https://www.baseball-almanac.com/law/Flood_v._Kuhn.shtml

[83] Goold. Derek. "On December 24, 1969, Curt Flood Mailed a Letter that Changed Baseball History." *STLToday,* 24 December 2021. https://www.stltoday.com/sports/baseball/professional/on-dec-24-1969-curt-flood-mailed-a-letter-that-changed-baseball-history/article_fe33784a-553c-52ba-87bb-ac981b077b37.html

[84] Will, George. "Dred Scott in Spikes," Syndicated newspaper article from November 21, 1993; reprinted in Will's *Bunts: Curt*

Flood, Camden Yards, Pete Rose and Other Reflections on Baseball (New York: Scribner, 1998).

[85] Birnbaum, Phil. "A Guide to Sabermetric Research." *SABR*. https://sabr.org/sabermetrics

[86] Keri, Jonah. "Nine Managerial Decisions that Helped Decide Game 2 of the NLCS." *FiveThirtyEight*, 13, October 2014. https://fivethirtyeight.com/features/nine-managerial-decisions-that-helped-decide-game-2-of-the-nlcs

[87] Keri.

[88] Associated Press. "Robot Umpires at Home Plate Moving Up to Triple-A for 2022." *ABC News*, 20 January 2022. https://abcnews.go.com/Sports/wireStory/robot-umpires-home-plate-moving-triple-2022-82381464

[89] Schmidt, Michael S. "Cardinals Investigated for Hacking Into Astros' Database." *New York Times*, 16 June 2015.

[90] Associated Press. "Christopher Correa, Former Cardinals Executive, Sentenced to Four Years for Hacking Astros' Database." *New York Times*, 18 July 2016.

[91] Bernstein, Dan. "Astros Cheating Scandal Timeline, From the First Sign-Stealing Allegations to a Controversial Punishment." *The Sporting News*, 24 July 2020.

[92] Passan, Jeff. "Ex-Astros Pitcher Mike Fiers: Team Stole Signs with Camera." *ESPN. 12 November 2019*. https://www.espn.com/mlb/story/_/id/28066522/ex-astros-pitcher-mike-fiers-team-stole-signs-camera

[93] Sheinin, Dave. "No Longer Sports' Dirty Little Secret, Tanking is on Full Display and Impossible to Contain." *Washington Post*, 2 March 2018.

[94] Kelly, Matt. "Every No. 1 Overall Draft Pick in MLB History." *MLB.com*, 6 December 2022. https://www.mlb.com/news/every-no-1-overall-mlb-draft-pick

[95] Rosenstein, Mike. "Yankees, Mets Each Have 1 Player Making More than Entire A's Roster After Sean Manaea-Padres Trade." *NJ.com*, 4 April 2022. https://www.nj.com/yankees/2022/04/yankees-mets-each-have-1-player-making-more-than-entire-as-roster-after-sean-manaea-padres-trade.html

[96] Blum, Ronald. "The Red Sox Are Over the 2022 Luxury Tax, but All Pale to the Big-Spending Dodgers." *Boston Globe*, 3 June 2022. https://www.bostonglobe.com/2022/06/03/sports/red-sox-are-over-2022-luxury-tax-all-pale-big-spending-dodgers

[97] Sheinin.

[98] The growth rate was calculated based on comparison of the 2022 estimate of vintage clubs (over 400) per the Tennessee Association of Vintage Base Ball, and the 2011 estimate of around 200 clubs as noted in James R. Tootle's book *Vintage Base Ball: Recapturing the National Pastime*

Chapter 6: Back to Basics: Reemergence of Vintage Base Ball

[99] Stewart, Doug. "The Old Ball Game." *Smithsonian*, October 1998.

[100] Brown, Maury. "MLB Sees Record 10.7 Billion in Revenues for 2019." *Forbes,* 21 December 2019. https://www.forbes.com/sites/maurybrown/2019/12/21/mlb-sees-record-107-billion-in-revenues-for-2019/?sh=553834825d78

[101] Tootle, James R. *Vintage Base Ball: Recapturing the National Pastime.* Jefferson, McFarland, 2011.

[102] Monti, Gary. Phone interview. Conducted by Jack Pelikan, 15 April 2022.

[103] Branson, Vicki. "Vicki Branson on the Founding of the Ohio Village Muffins". *YouTube,* 22 February 2014. https://www.youtube.com/watch?v=QSrmTDQjKWQ

[104] Andersen, Don. E-mail interview. Conducted by Jack Pelikan, 24 March 2022.

[105] Tootle.

[106] Andersen.

[107] Andersen.

[108] Schwartz, Joel. "Playing Baseball the Old-Fashioned Way." *Sports Illustrated*, 27 April 1987.

[109] Monti.

[110] Monti.

[111] Monti.

[112] Elmore, Ed. E-mail interview. Conducted by Jack Pelikan, 11 May 2022.

[113] Vintage Base Ball Association. "Code of Regulations (i.e., Bylaws)." https://www.vbba.org/bylaws. Accessed 24 May 2022

[114] Monti.

[115] Elmore.

[116] Andersen.

[117] Monti.

[118] Elmore.

[119] Andersen.

Chapter 7: Mountain Athletic Club (Fleischmanns, NY)

[120] Thorn, John. "Mangled Forms." *Our Game: The MLB.com/Blog of Official MLB Historian John Thorn.* 11 October 2016. https://ourgame.mlblogs.com/mangled-forms-b7f73a2e40d9

[121] Haber, Joel. "How Fleischmann's Yeast built the Jewish Catskills." *Jewish Community Voice.* 14 July 2021. https://www.jewishvoicesnj.org/articles/how-fleischmanns-yeast-built-the-jewish-catskills

[122] Thorn. "Mangled Forms".

[123] Randhawa, Manny. "Honus Wagner T206 Card Sells for Record $7.25 Million." *ESPN.* 4 August 2022. https://www.mlb.com/news/rare-t206-honus-wagner-baseball-card-sold-for-7-25-million

[124] Baseball Reference. https://www.baseball-reference.com/players/w/wagneho01.shtml

[125] "Honus Wagner". *Baseball Hall of Fame.* https://baseballhall.org/hall-of-famers/wagner-honus

[126] Thorn, John. "Honus Wagner's Rookie Year, 1895." *Our Game: The MLB.com/Blog of Official MLB Historian John Thorn.* 5 September 2017. https://ourgame.mlblogs.com/honus-wagners-rookie-year-1895-558e7a006f43

[127] Thorn. "Honus Wagner's Rookie Year, 1895".

[128] "Honus Wagner Stats." *Baseball Almanac.* https://www.baseball-almanac.com/players/player.php?p=wagneho01

[129] Thorn. "Mangled Forms."

[130] Severo, Richard. "Rash of Fires in Catskills Points Up Growing Decline." *New York Times.* 27 July 1976. https://www.nytimes.com/1976/07/27/archives/rash-of-fires-in-catskills-points-up-growing-decline-rash-of-fires.html

[131] Reischel, Julia. "In Fleischmanns recount, Morrell still wins, but only by 2 votes." *Watershed Post.* 17 March 2011. http://www.watershedpost.com/2011/fleischmanns-recount-morrell-still-wins-only-2-votes

[132] "Baseball Rule Changes: A Timeline of Major League Baseball Rule Changes." *Baseball Almanac.* https://www.baseball-almanac.com/rulechng.shtml

[133] Miller, Collin. Phone interview. Conducted by Jack Pelikan, 1 March 2022.

[134] Mountain Athletic Club Vintage Base Ball. *Facebook,* 24 Sep. 2019. https://www.facebook.com/page/341511739594891/search/?q=Keator%20Cup

[135] Associated Press. "Hurricane Irene One Year Later: Storm Cost $15.8 in damage from Florida to New York to the Caribbean." *New York Daily News,* 27 August 2012. https://www.nydailynews.com/new-york/hurricane-irene-year-storm-cost-15-8-damage-florida-new-york-caribbean-article-1.1145302

[136] Andre, Rebecca. "Irene Five Years Later: Eight Untold Stories from the Catskills Flood." *Watershed Post,* 3 September 2016. http://www.watershedpost.com/2016/irene-five-years-later-eight-untold-stories-catskills-flood

[137] Carola, Chris. "Suspenders, Yes. Gloves, No. Vintage Baseball Makes a Comeback in the Catskills." *Times Union,* 25 May 2021. https://www.timesunion.com/hudsonvalley/outdoors/article/Vintage-baseball-makes-comeback-in-Catskills-16197922.php

[138] Baseball Reference. https://www.baseball-reference.com/register/player.fcgi?id=kirke-002jud

[139] Miller, Collin. "Founders' Day & the Hon. Julius Fleischmann – Yeast Magnate, Mayor, Baseball Executive & Ballist." *Mountain Athletic Club.* 10 June 2020. https://www.macvintagebaseball.org/post/founder-s-day-the-hon-julius-fleischmann-yeast-magnate-mayor-of-cincy-baseball-exec-ballist

[140] Carola.

[141] Miller, Collin. "2021 Season in Review Part 1: Living History." *Mountain Athletic Club,* 27 November 2021. https://www.macvintagebaseball.org/post/2021-season-in-review-part-1

[142] Miller. Interview.

[143] Miller, Collin. "2021 Season in Review Part 2: M.A.C. Returns to Queen City 121 Years Later." *Mountain Athletic Club,* 9 January 2022. https://www.macvintagebaseball.org/post/season-in-review-part-2-121-years-later-m-a-c-returns-to-the-queen-city

[144] Frandsen, Nicholas. "Bovina Offense Rolls Through DelCo Historical Association Hay Fields; Improves to 10-1." *Bovina Dairymen,* 26 July 2021. https://www.bovinadairymen.org/post/bovina-offense-rolls-through-delco-historical-association-hay-fields-improves-to-10-1

[145] Mountain Athletic Club Vintage Base Ball. *Facebook,* 10 Oct. 2021. https://www.facebook.com/page/341511739594891/search/?q=yearning

Chapter 8: Akron Black Stockings

[146] Hamblin, Scott. E-mail interview. Conducted by Jack Pelikan, 2 September 2021.

[147] "Rubber Industry". Ohio History Connection. https://ohiohistorycentral.org/w/Rubber_Industry

[148] "Rubber Industry".

[149] McBane, Richard. *A Fine-Looking Lot of Ball-Tossers: The Remarkable Akrons of 1881.* Jefferson, McFarland, 2005.

[150] Wyss, Robert. "1869 Cincinnati Red Stockings Turned Baseball Into a National Sensation". *The Conversation.* 27 Mar 2019. https://theconversation.com/how-the-1869-cincinnati-red-stockings-turned-baseball-into-a-national-sensation-113299

[151] Peterjohn, Alvin K. "Baseball in Akron, 1879-81". *1973 Baseball Research Journal.* https://sabr.org/journal/article/baseball-in-akron-1879-81

[152] McBane.

[153] Peterjohn.

[154] "Stan Hywet Fact Sheet". Stan Hywet Hall & Gardens. https://www.stanhywet.org/sites/default/files/assets/docs/Stan%20Hywet_Fact%20Sheet.pdf

[155] Hamblin.

[156] Hamblin.

[157] Hamblin.

[158] Barnard, Matthew and Rudy Frias, hosts. "02-11 ROTB-Scott "Tiny" Hamblin – Akron, OH Black Stockings". *The Roller Out the Barrel Podcast. From Listen Notes,* 18 Oct 2020,

https://www.listennotes.com/podcasts/the-roller-out-the/02-11-rotb-scott-tiny-xJmvb0ECkMW

[159] Barnard.

[160] Hamblin.

[161] Hamblin.

[162] Hamblin

[163] Bowers, Jennifer. "Ohio Cup Brings Vintage Base Ball to Ohio Village". *NBC4i.com.*
4 September 2021. https://www.nbc4i.com/news/local-news/columbus/ohio-cup-brings-vintage-base-ball-to-ohio-village

[164] Hamblin.

[165] Akron Black Stockings.
https://www.facebook.com/AkronBlackStockingsBBC

[166] Hamblin.

Chapter 9: Lafayette Square Cyclone Base Ball Club (St. Louis, MO)

[167] Duggan, Chris. E-mail interview. Conducted by Jack Pelikan, 22 August 2021.

[168] The total of 12 refers to former players inducted into the Hall of Fame as Cardinals. Note that the St. Louis Cardinals have had 47 former players and 13 former managers/executives (with some overlap) reach the Baseball Hall of Fame (as of 2023).

[169] O'Dea, Janelle. "Youth Baseball Tournament in Cottleville a Sign of Strange New Normal."
St. Louis Post-Dispatch, 11 May 2020.

[170] Kittle, Jeffrey. "Henry Gratiot and Early St. Louis Ball Playing." *This Game of Games,* http://thisgameofgames.com/henry-gratiot-and-early-st-louis-ball-playing.html
Accessed September 2021.

[171] Morris, Peter. *But Didn't We Have Fun? An Informal History of Baseball's Pioneer Era, 1843-1870.* Chicago, Ivan. R. Dee, 2008.

[172] Kittel, Jeffrey. "19th Century St. Louis Baseball Grounds." *This Game of Games,* http://www.thisgameofgames.com/19th-century-st-louis-baseball-grounds.html
Accessed September 2021.

[173] Porter, William. "Out-Door Sports: Base Ball: Base Ball at St. Louis, Mo." *Porter's Spirit of the Times,* vol. 8, no. 21. 17 July 1860.

[174] American Battlefield Trust. "Vicksburg." https://www.battlefields.org/learn/civil-war/battles/vicksburg
Accessed September 2021.

[175] St. Louis Public Library. "The Great Cyclone of 1896". http://tornados.slpl.org
Accessed September 2021.

[176] Duggan.

[177] Duggan.

[178] Duggan.

[179] Holleman, Joe. "St. Louis Maroons Erased from Record Books." *St. Louis Post-Dispatch*, 7 December 2021.

[180] Duggan.

[181] Sampson, Bob. "Pioneers of Vintage Base Ball, No. VI: Debra Reid, many teams from Cooperstown, N.Y. to St. Louis Missouri and points between." 6 September 2020. https://www.facebook.com/groups/459820377408533/ 6 September 2020.

[182] Duggan.

[183] Wicker, Tony. E-mail interview. Conducted by Jack Pelikan. 17 January 2022.

[184] Duggan.

Chapter 10: Ohio Village Diamonds Ladies Base Ball Club

[185] Forquer, Jackie. E-mail interview. Conducted by Jack Pelikan, 6 April 2022.

[186] Annie Glidden Houts to John Glidden, April 20, 1866. http://digitallibrary.vassar.edu/fedora/repository/vassar:24406

[187] Wood, Frances. *Earliest Years at Vassar*. Poughkeepsie, Vassar College Press, 1909.

[188] "Girls Base Ball Clubs." *Utica Morning Herald,* 17 Oct 1867.

[189] Shattuck, Debra. "Women's Baseball in Nineteenth-Century New York and the Man Who Set Back Women's Professional Baseball for Decades." *SABR*. 2017. https://sabr.org/journal/article/womens-baseball-in-nineteenth-century-new-york-and-the-man-who-set-back-womens-professional-baseball-for-decades/#sdendnote7sym

[190] *The Revolution*, August 6, 1868.

[191] Tootle, James R. *Vintage Base Ball: Recapturing the National Pastime.* Jefferson, McFarland, 2011.

[192] "Female Club in Brooklyn." *Brooklyn Daily Eagle,* 10 September 1868.

[193] Clarke, Edward H. *Sex in Education; or, A Fair Chance for the Girls.* Boston, James R. Osgood and Company, 1873.

[194] Berlage, Gai Ingham. *Women in Baseball: The Forgotten History.* Greenwood Publishing Group, Inc., 1994.

[195] Kaneko, Gemma. "Three Fascinating Stories About Women Who Played Baseball in the 19th Century." *Cut4 by MLB.com*, 17 Jan 2017. https://www.mlb.com/cut4/3-fascinating-stories-from-debra-shattuck-s-book-bloomer-girls-women-baseball-pi

[196] Belson, Ken. "Apples for a Nickel, and Plenty of Empty Seats." *New York Times,* 7 Jan 2009.

[197] Rothenberg, Matt. "30 Years Ago, The AAGPBL Came to Cooperstown." *National Baseball Hall of Fame.* 2018. https://baseballhall.org/discover/women-in-baseball-exhibit-made-history-in-cooperstown

[198] Tootle.

[199] Ohio History Connection. "Handbook of the Ohio Village Muffins & Lady Diamonds Vintage Base Ball Program."

[200] Forquer.

[201] Ohio History Connection.

[202] Forquer.

[203] Forquer.

[204] Forquer.

[205] Forquer.

Chapter 11: Westward Expansion: Fort Verde Excelsiors (Camp Verde, AZ) & Whatcom Aces (Bellingham, WA)

[206] Helm, Bill. E-mail interview. Conducted by Jack Pelikan, 5 February 2022.

[207] Note: While Cleveland and New York were the first clubs to make Arizona their spring training homes, the Detroit Tigers played a pair of exhibitions against the Pirates and Cubs in Phoenix in 1929.

[208] Boardman, Mark. "The Camp Grant Massacre." *True West*, 4 March 2016.

[209] Locke, Irwin J. S. "Tucson Defeats Phoenix, 10-2; Old Pueblos Are Heavy Hitters." *El Paso Herald*, 28 April 1915.

[210] Sharpe, Abby. "It's Just Something Magical: Bisbee's Historic Warren Ballpark Facilitates Sports in a Small Town." *KOLD News 13*, 26 August 2021. https://www.kold.com/2021/08/26/its-just-something-magical-bisbees-historic-warren-ballpark-facilitates-sports-small-town

[211] "1908: The Merkle Boner." *This Great Game*. https://thisgreatgame.com/1908-baseball-history/

[212] Arizona Territories Vintage Base Ball League: Rules Page. http://arizonavintagebaseball.org/links-information

[213] Jernigan, Zachary. "Stubler Keeps History Alive." *JournalAZ.com*, 22 January 2016. http://www.journalaz.com/news/camp-verde/3532-stubler-keeps-history-alive.html

[214] Jernigan.

[215] Helm.

[216] Helm, Bill. "Mike Adrian: A Real Ace." *The Base Ball Players Chronicle.* Winter 2022. https://www.vbba.org/wp-content/uploads/2022/01/VBBA-2022-WINTER-Newsletter-.pdf

[217] Helm.

[218] Helm, Bill. "Arizona Vintage Baseballer Meets His Idol." *The Base Ball Players Chronicle. Winter 2022.* https://www.vbba.org/wp-content/uploads/2022/01/VBBA-2022-WINTER-Newsletter-.pdf

[219] Arizona Territories Vintage Base Ball League: Fort Verde Excelsiors Page. https://arizonavintagebaseball.org/leaguehome#/fort-verde-excelsiors

[220] Lineberger, Mark. "Sluggers Send Fans Back in Time." *JournalAZ.com.* 13 July 2011. http://www.journalaz.com/news/camp-verde/918-sluggers-send-fans-back-in-time.html

[221] Helm.

[222] Shine, Gregory P. *"The National Game is Decidedly 'on the Fly.'" The Rise of Organized Base Ball in the Portland and Vancouver Area in 1867.* Vancouver WA, National Park Service, 2006.

[223] Shine.

[224] Shine.

[225] Cartwright, Alexander. "Alexander Joy Cartwright IV Forms Pacific Northwest Vintage Baseball League." *PRWeb,* 20 February 2006. https://www.prweb.com/releases/2006/02/prweb347849.htm

[226] Anderson, Sarah. "Play (Really Old) Ball! One man's quest to set the national pastime back 150 years." *Seattle Met.* 27 Dec 2008. https://www.seattlemet.com/arts-and-culture/2008/12/0708-mud-baseball

[227] Helm, Bill. "Getting the Word Out: Drumming up Fan Interest in Vintage Base Ball." *The Base Ball Players Chronicle.* Fall 2021.

[228] Helm, Bill. E-mail interview. Conducted by Jack Pelikan, 5 February 2022.

[229] Helm.

[230] Helm, Bill. E-mail interview. Conducted by Jack Pelikan, 1 May 2022.

Epilogue: Those Were and These are the Days

[231] Brown, Maury. "MLB Sees Record 10.7 Billion in Revenues for 2019." *Forbes,* 21 December 2019. https://www.forbes.com/sites/maurybrown/2019/12/21/mlb-sees-record-107-billion-in-revenues-for-2019/?sh=553834825d78

About the Author

Jack Pelikan, CPA, CISA, CISSP, has over 15 years of experience in business and academia and is a member of the Society for American Baseball Research. While now a resident of Columbia, Missouri, Mr. Pelikan lived for nearly a decade in St. Louis' Lafayette Square neighborhood, a nationally renowned preservationist community known for its Victorian row houses and iconic Lafayette Park, the first city park west of the Mississippi and current home of two prominent vintage base ball clubs (St. Louis Perfectos and Lafayette Square Cyclone), where he witnessed the area's vintage base ball revival up close, taking in countless matches and learning the game and its rich 19th century heritage. Ultimately, the compelling yet unheralded stories behind the vintage game and Mr. Pelikan's unrivaled passions for sports history, research and storytelling were the catalysts for *Vintage Base Ball's Enduring Legacy*.

www.ingramcontent.com/pod-product-compliance
Lightning Source LLC
Chambersburg PA
CBHW070736170426
43200CB00007B/548